Investment Banking and Diligence

Investment Banking and Diligence
What Price Deregulation?

Joseph Auerbach and Samuel L. Hayes, III

Harvard Business School Press
Boston, Massachusetts

The paper used in this publication meets the requirements
of the American National Standard for Permanence of Paper
for Printed Library Materials Z39.48–1984.

Harvard Business School Press
© 1986 by the President and Fellows of Harvard College
All rights reserved.
Printed in the United States of America.
90 89 88 87 86   5 4 3 2 1

Library of Congress Cataloging-in-Publication Data

Auerbach, Joseph, 1916–
   Investment banking and diligence.
   Bibliography: p.
   Includes index.
   1. Investment banking—United States. 2. Securities—United States. I. Hayes,
Samuel L. II. Title.
HG4910.A94 1986   332.66′0973   86-319
ISBN 0-87584-171-6

For

Barbara Hayes and Judith Auerbach

Contents

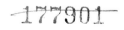

Acknowledgments

This book grew out of research the authors undertook with the support of the Division of Research of the Harvard Business School and the encouragement of its Director, Professor E. Raymond Corey, and his staff. Parts of it were originally circulated as a Harvard Business School Working Paper. Because of the apparent widespread interest in our central thesis and the helpful suggestions of a number of readers, including many persons on the faculty of the school and others, both in government and in private enterprise, we subsequently moved to expand the scope of the research into the present format—an examination of the initial concepts of regulation of the public offering of securities in the United States, its further development and impact on the securities industry, and its bearing on future regulation.

Alan Kantrow of the *Harvard Business Review* conducted valuable research for us, and particularly brought together historical material. We also received valuable research and source note assistance from John M. Case and Douglas D. Rohall. From the faculty staff, Ms. Abby Ourge and Ms. Helen Eiseler were of immeasurable assistance in typing and attending to a host of details in the course of writing this book, and Ms. Duncan Bauer and Ms. Rose M. Giacobbe were exceptionally helpful in the actual production of the finished manuscript. We are grateful to all of them.

We, of course, are solely responsible for everything which appears in the book.

Joseph Auerbach
Samuel L. Hayes, III

Boston, Massachusetts
January 1986

Investment Banking and Diligence

1
A Half-Century of Regulatory Experience

A great deal has changed in the securities market environment in the half-century since the passage of the Securities Act of 1933. While the forms of securities being offered have proliferated in number, responding to changes in investor tastes, the markets in which capital is raised have undergone an even more profound transformation. The volume of capital now being raised dwarfs the amounts deemed significant fifty years ago. The suppliers of capital have become agglomerated. Where formerly individuals were the most important source of new investment capital, with banks and insurance companies serving as supplementary sources, today individuals are a much reduced source of direct investment funds. Individual investors are now largely represented through pension funds, professional managers, trust departments, investment companies, and employers' savings and profit-sharing plans.

1

The changing sources of capital have been accompanied by changes in appetite. If the "traditional" sources of capital and taste in investments were those typical of the period from 1920 to 1950, the next thirty-five years saw a change not only in sources but also in investment preferences. In the period since World War II, investment success has increasingly been due to the efforts of portfolio managers, whose effectiveness is a result not only of acumen but of diligence as well. Although less in evidence as a direct investor, the individual saver remains an important source of funds for contemporary capital markets. The "rank-and-file" individual saver has simply adopted the methods of the historically affluent families, who have always employed professionals to represent them and guide their investment decisions. The 1950s saw the cyclical emergence of the "hot issue" initial public offering market. During the same period the professionally managed venture capital investment pools first appeared as a significant market force. These funds appeared both through the formation of closed-end public investment companies and privately formed limited partnerships.

While the growing institutionalization of the markets has been the overall, dominant phenomenon since the 1950s, subsectors of these markets have not evolved homogeneously. The new debt issues offered in the contemporary money markets are predominantly sold to large institutions with investment appetites stimulated by a constant influx of cash seeking employment. By contrast, new stock issues, as well as those equity issues that masquerade as debt, are not primarily institutional fare. Most institutions with obligations to individuals favor a portfolio with a balance between debt and equity that promotes both stability in investment value and reliability of income. Accordingly, the number of equity issuers meeting the requirements of mainstream institutional buyers is somewhat limited. The individual investor and a subgroup of aggressive growth institutions fill the gap thus created on the demand side of the market with their interest in the more speculative equities and as ready buyers of the less speculative issues that remain after having been picked over by the more conservative institutions.

Despite the impressive development of and important changes in the marketplace, much of the thinking that went into formulating the securities legislation, including the Securities Act of 1933 is still relevant fifty years later.[1] One practice that has not changed is the employment of the investment banker as the principal agency for raising corporate capital. In 1933, as now, an issuer could fix the terms, self-manage, and publicly sell its own issue of securities. It could, as now, forego an underwriting guarantee and sell its securities to the public, its employees, or existing security holders. (Indeed, the existence of preemptive rights of shareholders to avoid dilution—entitling them to a preferred opportunity to subscribe to a new issue of a company's securities—was far more prevalent then than now.) Or it could, as now, employ specially designed offering methods, akin to the contemporary Dutch auctions, installment plans on the British Telecom model, and other esoteric schemes.

In the United States, however, the basic technique, then as now, for raising capital speedily and efficiently has been the underwritten public offering. The underwriting might be an absolute purchase by a banker for resale or, infrequently, a "best efforts" commitment on an agency basis. Nonetheless, the underwriting has relied on a professional investment (or merchant) banker to define the terms of—and to price, manage, and sell—an offering of securities. This investment banking intermediary has, over the years, been charged with carrying out the Securities Act's intent of "regulation by information" through the banker's commitment to use "due diligence" to ensure that relevant information is in the hands of investors at the time of a securities offering.

We became particularly interested in how this information dissemination function was faring when in 1982 the Securities and Exchange Commission announced its experimental "shelf" registration option. Under the SEC's Rule 415 (specifically referred to as "temporary"), companies would be permitted to file a registration statement offering to the public an aggregate block of a class of securities, and then to sell those securities not at a designated time but as windows of opportunity opened over a maximum two-year span. Questions were immediately raised by investment bankers, legal scholars, and others about the effect of the new rule upon compliance with the due diligence requirements laid down by the Securities Act. Did the time constraints permitted under the Rule preclude adequate investigation of an issuer? Had conditions and circumstances changed so radically since the passage of the Act that the traditional investigation (mandatory in the view of many persons) for determining information material to the offering could be waived or substantially curtailed?[2]

It appears, from an informal survey of private litigation and the public records of SEC "stop order" proceedings that, since the promulgation of the Securities Act, fewer than one in a thousand effective registration statements have been the subject of litigation charging lack of due diligence by underwriters. Of course this statistic alone does not permit us to ascertain how many proposed registration statements and their disclosures were required by the underwriters to be modified, corrected, or expanded or were accepted only tentatively, subject to the securing of independent expert analyses, opinions, and certificates. We are convinced that prior to the adoption of the experimental Rule 415, the overwhelming proportion of proposed registration statements received such treatment. Furthermore, once filed with the underwriter's concurrence, the overwhelming proportion of registration statements were the subject of one or more of the so-called deficiency letters from the SEC staff suggesting the need for inclusion or omission of certain information. By law the commission does not approve a registration or become responsible for its comments. Accordingly, an issuer who disagrees with the contents of a deficiency letter would theoretically be free to start selling at will once the statutory twenty-day incubation period had elapsed. No sensible underwriter, however, would agree to commence an offering under such circumstances. The deficiency letter would not necessarily be evidence of omission of material fact (for the SEC staff might be wrong) but it would indicate the need for further investigation. As for the issuer acting on its own, in disregard of the deficiency letter, the commission could invoke stop order proceedings freezing any such financing move.

Underwriters have always interpreted the statute—as well as the concept of due diligence—to embody a public policy calling for mandatory rather than discretionary investigation. And many believe that they have benefited from behaving so. Prestige, standing, and reputation are marketing tools for the investment banker, as well as a prerequisite for recruiting quality personnel. Not being sued at all under the Securities Act has been a far more important objective for the investment banker than being able to demonstrate sufficient investigation to constitute a shield against financial loss from a suit actually having been filed.

In order to explore the possible implications and ramifications of the shelf registration phenomenon and its place in the entire scheme of public capital raising in the United States, it is essential to compare and contrast the economic, banking, and financing environments at the time when the regulatory arrangements for underwriting were formulated fifty years ago to those of the early 1980s, when the shelf rule was introduced.

In Chapter 2 we present a historical perspective on the securities industry in the period leading up to and including the Great Depression of the 1930s. Our research uncovered a wide variety of general sources of data and comment, but we could find no concise, focused articulation of that significant period in U.S. economic and social history as it related to the underwriting sector of the securities industry. Yet it seemed to us that such a focus would be a key to what subsequently transpired with respect to both the introduction of formal regulation and the impact that it had on industry structure over the half-century prior to the introduction of the temporary shelf registration rule.

In Chapter 3 we explore the important currents of thought and political opinion that influenced and shaped the debate in Congress during 1933 and 1934 which ultimately yielded the legislation that reorganized and constrained the securities industry. Principal attention is paid to the Securities Act of 1933. Its central precept, which has governed the process of public offerings of securities ever since that time, is that government can most effectively protect investors by regulating the flow of information on which a personal decision can be based. The implications and consequences of this concept, which we term "regulation by information," are then examined as we lay out the procedures by which underwriters exercise the due diligence required under the Securities Act.

Chapter 4 summarizes the guidelines and procedures customarily used by the securities firms in gathering the information about an issuer necessary for making an informed decision on the purchase offer. It is our impression that the general public and even a number of professional investors not directly involved in the investigation process are unaware of the exacting detail and calendar involved in the process.

A brief overview of the securities industry's evolution since the passage of the 1930s regulatory legislation is presented in Chapter 5. The changes, almost revolutionary in nature, in the composition and sophistication of capital suppliers and capital users are discussed. We then review the introduction of new, alternative mechanisms of capital raising hardly imagined when the regulation of the industry was initiated, and we give brief scrutiny to the evolution and development of other capital markets.

Chapter 6 follows another thread of the evolution of the securities markets: the impact of the changing composition of issuers, investors, and market liquidity on the practical implementation of the regulation by information mandate. We document the evolutionary moves by the Securities and Exchange Commission toward "integrated disclosure" under the two basic regulatory statutes, the Securities Act of 1933 and the Securities Exchange Act of 1934, which formed the most important basis for introducing the streamlined securities issuance procedure that ultimately took the form of shelf registration.

Chapter 7 then examines in detail the shelf registration procedure, identifying it as a logical sequel to the industry trends and disclosure developments discussed in Chapters 5 and 6. The registration process itself is explained, and this sector of underwriting activity is documented for the period since it was first introduced in early 1982.

In Chapter 8 we turn to an examination of profiles of both the companies that used this registration procedure during the initial trial period and the group of potential users now that the SEC has made this option a permanent one for qualifying issuers. Chapter 9 offers an exploration and analysis of the future implications of these developments for carrying out the mandate of the Securities Act of 1933. We make recommendations for modifying the qualifying rules now in effect in order to preserve the positive elements of the shelf procedure while minimizing the potential for revisiting the abuses of the past. The book concludes with a summary and an overview of the topics discussed.

NOTES

1. For a different approach to reviewing the history of the 1933 Act, see Homer Kripke, "Fifty Years of Securities Regulation in Search of a Purpose," 22 *San Diego Law Review* 257 (1984). He found that in the first forty years of the SEC there was an over-emphasis on the role of disclosure as a tool to aid "enforcement of the antifraud laws. . . rather than to assist affirmatively in securities selection or to strengthen the capital markets."
2. Like Professor Kripke, former SEC commissioner Roberta S. Karmel addresses the enforcement aspects of regulation in her book *Regulation by Prosecution* (New York: Simon and Schuster, 1982). We have been concerned not with the SEC's interpretation of its regulatory mission in its first forty years but with what appears to us to be a decision to pursue a deregulatory approach thereafter.

2
Rude Awakening

The chronicle of forces which led to the reform legislation of
the 1930s governing investment banking must go back to economic events leading up to the Great Depression. By early
1933 the bitter facts of economic collapse had become inex-
tricably linked in the public mind with the market crash of
1929 and, more broadly, with the increasingly feverish operations of high finance during the 1920s. October 1929 and its
aftermath on Wall Street heralded far more than a calamitous
decline in the value of the nation's paper wealth. What
crashed on Black Thursday and Tragic Tuesday was a deep-
seated public faith in the essential soundness of the whole
economic system and, especially, in the men and institutions
that had long dominated it. A democratic society, whatever
the formal basis for its call on the allegiance of its citizens,
derives its continued political power from effective compliance with the implied compact it shares with them. So too
with that society's economic power; its market economy can

flourish only when those who participate in it have faith in the institutions upon which the system calls and the people who guide it. Legitimacy in the economic sphere, as in the political, is not imposed from the top down; it is created from the bottom up.

In a pre–eighteenth-century economy, based on barter and media of exchange with intrinsic value, the tangibleness of transactions provided a basis for communal life and the growing demand for goods and services. In a more advanced economy, however, based on intangible transactions and paper symbols of value, an acceptance of these more abstract symbols of community had to precede and underlie economic activity. In 1929 the crash of what had been considered a mature economic system of world rank shook that necessary sense of community to its foundation. As a rudely awakened public came to understand exactly what the self-appointed stewards of their economic well-being had been doing, they pointed with anger and a sense of betrayal to what they saw as gross violations of the ethic of stewardship. In such a climate faith evaporates, and with it the perceived legitimacy of a financial structure built on paper. Concurrently, barely a decade had elapsed since the installation in Russia of the societal structure called communism, an economic-political system previously both scorned and feared in its theoretical concepts by many business and intellectual leaders, both in the United States and Europe.

The public's first reaction to the crash was to seek to defend the system if at all possible, while finding the rascals who had betrayed it. The violations of stewardship which were found and documented "indicated a system as a whole that had failed to impose those essential fiduciary standards that should govern persons whose function it was to handle other people's money. Thus, virtually all of the players in the competitive equation of the financing industry—investment bankers, brokers and dealers, corporate directors, lawyers, accountants—found themselves the object of severe criticism from an American public (including a large number of securities investors) that had theretofore regarded the financial community with a respect that had approached awe."[1]

But it was not enough merely to punish the malefactors (if that were, in fact, legally possible). The system was demonstrably no longer invincible. Complicating the analysis was the need for speed owing to the political costs of procrastination. In order to understand the remedies sought by the country's political leadership in the wake of economic collapse, it is useful to understand as well the economic environment of the time and the competitive factors then operating in the U.S. securities markets.

MARKET ENVIRONMENT

As the industrial momentum of the United States grew, so did the size and scope of its business sector, and of local and national governmental sectors as well. The merger wave of 1898–1902 had brought with it a consolidation of what had in many instances been fragmented local or regional industries. This consolidation was fostered by the spanning of the continent by the railroads. The telegraph, and in the 1920s the radio, ushered in the age of national marketing. Gross national product in 1958 dollars rose from $77 billion in 1900 to $184 billion in 1930. During the period 1920–28, gross national product grew at an impressive average annual compound rate of 4.3 percent.[2]

Private Sector Capital Users.   While a national industrial consolidation was taking place, the number and size of incorporated businesses was also growing, reflecting the expanding economy during much of this period. Among large manufacturing businesses, for example, assets more than tripled between 1914 and 1930. Although consistently more than half of the growth in corporate assets was accomplished through internal depreciation set-asides and retention of profits,[3] a substantial part was provided by external borrowing (both short and long term) and, particularly during the late 1920s, by the issuance of new equity securities.[4]

The period from World War I to 1930, however, was not generally characterized by capital structures with high debt burdens. The average corporate debt-to-capitalization ratio (usually referred to as its financial leverage) was only 21 percent in 1926 and 24 percent in 1930.[5] The percentage of debt was even lower in 1930 for the manufacturing sector (10 percent) but, as might be expected, higher in the utilities sector (42 percent) as well as in the finance, insurance, and real estate sectors (27 percent).[6] Thus, while substantial amounts of new funds were being raised publicly, it was not generally at the expense of overlevered corporate capital structures.

Government Capital Users. Financing demands were also growing in the government sector, both domestic and foreign. Substantial deficits during World War I had necessitated a large U.S. bond funding program that had drawn a number of new investors into the public marketplace for the first time.[7] In the wake of the war, there was also an acceleration in the public issuance of securities for city and state capital improvements.[8]

The United States had been a net importer of capital prior to 1900, but by the end of World War I the country had become a capital exporter. A number of foreign governments, as well as large off-shore private sector projects, successfully sought financing in New York, often at the bidding and encouragement of the U.S. State Department, which apparently saw the accommodation of these foreign borrowers as an important element in the management of foreign policy.[9]

The Investor Group. The size and composition of the domestic U.S. investor community was itself changing and expanding. Prior to World War I, the wealthy individual had been the most important source of both debt and equity capital,[10] but subsequent events and trends worked to change that. For one thing, a relatively high income tax surcharge had driven effective tax rates on incomes of more than $100,000 to 31 percent,[11] and this in turn had driven wealthy investors away from dividend-paying equity securities and into a variety of tax avoidance schemes, especially insurance policy vehicles with deferred tax recognition of investment earnings. Consequently, wealthy individuals' share of corporate equity securities continued to slide until 1921, when it leveled off. The surtax was also subsequently reduced.[12] Meanwhile, the institutional investor community was of relatively limited scope and influence, at least until the end of the 1920s. True, the assets of insurance companies were growing at an impressive rate (but from a very small base as shown in Table 2-2), reflecting a growing preference among individuals of more modest income for this systematic savings vehicle, as well as the influx of funds from the wealthy. The only other important institutional investors during this period were the commercial banks, which were also a dominant influence in financing (or facilitating the financing of) both private and public sector capital needs.

A particularly important trend in the early twentieth century was the emergence in the public markets of individual investors of modest means. It is likely that the Liberty Bond campaigns during World War I helped make these individuals comfortable with the notion of putting their money into the securities markets, much as the government's bond financing during the Civil War had helped create a national market for railroad securities as individuals liquidated much of their government bond holdings.[13] Because of the reluctance of wealthy individuals to invest during the period after the war, corporations actively solicited their customers and employees to buy their equity securities. While statistics show that individuals at first invested more heavily in debt than in equity securities, by 1927 they had shifted to corporate equities.[14] It has been estimated that by the end of the 1920s there were some 18 million individual investors holding an increasingly diversified portfolio of securities.[15] At this time, then, the holdings of individual investors constituted the overwhelming majority of public equity securities (see Table 2–1) and about 50 percent of public debt securities (see Table 2–2).

INTERMEDIARIES AND CAPITAL FLOWS

Among the principal financial intermediaries in the securities markets which operated during the period after 1900, the historically dominant private banks are particularly noteworthy. Like their antecedent British and continental merchant banks, they were empowered to undertake a broad array of financing and investment activities, but chose to focus most of their energies both on the financing needs of substantial private sector corporations and foreign government entities and on the various banking requirements of wealthy individuals. The other important group of financial intermediaries operating in the markets at this time were the commercial banks, which traditionally focused on taking deposits from and extending loans to a variety of customers and clients, depending on geographical location and targeted market. Many of these banks assumed an active role in the securities business rather later than the private banks.

Although both groups of competitors were empowered to pursue similar lines of business, the securities industry in the period after World War I was far from homogeneous. It was characterized by a hierarchical structure that had been confirmed among European merchant banking firms since at least the 1780s. At the apex of the hierarchy were a few private banking houses that had figured prominently in private and public sector financing from immediately after the Civil War until World War I. This group included J. P. Morgan, Drexel & Co. (the Philadelphia affiliate of Morgan), and Kuhn Loeb & Co. A number of other securities firms with origins in Boston (an important early location of investable capital), Philadelphia, and Baltimore, as well as New York, also participated in this market. A second segment of the securities issuance competitor group was composed of the commercial banks which had actively developed their corporate and investor activities.[16]

The traditionally dominant private banks enjoyed the bulk of the originating business in the early postwar period. It was only as the 1920s wore on that the commercial banks' managerships (and participations) picked up to a point where they almost equaled those of the private banks, as shown by Table 2-3. This did not reflect a major shift of client loyalty away from the private banks. Rather, it reflected the commercial banks' successful efforts to generate financing business from issuers whose quality (or prodigious capital appetite) made them less attractive to the private banks.

Taken together, the financial resources of all reporting banks, private and commercial, grew from roughly $53 billion

Table 2-1

Ownership of Financial Intermediaries in Domestic Corporate Stock Outstanding (*percent*)

Intermediaries	1900	1912	1922	1929	1933	1939	1945	1949	1952
1. Commercial banks	0.8%	0.9%	0.9%	0.8%	1.6%	0.8%	0.3%	0.3%	0.2%
2. Mutual savings banks	0.3	0.1	0.1	0.1	0.2	0.2	0.1	0.1	0.2
3. Private life insurance companies	0.5	0.3	0.1	0.2	0.9	0.7	0.8	1.3	1.3
4. Faternal insurance organizations	..	..	..	..	0	0	0	0.1	0
5. Private noninsured pension funds	..	..	..	0.1	0.2	0.3	0.3	0.6	0.9
6. Fire and marine insurance companies	0.9	0.6	0.5	0.8	1.1	1.3	1.4	1.7	1.6
7. Casualty and misc. insurance companies	0.1	0.1	0.1	0.2	0.4	0.5	0.5	0.7	0.6
8. Savings and loan associations	..	..	..	..	0	0.1	0.1	0.1	0.2
9. Credit unions	..	..	0	0	0	0	0	0	0.1
10. Investment companies	..	..	0.1	1.5	1.6	1.5	1.6	1.9	2.6
11. Government lending institutions	..	0	0	.0	0.4	1.0	0.3	0.1	0
12. Personal trust departments	4.9	7.6	11.0	8.6	12.8	16.0	14.3	15.4	12.8
Total holdings by intermediaries	7.6%	9.6%	12.9%	12.3%	19.3%	22.2%	19.6%	22.2%	20.5%
Total outstanding (billions)	$12.3	$32.1	$57.1	$146.9	$62.5	$81.1	$126.2	$129.9	$195.0

Source: Raymond W. Goldsmith, *Financial Intermediaries*, National Bureau of Economic Research, Princeton University Press, 1958, p. 225.

Table 2-2

Ownership of Financial Intermediaries in Domestic Corporate Bonds Outstanding (*percent*)

Intermediaries	1900	'1912	1922	1929	1933	1939	1945	1949	1952
1. Commercial banks	9.8%	11.5%	13.9%	12.1%	10.7%	10.2%	10.6%	8.0%	6.7%
2. Mutual savings banks	6.4	5.5	5.1	5.2	5.5	4.1	3.5	5.2	4.9
3. Private life insurance companies	7.9	9.1	9.2	12.0	13.3	24.7	37.3	54.6	58.0
4. Fraternal insurance organizations	0	0.1	0.1	0.2	0.3	0.4	1.7	1.7	1.8
5. Private noninsured pension funds	..	..	0.2	0.8	1.1	1.7	3.9	7.1	8.9
6. Government trust funds	..	0	0	0	0.1	0.2	0.5	0.5	0.8
7. Fire and marine insurance companies	1.4	1.6	2.0	2.1	1.6	1.1	0.7	0.7	0.6
8. Casualty and misc. insurance companies	0.3	0.4	0.6	1.2	1.0	0.9	0.8	1.0	1.3
9. Savings bank life insurance departments	..	..	..	0	0	0	0	0	0
10. Investment companies	..	..	0.1	0.3	0.2	0.4	0.8	0.4	0.6
11. Personal trust departments	8.7	8.0	14.9	17.3	13.0	20.9	13.4	10.2	9.9
Total holdings by intermediaries	34.5%	36.2%	46.1%	51.3%	46.7%	64.6%	73.0%	89.5%	93.6%
Total outstanding (billions)	$6.9	$17.5	$24.2	$39.0	$38.5	$33.5	$27.0	$39.3	$50.4

Source: Raymond W. Goldsmith, *Financial Intermediaries*, National Bureau of Economic Research, Princeton University Press, 1958, p. 224.

Table 2-3

Percentage origination of Bond Issues By All Houses 1927–1930

	1927	1928	1929	1930
Nat'l Banks Affil.	10.1%	15.6%	24.6%	27.6%
Other Bank Affil.	2.7	7.7	16.9	11.6
Com'l Banks and Trust Co's	9.2	6.2	4.0	5.4
Subtotal	22.0	29.5	45.5	44.6
Total Bank Trust Affil. Private Bankers	78.0	70.5	54.5	55.4
Total	100.0%	100.0%	100.0%	100.0%

Source: W. Nelson Peach, *The Security Affiliates of National Banks*, reprint, Baltimore, MD.: Johns Hopkins Press, 1983, p. 109.

in 1920 to a peak of $74 billion in 1930, a 40 percent increase, before falling back drastically to $51 billion in 1933.[17] For the period 1920–30, this rate of growth in all classes of bank assets was more than double that of the nation's population. At the same time, the banking industry as a whole was experiencing a process of consolidation, as evidenced by a decrease in the total number of banks,[18] coupled with an increase in bank branches. By 1933 the national total of 14,771 banks was down sharply from more than 31,000 in 1921. Branches, however, had risen from 1,455 in 1921 to 2,786 in 1933.[19] As the comptroller of the currency noted in 1929, "Banking is following in the wake of the trend in business in general toward larger operating units with stronger capital funds and more experienced and highly-trained management."[20] In practice, this also meant that a growing proportion of banking resources found its way into the hands of financial institutions based in the larger cities. In 1929 some 250 such banks controlled nearly half ($33 billion out of a total of $72 billion) of all banking resources.[21]

How did these developments relate to the operation of the securities market? Holding these supplies of capital, banks had themselves invested substantial resources in the stock market and had also financed the investments of others by making loans for that purpose. The commitment of individual savings to new securities issues paralleled the credit directed for that purpose by the banks. In 1920 the dollar volume of new issues (less refunding) represented some 23 percent of all available savings; by 1930 the comparable figure had risen to 59 percent (see Table 2-4).

The data cited up to this point have a significant bearing on subsequent events. During the 1920s and early 1930s, America's financial activities were becoming more concentrated, and the flow-through of resources was becoming increasingly channeled to the securities markets. These data square well with both the dollar volume of new securities issues (see Table 2-5) and the trading volume of outstanding securities on the New York Stock Exchange (see Table 2-6), by far the nation's largest market. The extent to which the United States functioned during this period as a capital-exporting nation, however, is not reflected. Tables 2-7 and 2-8 give details of foreign stock and foreign government bonds issued in the United States from 1920 to 1929, and the growing importance of these foreign financings in the overall volume of capital issues in the United States.

With so large an exposure to debtors abroad, domestic creditors were linked in a new way to the fortunes of governments and economies elsewhere. For much of its earlier history, the United States had been a net importer of foreign capital. With the shift to net capital exporter after World War I,[22] it became increasingly difficult for domestic capital suppliers to retain their old immunity to financial troubles in other parts of the world.

Thus, during the 1920s there were profound structural changes in the U.S. securities industry. New sources of capital, new groups of investors, and new issuers all sought to participate in the booming market for securities. And there were accompanying shifts in the way in which the work of investment banking was done.

Syndications. Throughout the nineteenth century and essentially up to the end of World War I, the volume of savings

Table 2-4

Estimated Savings Compared with New Security Issues: 1920–1932 (*In Millions of Dollars*)

	Savings				New Capital Issues Less Refunding	Percent of Savings Represented by New Issues
	Corporate	Non-Corporate	Individual	Total Savings		
1920	6,039	3,387	6,662	16,088	3,635	23
1921	3,732	6,043	5,150	14,925	3,576	23
1922	5,634	3,737	5,504	14,875	4,304	29
1923	6,332	494	6,680	13,506	4,304	32
1924	5,557	4,639	7,113	17,309	5,593	32
1925	6,555	1,952	7,326	15,835	6,220	38
1926	6,340	3,447	8,163	17,950	6,344	31
1927	5,913	4,126	9,583	19,622	7,776	40
1928	6,591	1,639	11,233	19,463	8,050	41
1929	6,749	3,532	12,408	22,689	10,183	49
1930	3,775	724	7,369	11,868	7,023	59
1931	-1,102	-1,223	5,268	5,389	3,115	38
1932	-2,149	-4,782	3,931	6,564	1,192	18

Source: Alfred L. Bernheim & Margaret G. Schneider, eds. *The Security Markets*, 1936, The Twentieth Century Fund, New York, p. 66.

Table 2-5

Corporate Security Issues: 1919–1934 (*In Millions of Dollars*)

Year	Bonds and Notes	Preferred Stocks	Common Stocks	Total Corporate Securities
1919	1122	793	753	2668
1920	1750	483	555	2788
1921	1994	75	200	2270
1922	2329	333	288	2949
1923	2430	407	329	3165
1924	2655	346	519	3521
1925	2975	637	610	4223
1926	3354	543	677	4574
1927	4769	1054	684	6507
1928	3439	1397	2094	6930
1929	2620	1695	5062	9376
1930	3431	421	1105	4957
1931	2028	148	195	2372
1932	620	10	13	644
1933	227	15	137	380
1934	456	3	31	490

Source: U.S. Bureau of the Census. *Historical Statistics of the United States: Colonial Times to 1970.* 2 vols. Washington: Government Printing Office, 1975. Series X 510-515, p. 1006.

available for investment was inadequate to meet the expanding demands of business enterprise for new capital. As a consequence, a considerable period of time—sometimes as much as a year or two—usually elapsed between the first offering of an issue and the disposition of the last of these securities to the investing public.[23] This was, in effect, an era of de facto "shelf" securities offerings. One result of the greater availability of capital after the end of the war was to make possible a more rapid process of flotation. At the same time, however, the modifications of syndicate operation that had, in the years before the war, been responsive to the lack of capital continued to flourish under quite different circumstances. In practice, this meant that efforts to make syndicates larger (in order to share more widely the heightened risks of long flotations), simpler (in order to pass risks along more quickly), and faster-acting (in order to try to reduce risks al-

Table 2-6

Volume of Sales on New York Stock Exchange: 1919–1934 (*Money Figures in Millions of Dollars and Stocks in 1,000,000 Shares*)

Year	Stocks	Bonds, Principal Amount			
		Total	Corporate	U.S. Government	State, Muni, and Foreign
1919	317	3,809	622	2,901	286
1920	227	3,977	827	2,861	289
1921	173	3,324	1,043	1,957	324
1922	259	4,370	1,905	1,873	592
1923	236	2,790	1,568	796	425
1924	282	3,804	2,345	877	582
1925	454	3,384	2,332	391	661
1926	451	2,987	2,004	262	721
1927	577	3,269	2,142	290	837
1928	920	2,903	1,967	188	749
1929	1,125	2,982	2,182	142	658
1930	810	2,764	1,927	116	721
1931	577	3,051	1,846	296	908
1932	425	2,967	1,642	570	755
1933	655	3,369	2,099	501	769
1934	324	3,726	2,239	885	602

Source: U.S. Bureau of the Census. *Historical Statistics of the United States: Colonial Times to 1970.* 2 vols. Washington: Government Printing Office, 1975. Series X 531-535, p. 1007.

together) generated increasing force. The new trends in syndicate operation burst through the barriers posed by former practice like a flood finding a weak spot in a dam.

Adding to the force of these changes were the competitive circumstances of many of the investment houses themselves. Although the more established apex issuing houses had ample requests for their services, the newer or smaller firms seeking to break into the business or move up within the industry's pyramidal structure could do so only by tapping pockets of supply and demand not already buttoned up. It was no accident that it was upstart Halsey, Stuart and not, for example, the House of Morgan, that plunged so deeply into the flotation of public utility bonds and the pyramidal expansion of the Insull utility empire. Nor was it an accident that it was Halsey, Stuart that pioneered the use of radio advertising, a

Table 2-7

Foreign Common Stock and Foreign Government Bonds Issued in the
United States, 1920–1929 (*In Millions of Dollars*)

Year	Stocks	Bonds
1920	7	439
1921	0	532
1922	0	660
1923	10	303
1924	0	912
1925	10	818
1926	11	673
1927	9	1,023
1928	41	875
1929	34	253

Source: Ilse S. Mintz, *Deterioration in the Quality of Foreign Bonds Issued in the United States, 1920–1930* (New York: National Bureau of Economic Research, 1951), p. 28.

private wire system, formal training for salesmen, and a system of partial payment for investors.[24] Of course, some of the older houses—Kidder, Peabody for one—could not resist either the allure of these new activities (especially, in Kidder's case, investment trusts) or the growing investor preference for common stocks over the more familiar bonds.[25]

Quality Discrimination.   Taken together, these developments did much to alter the way the industry worked. In the first place, as syndicates grew larger, they also became more streamlined: that is, their traditional organization as a portfolio of different functional groups began to give way to a simpler twofold division into underwriters and selling groups. Second, as fees for underwriting services declined, it became increasingly attractive for the underwriters themselves to become more extensively involved than they had been in distribution, either directly or through affiliated organizations. Third, as the smaller individual investors became the dominant buying force in the market, particularly for equities, there arose rapid advances in the high-powered sales techniques needed to reach them. And fourth, as demand fed on itself to create even greater demand, investment houses were faced with the constant challenge of finding enough product to sell.

Table 2-8

Foreign Capital Issues Compared with Total Capital Issues Offered in the United States, 1920–1929 (*In Millions of Dollars*)

Year	New Foreign Issues	Total New Issues	Foreign in Percent of Total
1920	485	3,635	13
1921	631	3,577	18
1922	728	4,304	17
1923	413	4,304	10
1924	1,001	5,593	18
1925	1,072	6,220	17
1926	1,130	6,344	18
1927	1,302	7,776	17
1928	1,246	8,050	15
1929	779	11,604	6

Source: Allin W. Dakin, "Foreign Securities in the American Money Market, 1914–1930," *Harvard Business Review* (January 1932), p. 229.

Where commissions were still large or where the need for new product was urgent, bankers did what they could to drum up new domestic or foreign securities for sale, whatever their investment quality. As one critic of these developments pointed out, during the 1920s, "bankrupt German municipalities and disrupted German industries had not to beg foreign bankers for advances; they were actually beseiged by those bankers until they accepted loans."[26] Above all else, a new importance was placed on speed which, according to both critics and supporters, was now "of the essence in the security distribution process, since underwriter and retailer both sought to avoid as far as feasible the risk of adverse price movements. . .[and regarded] their function almost entirely as one of distribution rather than risk bearing."[27]

The flood of changed industry practice was, indeed, best represented by this unprecedented concern for speed, a concern that was not entirely healthy. In the opinion of Paul Gourrich, an early director of the research division at the SEC (and previously the chief economist at Kuhn, Loeb):

The outstanding characteristic of investment banking during the 'twenties probably was the speed of distribution. It appears that there was a definite tendency for the policy of investment bankers to be dominated by the knowledge of the fact that the mechanisms of syndication would permit rapid and effective selling, at times regardless of the quality of issues. In part, this was possible because all the participants in syndication and the ultimate buyers placed much reliance on the originating and participating bankers and their judgments in choosing a new issue. When this judgment was directed by thoughts of immediate profits, when investment bankers made their decisions to associate themselves with the distribution of an issue not on the basis of conservative appraisals but rather because of the clamor of their distributing organizations for securities, when, in other words, the "tail" began to "wag the dog," this reliance on the originating banker was unsound. In fact, this faith, instead of protecting the investor, led him astray.[28]

Two points here are worth special note. By the time of the 1933 Act, industry practice appeared to many to be driven less by the desire to make a fair profit from underwriting and distributing sound, well-researched securities to the public than by the need to help keep the pipeline of distribution filled with securities no matter what their underlying value. Furthermore, the reason why it was such a bad thing for the tail to wag the dog was not simply that the practice occasionally brought to market securities that did not deserve public confidence. More important, it undermined the quality and timeliness of the information upon which bankers, analysts, and investors depended. Thus, Gourrich commented:

> the ease of selling poor quality and overpriced securities was enhanced by the frequent absence of adequate information for buyers of securities and for security analysts and experts, who might aid buyers in reaching considered judgments. Sometimes, the information was not even available to the bankers, so that their judgment, though honest, might not have been based on enough information to be accurate; in many cases, whether or not the information was available to the firm, it was not disclosed to the public in an unambiguous manner. It is because of the many instances of these conditions which were revealed when, with the depression, the light of publicity was directed to these transactions, as well as the more shocking examples of suppression of factual data, that the Securities Act, based upon the principle of adequate disclosure, was passed.[29]

Credit Information Dissemination. The complex relationships among originators, underwriters, and distributors that had long characterized the work of investment banking syndicates depended, in no small measure, on the trust that syndicate members put in the research and judgment of the originating house. It was far too expensive a proposition for each syndicate participant to do its own analysis of a security's underlying value. As a result, they all regularly agreed to the extra fees and special terms for such management service as the originating houses demanded. During the 1920s, however, as these participants found themselves handling ever larger volumes of securities, they put more reliance and pressure on the syndicate manager's ability to generate and disseminate information than it was able to bear. This effect was both unintentional and undesired, but it followed directly from the participants' urgent calls for more product to sell.

As in the vertical chain of most industries, one organization's need is another's point of leverage. Although the syndicate members depended heavily on syndicate managers for investigations and services, they were usually in no position to discipline the managers for shortfalls in performing these functions. It was not that new increased demand suddenly made it impossible for originating houses to pass along fully adequate information about new issues. These prestigious houses had long used their commanding position in the industry generally, and at the apex of individual syndicate pyramids specifically, to dictate terms of participation to others. If a smaller house wanted to be included in future syndications, it had little choice but to accept the opportunities—and the terms—offered by apex firms. Pressed to accept a new participation, and with very little time to decide, a regional broker in, say, Chicago, had no way to evaluate the merits of the security in question or the completeness and accuracy of the information passed along about it. The faster operation of syndicates and the pressures for heightened volume thus exacerbated an existing structural problem.

Making the problem even worse was the surging interest of the market in stocks rather than bonds during the latter half of the 1920s. Investment Banker Association members, accustomed " 'to look carefully at the intrinsic value of properties and to have their buying. . .on a safe margin against these values,' discovered they now needed new data on management and projected earning power rather than on real property and tangible values. . .'We, here, and our customers,' said one member, 'are groping around to find out what our equities are worth. . . .There is no yardstick for us to go by.' Another member felt certain 'we are densely ignorant of our own business.' "[30] The boom in equity financing, with its attendant demands for a new kind of information about corporate operations, underscored the chaos of accounting principle and practice, the inadequacy of listing requirements on the major exchanges, and the gross lack of comparability among corporate balance sheets and income statements.

To gain a perspective on this "information gap," one must understand the nascent state of uniform public accountancy that existed prior to the promulgation of accounting regulations by the SEC under the auspices of both the 1933 and the 1934 Acts. Although the double entry bookkeeping system had been invented in the fifteenth century, accounting as a recognizable profession emerged only in the wake of the industrial revolution in Europe and the subsequent extensions of commercial, financial, and political hegemony to far-flung colonial empires. Records suggest that the earliest accounting professionals came from Scotland and that they were employed widely in both the British private sector and in the government's administration of the colonies. Their introduction into the United States came in the late 1800s, when they were sent over to inspect investments of British capitalists and to handle bankruptcies. Some stayed on, forming the initial cadre of U.S. accountants. Their activities were largely concerned with the internal control of company affairs. Since there were few standardized conventions that could provide a basis for comparison among companies, the public accountants were dominated largely by those companies who retained them. They usually cooperated with their clients and, not infrequently, submitted reports to accord with whatever face management wanted to present to the outside world, misleading or not.

By the 1920s, accurate and timely information was more

crucial than ever before, but this was precisely what traditional business practice, exacerbated by the competitive circumstances of the time, had made impossible. The great crash of 1929 produced a crisis of legitimacy. Neither the confidence nor the faith upon which legitimacy rests could be restored by a simple act of belief. What was needed was information, but information was not forthcoming. As early as 1920, some observers understood quite clearly what this meant. Morgan banker Harold Stanley said at the time, "Unless the bankers who sell the highest grade of securities give at least such information as an intelligent investor requires. . .the demand for this information may lead to a national registration plan of some kind which will oblige companies, issuing securities, to put on a public record information probably in greater detail than bankers or investors would ordinarily require."[31]

The further these issuing institutions rode the speculative boom and the more actively they piled assets on a shaky foundation of faith and credit, the less thoroughly they researched or acknowledged the underlying values of those assets. In short, the more outwardly successful they were, the more they appeared to their critics as little other than huge engines for the collection of fees, charges, and unearned profits. The great reorganization of the Insull utility empire early in 1929 into two super holding companies immediately gave the Insull family the then huge profit on paper of some $24 million.[32] This passed beyond mere stock watering to out-and-out inundation. Or, consider the central role played by the investment trusts in enticing small investors into the market for foreign bonds. By December 1931, the average market price for the bonds of fourteen Latin American nations had fallen to 26 percent of their face value; Peru's bonds had fallen to less than 7 percent.[33] As later events would show, the active merchandising of these securities had clearly been based on marketing decisions made without the careful analysis and reporting of value factors which prudence required. To the contrary, financial institutions often suppressed negative reports of the issuing country's likely ability to make good on its debts. The true appeal of these bonds had simply been to provide merchandise to generate the extraordinary fees they brought to issuing and distribution houses.

It was not only these new institutions and their opportunities for abuse that raised public concern. Instances were plentiful of insider trading and outright fraud across the spectrum of respectability, and "bucket shops" and "boiler rooms" still plied their trade with little concern for sanctions or opprobrium. There were few requirements for listing securities on the major exchanges, and there was great resistance to increasing or enforcing existing ones. Excessive profits were being made in securities-related businesses; and as the Gray-Pecora Senate hearings in 1933–34 made clear, not all the institutions and individuals making them were paying their fair share of taxes.[34] There were securities pools to manipulate markets in order artificially to inflate or deflate securities prices. There were preferred lists, through which investment houses rewarded their friends with certain profits on sweetheart deals. There was easy credit to fuel all this speculation and manipulation. When further stimulation of market activity was desired, stories were planted in the financial press to sing the praises of this or that security.

An industry that had been allowed by public trust to police itself revealed at last a structural inability to keep its own house in order. The problem lay not simply in the gross misconduct of some individuals. It extended to the very way in which the industry went about its business. If there was to be meaningful reform, it would have to be imposed from outside. What really needed changing was not so much a set of outdated practices as an attitude, a view of how things should operate, an understanding of what was acceptable and in the public interest.

Though it had grown impolitic to say so in public, the sentiments of Henry O. Havemeyer, head of the American Sugar Refining Company, more than ever characterized the attitude of the nation's industrial and financial stewards. Or so it seemed to their critics, especially after the market crash in 1929. Questioned by a member of the *ad hoc* Industrial Commission in 1899, Havemeyer denied that the public had any right to know the true earning power of organizations in which they might purchase stock. Said Havemeyer, "Let the buyer beware; that covers the whole business. You cannot wet-nurse people from the time they are born until the day they die....They have got to wade in and get stuck and that is the way men are educated and cultivated."[35]

If contemporaries had some difficulty in perceiving the momentous implications of the events unfolding around them, it was probably, as Alfred D. Chandler, Jr., has suggested, because of the unequal pace at which large-scale industry and government had evolved in the United States.[36] In Europe, the development of modern integrated firms and the managerial hierarchies needed to run them took place against the backdrop of a government structure that was itself already well advanced. In the United States, the situation was quite different. The first true appearance of Chandler's "visible hand" of managerialism occurred in the private sector, not the public. From the late nineteenth century until World War I, the sheer difference in scale between the major structures of business and the much more modest government apparatus for monitoring them effectively precluded any close or consistent regulation.

The tradition of reform out of which the Securities Act of 1933 emerged was thus in an important sense a response to the simple fact that, in historian Michael Parrish's neat summary, "Americans created a de facto national economy, capitalist in style and corporate in form, before they devised responsible institutions, public or private, which could govern that economy with a modicum of justice and foresight."[37] Not surprisingly, given this pattern of development, a major aspect of that reform tradition had to do with a deep and abiding suspicion of the great size of modern enterprise. Perhaps the most articulate spokesman for this view was Louis Brandeis, who challenged with force and spirit what he saw as the "curse of bigness" in the American economy. To Brandeis and his followers, the very fact of large-scale, concentrated enterprise was the cause of the economy's lack of equity and failure of performance.[38]

In the years leading up to the 1933 Act, this general attack on the "curse of bigness" found a ready target in the nation's system of high finance. According to Ellis Hawley, the Brandeis faction "knew how the investment bankers had first fastened their control upon American industry in the 1890s, how this control had been broadened and solidified through a vast network of interlocking directorates, gentlemen's agreements, and communities of interest, and how the bankers had come to dominate both the capital-supplying and capital-using institutions."[39]

Whatever the merit of their deep-seated fears of a conspiracy against the public interest among the big financial powers, the reformers did understand, if only indirectly, the nature and significance of the structural changes which had been unfolding in the American economy. If the economy were likened to an ocean-going ship, it is fair to say that, in earlier years, the internal sections of that ship had been set off from each other by an elaborate series of bulkheads and watertight compartments. A nation still predominantly rural and agricultural, still divided into distinct regions of business activity, was protected against the worst effects of economic calamity by the very degree to which its various clusters of enterprise were separate from each other. Damage in one quarter need not inevitably spill over into all others.

By the first years of the twentieth century, however, these bulkheads had begun to disappear at an increasing rate. Great advances in transportation, distribution, and communication, as well as in the horizontal and vertical scale of individual firms, ever more quickly replaced the old buffers of time, distance, inefficiency, and lack of coordination. Compared with the global financial markets of the 1980s or the electric power grids that are now designed to treat large sections of the country as a single interconnected unit, the early linkages were still quite rudimentary. Compared, however, with the historical experience of the 1800s, they represented a major shift in economic structure. Implied in Brandeis's attack on the "curse of bigness" was an appreciation, not yet fully developed, of the harm that could be done throughout an integrated economy by shoddy practice in any one sector of it.

NOTES

1. James M. Landis, "The Legislative History of the Securities Act of 1933," 28 *George Washington Law Review* 30 (1959).
2. U.S. Bureau of the Census, *Historical Statistics of the United States: Colonial Times to 1970*, series V 271–284, p. 940; U.S. Bureau of the Census, *Historical Statistics of the United States: Colonial Times to 1970, National Income and Wealth*, series F 31, p. 226.
3. Fifty-five percent growth was thus generated from 1901 to 1912, 60 percent from 1913 to 1922, 54.6 percent from 1923 to 1929, and virtually 100 percent from 1930 to 1939. Raymond W. Goldsmith, *Financial Intermediaries in the American Economy since 1900*, National Bureau of Economics Research (Princeton, N.J.: Princeton University Press, 1958), pp. 224–225.
4. Of external funds raised from 1913 to 1922, about equal proportions came from public issues of debt/equity, on the one hand, and various private external debt sources, including trade credit, bank loans, mortgages, and other accruals. During the period 1923–29, however, the amount of publicly issued debt and equity was three times as large as private external debt sources.
5. U.S. Bureau of the Census, *Historical Statistics of the United States: Colonial Times to 1970, Business Enterprise,* series V 108–140, p. 926.
6. U.S. Bureau of the Census, *Historical Statistics of the United States: Colonial Times to 1970, Business Enterprise,* series V 167–181, p. 928.
7. A historically extraordinary amount of savings was channeled into U.S. government securities during World War I: in 1917, $3.4 billion out of total personal savings of $9.4 billion; in 1918, $8.67 billion out of a total of $12.99 billion; and in 1919, $3.15 billion out of a total of $9.3 billion. U.S. Bureau of the Census, *Historical Statistics of the United States: Colonial Times to 1970, National Wealth and Savings,* series F 638–667, p. 267.
8. Ibid.
9. See, for example, Vincent P. Carosso, *Investment Banking in America* (Cambridge, Mass.: Harvard University Press, 1970), p. 248.
10. Gardiner C. Means, "The Diffusion of Stock Ownership in the United States," 44 *Quarterly Journal of Economics* 586–588 (August 1930).
11. U.S. Bureau of the Census, *Historical Statistics of the United States: Colonial Times to 1970, Government Employment and Finances,* series Y 412–439, p. 1111.
12. Means (see note 10) hypothesizes that these wealthy individuals also found alternative legal vehicles, such as holding companies, to increase their influence over corporate enterprises even as their actual equity holdings were declining.
13. Samuel L. Hayes, III, Michael Spence and David Marks, *Competition in the Investment Banking Industry* (Cambridge, Mass.: Harvard University Press, 1983), p. 11.
14. Means, "The Diffusion of Stock Ownership in the United States," pp. 565, 595.
15. Ibid.

16. See, for instance, Sheridan A. Logan, *George F. Baker and His Bank, 1840–1955* (Lunenburg, Vt.: The Stinehour Press, 1981), p. 156.
17. U.S. Bureau of the Census, *Historical Statistics of the United States: Colonial Times to 1970*, series X 580–587, p. 1019.
18. Ibid.
19. U.S. Bureau of the Census, *Historical Statistics of the United States: Colonial Times to 1970*, series X 731–740, p. 1036.
20. Carosso, *Investment Banking in America*, p. 242.
21. U.S. Treasury, *Annual Report*, 1929: p. 679; Carosso, *Investment Banking in America*, p. 242.
22. Carosso, *Investment Banking in America*, pp. 246–247.
23. Ibid., p. 68. See also Willard E. Atkins et al., *The Regulation of the Security Markets* (Washington, D.C.: Brookings Institution, 1946), p. 27.
24. Ibid., p. 260.
25. Vincent P. Carosso, *More Than a Century of Investment Banking* (New York: McGraw-Hill Book Company, 1979), p. 43ff.
26. Robert Valeur, "Foreign Investments in Germany and the Problem of Inter-Government Debts," *The Annals* 173 (July 1934): 32–33; Carosso, *Investment Banking in America*, p. 262.
27. Jules Bogen, "Changed Conditions in the Marketing of New Issues," *Journal of American Statistical Association*, 33 (March 1938): 32.
28. Paul P. Gourrich, "Investment Banking Methods Prior to and Since the Securities Act of 1933," 4 *Law and Contemporary Problems* 44, 52 (1937).
29. Ibid.
30. Michael E. Parrish, *Securities Regulation and the New Deal* (New Haven, Conn.: Yale University Press, 1970), pp. 32–33.
31. Ibid., p. 34.
32. Joel Seligman, *Transformation of Wall Street: A History of the Securities and Exchange Commission and Modern Corporate Finance* (Boston: Houghton Mifflin, 1982), p. 22.
33. Ibid., p. 10.
34. See, for example, Seligman, *Transformation of Wall Street*, chap. 1 passim.
35. Thomas K. McCraw, *Prophets of Regulation* (Cambridge, Mass.: Harvard University Press, 1984), p. 166.
36. Alfred D. Chandler, Jr., "Government vs. Business: An American Phenomenon," in *Business and Public Policy*, ed. John T. Dunlop (Boston: Division of Research, Harvard Business School, 1980), pp. 1–11.
37. Parrish, *Securities Regulation*, p. 3.
38. See the discussion of Brandeis in McCraw, *Prophets of Regulation*, chap. 3.
39. Ellis W. Hawley, *The New Deal and the Problem of Monopoly* (1966; reprint, Princeton, N.J.: Princeton University Press, 1969), p. 304.

3
Legislative History

The previous chapter has already chronicled how by the early 1930s the country had lost confidence in the financial system and the people who led it. The national election campaign in 1932 stressed issues not only of the banks and banking systems but of the entire financial system. The national political leadership promised to "fix" the myriad financial ills which beset the current system. The intent of the legislative strategy following the 1932 election was to set up a mechanism to regulate the evils, but in a manner unlike prior models of regulation, such as the Interstate Commerce Act, which even then had been in effect nearly fifty years.

HERITAGE AND OBJECTIVES

Administrative law, as distinguished from judicial proceedings, arose as a means of protecting aspects of the public interest not otherwise protected by the judicial system. For example, in an era that encouraged railroad expansion, a quasijudicial body, the Interstate Commerce Commission, was created to regulate that industry's private excesses, prevent public exploitation, and secure competition. The commission, however, was not envisioned solely as a limited-jurisdiction specialized court, dealing specifically and exclusively with railroad matters by adjudicating issues on an adversarial basis. Rather, while it was to function somewhat like a court in reaching an appealable decision that satisfied constitutional requirements of due process, the adjudicative body was to consist of a group of persons knowledgeable in the field, assisted by a permanent staff of experts; its mandate was to implement certain policies and standards established by Congress.

The very same decade—the 1880s—which saw the emergence of this sophisticated approach to regulation also produced the Sherman Act. The act was intended not to regulate a particular industry in the manner of the Interstate Commerce Act but to establish a public policy under which all industry would be monitored by the executive branch through the Attorney General. Not until the passage of the Clayton Act in 1914 was Congress to enlarge the scope of these initial antitrust concepts, and then, concurrently, establish another quasijudicial body—the Federal Trade Commission—to achieve public policy objectives. The FTC was created as a regulatory agency, analogous in many respects to the Interstate Commerce Commission, particularly in its combined administrative-judicial purpose, but it was more concerned with creating standards than with resolving disputes between adversaries.

However, this historical approach would not by itself remedy all of the perceived problems in capital-raising. The deposit-taking banks had not only been making conventional business and personal loans but, as was noted in Chapter 2, had also been increasingly active participants during the 1920s in underwriting syndicates. They had not been averse to utilizing their depositors' funds to back not only their securities underwriting commitments but also to engage in subsequent securities trading, sometimes with disastrous consequences. This free-wheeling banking activity was considered to have produced both unacceptable practices in issuance of securities as well as dangers to the safety of the public's savings. The problem was met by passage of special legislation—the Glass-Steagall Act, discussed later in this book. This act was written to separate what was regarded as essentially "commercial banking" (that is, deposit-taking and loan extension functions) from investment banking (that is, principally corporate securities-related activities).

This combination of regulation by prohibition (the Glass-Steagall Act) and regulation by information (the Securities Act of 1933), it was believed, would achieve a comprehensive overhaul of the procedures for the public issuance of securities and thus restore economic vitality and public support for the capital-raising mechanism.

The 1932 presidential election involved academics and professionals on a broad scale. In part they realized their personal stake in restoring the viability of the economic system. And they felt a combination of pride and conviction in their own intellectualism as a resource for solving economic and social problems. They responded enthusiastically to an urgent appeal by the newly elected president, Franklin D. Roosevelt, to bring their talents to bear on these problems. The process of gestation involved in creating a "brain trust," the satisfaction derived from serving in a "kitchen cabinet," and the accompanying direct and intimate access to the political decision makers were intoxicating. The desire to do one's best for one's country with a disregard for the trappings of public recognition and credit was not only wholly acceptable but, indeed, stimulated by the president's admonition that he sought players who did not disdain anonymity. Rejecting the earlier formula of absolute administrative regulation with quasijudicial sanctions, or absolute judicial regulation, these new players found their answer in a partial employment of the administrative agency function, but with a new approach to carrying it out.

Thus, they ultimately established an administrative formula that regarded "light" itself as regulation—a system of regulation by information. This regulatory concept having been formulated, the search for models after which the legislation could be patterned was less significant. The challenge facing the lawmakers in drafting the Securities Act was not, in the first instance, to lay out more tamper-resistant mechanisms of corporate finance. Traditional regulation could have achieved that easily, but at a price to the system's economic flexibility. The task was, rather, to devise a system for channeling capital into economic activity that was most likely to restore—and sustain—public confidence in the financial system itself,[1] while preventing a recurrence of the crisis that had made regulation necessary.

With this restoration of confidence would come a renewal of the system's badly shaken legitimacy; without the renewal of legitimacy, no flow of funds could reinvigorate the economy. Joseph P. Kennedy, first chairman of the SEC, made this point to the nation late in 1934. "We have two major objectives in our work," he said. "One is the advancement of protection of decent business; and the other—even more important—is spiritual, and I do not hesitate to employ that word in connection with finance. We are seeking to recreate, rebuild, restore confidence. . .we do not have to compel virtue; we seek to prevent vice. Our whole formula is to bar wrongdoers from operating under the aegis of those who feel a sense of ethical responsibility."[2]

Regulation by Information. By stressing the importance of legitimacy, we do not intend to support the extravagant argument, still heard in some quarters, that irresponsible financial dealing was the direct cause of the crash, which in turn was the direct cause of the depression. To the contrary, our intent is simply to underscore the key problem with which the drafters of the 1933 Act thought they had to wrestle—namely, a widespread loss of confidence in the financial system itself. To that task they brought a set of potent tactical innovations in administrative law and procedure. But they also brought a novel strategy with which to guide those tactics. To rebuild faith in the legitimacy of that system, they would expose its inner workings to intense public scrutiny by compelling the disclosure of material information about new securities. They would regulate the securities industry not by breaking it up or by promising to safeguard investors against the inevitable risks of capitalist enterprise, but by forcing it to disclose relevant information.[3]

Thus, the concept of regulation by information proposed by the Securities Act of 1933 was the solution to an example of what the historian Ellis Hawley has called the central dilemma of twentieth-century American reform: "the difficulty of reconciling a modern industrial order, necessarily based upon a high degree of collective organization, with democratic postulates, competitive ideals, and liberal individualistic traditions inherited from the nineteenth century."[4] With the economy in chaos, there were strident calls for national planning and public guarantees that new investments would be protected. With the self-interested doings of the nation's financial stewards a matter of record, there were equally insistent calls for dismantling, or at least radically trimming, the apparatus of high finance. In its approach to securities regulation, however, the 1933 Act resisted the allure both of statism, which beguiled so many other industrial economies during the 1930s, and of a nostalgic retreat into the nineteenth-century past of smaller-scale enterprise. By following a course of regulation by information, it denied neither democratic values nor the realities of a modern economy. Instead, it created the necessary incentives for each to serve the other.[5]

The Securities Act of 1933 was a prime instrument of a genuinely conservative revolution in the nation's system of finance. It was a ground-breaking novelty within the next year to have an established, specialized regulatory authority to oversee the securities industry, the Securities and Exchange Commission being created as part of the 1934 Act and replacing the Federal Trade Commission as the administrator of the 1933 Act. By contrast with parallel developments in the regulation of banking, for which there was ample precedent at both the state and federal levels, Michael Parrish has pointed out that "no fund of continuous, national administrative experience informed the original conception of federal securities regulation. No machinery comparable to the Federal Reserve served as a focus for reform and reorganization."[6] It is important to note that the reform effort did not aim at a root-and-branch upheaval in the process of floating new securities. Much as Thomas Reed Powell, a Harvard Law School colleague, said of Felix Frankfurter, the acknowledged intellectual mentor and sponsor of that effort, the Act merely tried "to make capitalism live up to its pretensions."[7]

It is important, however, to remember that the framers of the 1933 Act were not addressing a previously unknown set of difficulties only newly and suddenly thrust upon an investing public by the happenstance of a great economic crisis. They were—and consciously knew themselves to be—grappling with a thorny collection of issues that had been plaguing legislators and regulators since before the turn of the century. In no small measure, their allegiance to the idea of a federal regulatory effort based on the principle of letting in the light grew out of their analysis of why and how past efforts had failed. To see more clearly what they were trying to do in the 1933 Act, let us look briefly at the body of historical experience of which they themselves were aware.

Blue Sky Laws.   What they saw, first of all, was a crazy quilt of "blue sky" legislation at the state level, a morass of legal theory, parochial interest, and administrative practice. With the intent of protecting local investors from the worst excesses of shady operators, various state legislatures had followed the example of Kansas, which in 1911 had passed a measure to regulate the in-state sale of securities by out-of-state issuers.[8] Under the federal system, each state could protect its own residents, but no state could extend the thrust of its legislation to the residents of any other state. To some extent, support for this local protective regulation came from in-state dealers and businessmen who wanted to shield themselves from potential competition for clients and investment dollars. In general, though, the blue sky laws were a perfectly understandable response, in the absence of any federal regulation, to a long list of abuses and the resulting loud public cries for protection. Whatever the soundness of its motives, however, the blue sky method of regulation proved inconsistent, inadequate, and impossible to administer.

Some states attacked their problem by regulating the process by which out-of-state securities were approved for sale—a kind of registration procedure. This and other techniques, sometimes in combination, took a wide variety of forms: regulation of the dealers who sold securities; determination of the investment value of the securities themselves; disclosure of information about the solvency and business prospects of the issuer; insistence on guarantees that the investment would retain its value; and a definition of fraud based on misrepresentation of fact. In practice, each blue sky state developed its idiosyncratic mix of these approaches. Neighboring states, deemed more important centers of finance, were tempted to be more sophisticated in their regulatory schemes. To a major corporation (and its investment banker) seeking funds on a national basis, the resulting checkerboard of laws and regulations yielded a procedural nightmare. To an investor, it meant that even certain high-grade securities might not be available at all, or only through such subterfuge as claiming a fictitious residence. For an unscrupulous operator the analogy to the bootlegger of the 1920s is apparent; it simply multiplied the chances for success.

To make matters even more complicated, each state would draw up its own list of categories of securities that were to be exempt from such regulation and then would usually leave the relevant judgments in individual cases to political appointees who were, if honest, overworked and understaffed, and if not, were easy targets for bribery and favoritism. To the president of the Cleveland Bar Association, for example, the Ohio statute was a "welter of exceptions and definitions. . .a piece of dictionary gone mad." With a law so badly drawn and an administrative system so poorly designed, regulation was little more than a "matter of expediency and a battle ground between the selfishness of the bureaucrat and the selfishness of the security dealer." In such an environment, "no precedents will be established. One administrator will succeed another and the lawyer will continue in the dark."[9]

Proposals for National Oversight. When the framers of the 1933 Act looked beyond these blue sky laws to the many abortive proposals for federal legislation, what they found was an equally unresolved set of ideas. Some proposals favored relying on simple antifraud statutes. Others were based on such concepts as the licensing of securities or dealers or both, the use of federal postal laws to prevent abuses, the after-the-fact punishment of those who had foisted bad securities on the public, and the federal enforcement of state laws. Indeed, in this body of legislative suggestions there was no general agreement on the proper object, timing, or mechanism of securities regulation, no agreement on the sanctions to be employed, no consensus on the role of the federal government. Much like the blue sky laws, these proposals did little more than sketch out a variety of competing approaches, without ever making clear the standard by which the best approach could be chosen.

Nor could sound guidance be found in the positions taken by the relevant professional organizations of the time. The Investment Bankers Association (IBA), created in 1912, was not able to overcome the local and regional differences among its members during its first two decades sufficiently to adopt and support a consistent policy on regulatory matters. To the extent that it tried, it opposed licensing statutes at the state level, pushing instead for the application of antifraud laws and then throwing its weight behind the idea of federal action based on Great Britain's Companies Act. When an improving economy and the growing belief that the states could be induced to rethink their blue sky laws made federal intervention less attractive, the IBA backed off, eventually working to defeat such legislation in Congress.[10]

Less helpful and even more obstructionist were the stock exchanges themselves, especially the New York Stock Exchange (NYSE), private organizations to which the states had allowed an immense and unprecedented grant of de facto authority to regulate securities in the public interest. Bound by few rules but their own, the exchanges gave way grudgingly to increasing public demands for tighter listing and issuance requirements and for prohibitions on the lucrative but frequently shady dealings—the bear raids, the pools, the inside trading—by which it seemed to many observers that a self-perpetuating financial elite kept itself in funds. One of the great spectacles of the 1920s and early 1930s was the NYSE's president, Richard Whitney, stoutly rejecting all pleas for remedial action, even from the White House, until he was forced to make small concessions by the direct threat of legislative intervention. In Whitney's view, the NYSE was "a perfect institution."[11] Others were not quite so sure. William O. Douglas, speaking as chairman of the SEC, called the NYSE a "private club" with "elements of a casino."[12] From his august perch, however, Whitney blandly denied the existence of bear raids, dismissed the market effects of short sales, and held off as long as possible the relentless external pressure for change—what *Business Week* called the "political need for a burnt offering."[13]

Arrayed before the framers of the 1933 Act was this panorama not only of institutional failure and legislative vacuum but also of the political realities of the first months of the New Deal. In his speech accepting the Democratic party nomination, Roosevelt had promised to pursue a strategy of letting in the light. Influenced by the thinking of Louis Brandeis and his followers, Roosevelt saw a genuine threat to the inviolability of private property in the degree to which a small group of powerful financial interests were dominating the nation's economy and manipulating the value of securities in the stock market. During an August 20, 1932, speech at Columbus, Ohio, for example, FDR called upon the government to "counterbalance this power" and "protect private property from ruthless manipulation in the stock market and corporate system."[14] For Roosevelt, then, there was little doubt that the federal government did have a significant role to play in regulating the securities markets, a counterbalancing role designed to offset the exercise of power concentrated in private hands.

Against more extensive calls for government action, however, Roosevelt drew the line. Washington could not—and should not—try to guarantee the soundness of individual investment decisions or safeguard investors against the possibility of loss. What it could do was make certain that potential investors had available to them all relevant information. It could also put a stop to the State Department's controversial practice, already the target of strong criticism from Carter Glass and Hiram Johnson in the Senate, of informally approving the sale to domestic investors of the debt instruments of foreign governments. As the value of these instruments plummeted, it became obvious that the State Department's implied endorsements were badly misleading the public. There must be an end, Roosevelt argued, to "international bankers and others [selling] foreign securities. . .on the implied understanding that these securities have been passed on or approved by the State Department or any other agency of the Federal Government."[15]

Underlying these calls for a change of policy early in the New Deal and for a system of regulation able to defend the public against the kind of operator FDR stigmatized as "the reckless promoter, the Ishmael or Insull whose hand is against every man's,"[16] there ran a deeper, unifying concern. It was not just that Roosevelt and his advisers believed that unscrupulous wheeler-dealers had found new ways to fleece the public or that the government had unintentionally lent credibility to some of their efforts, troubling as all this was. It was not just that the unequal concentration of power over economic matters could no longer be quietly accepted. Nor was it that easy credit had exacerbated the financial system's impulse toward less and less responsible modes of speculation.

The concern was that the system increasingly appeared to serve not the legitimate and essential end of funneling capital to needy productive enterprise, but, rather, the artificial objective of creating and distributing securities as an end in itself, without regard for social considerations. In their view the only purpose of this objective lay in raking off fat profits from the transactions thus created. Much as an unethical securities broker may churn an individual client's account simply to generate commissions, so the nation's financial nexus seemed more and more a giant churn that produced little of social value—unless lining the pockets of promoters and middlemen was deemed desirable. As Roosevelt insisted during his Columbus speech, "Every effort [will] be made to prevent the issue of manufactured and unnecessary securities of all kinds which are brought out merely for the purpose of enriching those who handle their sale to the public."[17]

STRUCTURE AND PHILOSOPHY OF THE LEGISLATION

A close reading of contemporary practice and historical background led the framers of the 1933 Act to seek to restore legitimacy to the nation's financial system by mounting a two-pronged assault: first, on the traditional reluctance of the securities industry to disclose relevant information in a timely fashion; and second, on those recent changes in the industry's structure that made relevant and timely information ever harder to come by at a time when that need was becoming ever more urgent. Thus the strategy of regulation by information had a double objective: to provide the necessary incentives, individual as well as institutional, for adequate disclosure; and to provide the appropriate link between those incentives and the evolving patterns of business needs and financing resources.

Framing the Securities Act of 1933. What arose out of these concerns and the weighing of various means of dealing with them was the filing of legislation which, in its final form, became the Securities Act of 1933.

The 1933 Act never involved the panoply of reforms that emerged a year later as the Securities Exchange Act of 1934. The 1933 Act had only one objective: to set down the rules by which an issuer could sell new securities to the public. In essence, it directed that when an issuer or related person sold securities, the sale had to be accompanied by a publicly filed sales document, or prospectus, laying out, in accordance with government specifications, all of the information deemed material to an investor's decision to purchase.[18]

The 1933 Act established civil liabilities in the event of a false sales document. It is here that the technique of regulation by disclosure came into full flower in the act's wording: "In case any part of the registration statement. . .contained an untrue statement of a material fact or omitted to state a material fact required to be stated therein or necessary to make the statements therein not misleading, any person acquiring such security" may sue those responsible. The latter were defined as including: every person who signed the registration statement; every director of or partner in the issuer; every accountant, engineer, appraiser, or other expert who consented to being named in the registration statement; and every underwriter of the security.[19]

In all events under section 11 of the 1933 Act, the *issuer* would be unconditionally liable for any misstatement or omission. The securities underwriters would be conditionally liable, unless it could be shown that they had exercised the necessary care in their own independent review— that is, that they had conducted a "reasonable investigation"—and could thus be excused from any liability or penalty.[20] The requirement of section 11 for a "reasonable investigation" became known colloquially as the "due diligence" provision.

It is important to note that the 1933 Act rejected the concept contained in a number of the blue sky laws formulated earlier by various states which required a public agency to pass on the *quality* of the security or its issuer. Rather, it limited itself to ensuring a thorough exposure of the facts material to an investment decision, and left it to the investor to draw appropriate conclusions.

Thus, this reform legislation was essentially limited to establishing the concept of regulation by information that had become a central part of the philosophy of the New Deal's brain trust. It was coupled with sanctions rejecting the common law concept of *caveat emptor* in all securities dealings, reversing the principle to "let the seller [not the buyer] beware." The seller was to be bound by the information disclosed, or which should have been disclosed, rather than what the buyer asked or failed to ask.

This philosophical approach sought to ensure that a party involved in the issuance, such as an underwriter, would undertake "reasonable investigation," or be responsible for its absence, on behalf of the investor, who would not, therefore, need be unduly cautious.[21] The buyer of publicly offered securities no longer had to fear the seller's possible puffing, exaggerations, omissions, or untruths. Moreover, since the crux of disclosure under the act was to be the "reasonable investigation" by persons *other* than the issuer, the buyer could rely on those persons as well as the issuer for protection and responsibility.

The history of the act reveals no narrow definition of what constitutes "reasonable investigation." In his message to Congress seeking the legislation, President Roosevelt stated a public purpose that clearly involved fiduciary concepts: "What we seek is a return to a clearer understanding of the ancient truth that those who manage banks, corporations and other agencies handling or using other people's money are trustees acting for others."[22]

The Effective Date. In its original enactment, the Securities Act provided that the "effective date of a registration statement shall be the twentieth day after the filing thereof."[23] Since this provision obviously permitted no flexibility to account for differences among issuers, issues, and varying kinds of "reasonable investigation" which might be required by underwriters, the section was amended in 1940 to give the commission authority to shorten the period, "having due regard to the adequacy of the information respecting the issuer theretofore available to the public and to the public interest and the protection of investors."[24]

In the House debate on the 1940 amendment to the Securities Act, the following colloquy, led by Sam Rayburn, who in 1933 had been the House manager of the legislative process leading to the Securities Act, occurred:

> Mr. Speaker, there is no clause in the Securities Act, as Members of the House who were here at the time it was passed will recall, that caused more controversy than this one thing and there was no abuse in the country that was more necessary to correct than that which we sought to correct by this 20-day clause. And may I say to the gentleman from Illinois that this is not a repeal of the 20-day clause. That clause remains in the statute. This simply gives the Commission authority to relax the 20-day clause if, under the circumstances, they think it wise and in the public interest to do so. I am certain that the Committee on Interstate and Foreign Commerce would not at this time recommend the repeal of the clause, but they are acting in this capacity simply to give the Commission authority to relax the rigidity of the clause.

Mr. Cole of Maryland: Mr. Speaker, the gentleman is correct.

Mr. Sabath of Illinois: This gives the Commission that power, and naturally they will use the power whenever they feel that conditions warrant it, and I hope it will not be abused by the Commission. I have the utmost confidence in the Commission today.[25]

It is not clear from the legislative history why such a delay in the effective date was considered necessary. The issuer as a practical matter files a registration statement only when it is satisfied with the content and is willing to accept financial responsibility for it. None of the legislation that predated the Securities Act established a public policy need for a delay in the registration's legal effectiveness after its filing. Yet the law without reference to concept or precedent insisted on barring the commencement of the public offering until after a required incubation period. This delay provision may have been inserted because Congress considered that persons other than the issuer (primarily the underwriters) might need time to review the registration statement prior to its becoming effective.

The significance of requiring time for reasonable investigation of the registration statement by someone finds a counterpart in two of the concepts underlying the Securities Act: first, that the government is not responsible in any way for the truth of the registration statement and indeed not required to make any investigation of its content; and second, that the burden of material accuracy falls entirely on those whom the law makes liable for failure of adequate disclosure. Congress's concern both in 1933 and 1940 seems to have been that since the government was not making an investigation, time for others to do so was essential.

"Due Diligence" as a Fiduciary Concept. If "due diligence," as construed by the commission and the securities industry a half-century later in the context of deregulation, is not understood to embody fiduciary values, then there is a significant danger that the purpose of the required "reasonable investigation" is apt to be obscured. Interestingly, the word *diligence* (or the phrase "due diligence") does not even appear in the operative regulatory sections of the Secu-

rities Act.[26] Provisions of the act that apply to the definition of an underwriter, the prohibitions against the offering or sale of unregistered securities, the registration requirement, the required basic information in the statement, the effectiveness of the statement, the required content of the prospectus, and civil liabilities on account of falsity in the statement nowhere contain the word *diligence* or make any reference to it.[27]

The only specific use of the word *diligence* in the Securities Act occurs in a context wholly unrelated to the burden in the legislative scheme of the provisions relating to disclosure, investigation, and penalty. The reference appears in a section which provides a period of limitations on bringing suit for a violation.[28] That is, it prescribes the period during which an injured purchaser must pursue civil liability rights against a seller under the act or forfeit the possibility. This period is set at one year (originally two years) after the discovery of the untrue statement or omission, or after such discovery of the failure of disclosure would have been made if "reasonable diligence" had been exercised.[29]

Since Congress knowingly prescribed diligence as an essential element in placing a burden of timely action on the victim of the violation, why did it not employ the same locution to satisfy the test of reasonable investigation so that persons other than an issuer could avoid legal liability for violation? Can one infer that this difference in language between sections dealing with statutory violations was intended? The answer must lie in the legislative history of the Securities Act and clearly depends on interpretation, since the debates as well as the statute provide no direct information.

The accepted dictionary definition of *diligence* at the time of the original enactment of the Securities Act was "the attention and care required of a person in a given situation."[30] Diligence was considered the opposite of negligence. For diligence to be "due" (that is, adequate), it must be capable of satisfying an obligation or requirement; it should be of a nature appropriate to the need.[31]

We can infer from the legislative history that it was not the objective of the drafters of the Securities Act merely to require observance of a standard embodying this definition of due diligence. The context in which Congress was acting had a bearing on the failure to employ such a familiar phrase. In 1933 the federal government was wandering into hitherto virgin territory, and the drafters were fully aware (as demonstrated by the debates) that they were encroaching on the presumed constitutional rights of the states. Particularly among the states involved in securities and commercial matters, we have already noted that the blue sky laws, with the universal intention of preventing fraud, took on all shapes and forms. Congress, however, favored federal rights enforceable in federal courts precisely because the blue sky laws neither crossed state boundaries nor established sufficient protection against fraud for the buyer of securities. We can assume, then, that Congress intended to adopt a legal standard to which the required reasonable investigation of the statutory scheme would specifically relate for determination of compliance or violation.

The House version (H.R. 5480) of the Securities Act was submitted by Sam Rayburn of Texas on May 4, 1933, on behalf of the Committee on Interstate and Foreign Commerce.[32] He paraphrased the aims set forth by the president's message. The bill was, he said: "A demand that the persons, whether they be directors, experts, or underwriters who sponsor the investment of other people's money should be held up to the high standards of trusteeship."[33] Rayburn proceeded to define what he meant by those words: "Honesty, care, and competence are the demands of trusteeship. These demands are made by the bill on the directors of the issuer, its experts and the underwriters who sponsor the issue."[34] In describing the scope of the bill to the House, Rayburn said, "The underwriters of the offering, are jointly and severally liable to any buyer for rescission of any sale or for damages, if the registration statement. . .is false or misleading and the defendant *cannot prove both that he did not know and by the exercise of due care could not have known* of such false or misleading character."[35]

As we previously noted, when Rayburn spoke in 1940 in favor of the amendment to authorize the commission's discretion to shorten the twenty-day incubation period for effectiveness of the registration statement, he stressed the significance given the delay provision by Congress in 1933. Rayburn had described the pertinent clause to the House as follows: "The compulsory [then thirty-day] inspection period. . .is deliberately intended to interfere with the reckless traditions of the last few years of the securities business. It contemplates a change from methods of distribution lately in vogue which attempted complete sale of an issue *sometimes within one day or at most a few days. . . .*This has resulted in the demoralization of ethical standards as between these ultimate sales outlets and the securities-buying public."[36]

Without employing the word *diligence* at any point, but frequently referring to "care," Rayburn summarized the intent of the then existing version of section 11 of the 1933 Act, saying that it would permit recovery from "those who have participated in such distribution" and have "failed to take due care in discovering" an untrue statement or omission. He repeated the phrase "due care" by saying that "all who sell securities. . .who cannot prove that they did not know—or who in the exercise of due care could not have known. . .of such misstatement or omission, are liable." The effect of these provisions, he stressed, was that "this throws upon originators of securities a *duty of competence as well as innocence.*"[37] This language would appear now, and must have been understood then, to be "trustee talk"—meaning that it called for prudence rather than simple diligence.

Indeed, unlike Rayburn's comments, the debate on the bill in the House did see a number of specific references to diligence in the context of section 11 by members of both parties. Representative Mapes of Michigan, spokesman for the minority on the bill, referred to the provision that directors of an issuer would not be liable "if they can show the exercise of good faith and reasonable diligence."[38] In affirming that a purchaser should be entitled to the return of a misrepresented security's purchase price, Mapes was unwilling even to make an exception for the director who, "in the exercise of due diligence, did not know the statement of fact to be untrue."[39]

Representative Parker of New York was of a different view. "Send them [the directors] to jail if the misstatement is willful. But if it is a statement founded on a mistake made by somebody else after the use of due diligence, I do not believe they should be held personally responsible. "[40] At a later point, Parker enlarged on his reference to diligence: "When you make a man liable for a misstatement when he has employed the very best accountants he can get, the very best engineers he can get, and then he sits in his office with the board of directors and they go over these figures *and use the utmost diligence* in setting forth what is correct, I believe they should. . .not be held."[41]

Representative Chapman of Kentucky also used the word *diligence* in the debate, but in a manner that seems clearly to lean toward Rayburn's trustee or fiduciary interpretation of the intent of section 11, by specifically referring to prudence: "The burden of proof is placed upon [the directors] to show that after the exercise of *the degree of diligence expected of reasonably prudent men* they 'had reasonable ground to believe and did believe.' "[42]

The House and Senate in due course adopted different versions of the Securities Act; they were particularly far apart in their concept of personal liability. Both bills referred to "care" rather than "diligence." The Senate bill imposed liability on the issuer, its directors, its chief executive officer, and its chief financial officer "*without regard* to whatever care they may have used for the accuracy of the statements made in the registration statement."[43] The House bill, by contrast, "measured liability for these [registration] statements in terms of reasonable care, placing upon defendants [other than the issuer] the duty. . .of proving that they had used reasonable care to assure the accuracy of these statements."[44]

After conference, the Senate accepted the standards imposed by the House bill, and Rayburn reported to the House in connection with final passage of the bill that "the standard by which reasonable care was exemplified was expressed in terms of a fiduciary relationship. A fiduciary under the law is bound to exercise diligence of a type commensurate with the confidence, both as to integrity and competence, that is placed in him."[45]

This statement appears to contain the only reference to diligence Rayburn made in managing enactment of the Securities Act. Even as used, it relates specifically to reasonable investigation only in the context of describing the nature of a trustee's obligation under common law. Rayburn's stress on the fiduciary relationship was not inadvertent. He referred again and again during the legislative history of the Securities Act to what he considered to be the trusteelike function implicit in the public sale of securities. Diligence in the legislative history, based upon Rayburn's references as the bill's manager, seems clearly intended to mean the diligence incumbent upon a trustee, and was not employed as a dictionary antonym to negligence.

Rayburn's further statements regarding the fiduciary relationship indicate that he was not thinking simply in terms of the procedures and standards of the prototypical common law trustee–beneficiary relationship familiar from nineteenth century English novels involving the peculations of the family solicitor or the recluse uncle. Rather he had in mind the sophisticated process carried out both by individuals and through banks, as professional trustees. He said: "This does not, of course necessitate that. . .[the fiduciary] shall individually perform every duty imposed upon him. Delegation to others of the performance of acts which it is unreasonable to require that the fiduciary shall personally perform is permissible. Especially is this true where the character of the acts involves professional skill or facilities not possessed by the fiduciary himself."[46]

Diligence and the Securities Exchange Act of 1934.   The significance of Rayburn's views expressed in the spring of 1933 as to the intent of section 11 of the Securities Act was emphasized the following year when, together with Senator Fletcher, he became a sponsor of what was subsequently enacted as the Securities Exchange Act of 1934 (and then generally referred to as the Fletcher-Rayburn Bill).[47]   The

1934 Act was designed to complete a regulatory scheme of which the 1933 Act was a foundation.

In a message to Congress dated February 9, 1934, President Roosevelt stated:

> In my message to you last March proposing legislation for Federal supervision of national traffic in investment securities I said: "This is but one step in our broad purpose of protecting investors and depositors. It should be followed by legislation relating to the better supervision of the purchase and sale of all property dealt with on exchanges."
>
> This Congress has performed a useful service in regulating the investment business on the part of financial houses and in protecting the investing public in its acquisition of securities.
>
> There remains the fact, however, that outside the field of legitimate investment naked speculation has been made far too alluring.[48]

The 1934 Act was passed June 6, 1934. Section 18(a) contained a conceptual parallel to section 11 of the Securities Act, providing with regard to any statement in reports and documents filed under the 1934 Act (such filing being the essence of its statutory scheme) that if the "statement was at the time and in the light of the circumstances under which it was made false or misleading with respect to any material fact[the maker of the statement] shall be liable. . .unless [the maker] shall prove that he acted in good faith and had no knowledge that such statement was false or misleading."[49]

Again, as in the case of the 1933 Act, there were differences between the House and the Senate versions of the proposed 1934 Act. The phrase "acted in good faith" appears, as noted above, in the final bill, whereas the original proposal provided for a test of "the exercise of reasonable care."[50] The debate, however, does not appear to have involved the use of the word *diligence.*

The 1933 Act and the Fiduciary Concept. A rich source of information concerning the concepts of disclosure and diligence can be found in Title II of the 1934 Act, which became the vehicle for concurrently amending the Securities Act and creating the Securities and Exchange Commission. In a letter dated May 2, 1934 (introduced by Senator Fletcher into the *Congressional Record*), James M. Landis, then commissioner of the Federal Trade Commission (which administered the 1933 Act until the 1934 Act created the SEC), wrote regarding proposed amendments to the Securities Act:

> The present section 11(c) fixes as the standard of reasonableness the standard required of a person occupying "a fiduciary relationship." This definition has apparently created considerable consternation, and I would be agreeable to a change which would state the meaning of a fiduciary relationship in commonly accepted legal terminology. I do not, however, believe that a definition of the standard of reasonableness as a fiduciary standard should be omitted from this section of the Act.[51]

Rayburn and Fletcher explained to their respective chambers the effect and intent of the amendments to the 1933 Act being proposed in Title II of the 1934 Act legislation as follows:

> *Rayburn:* The amendment to section 11(c) removes possible uncertainties as to the standard of reasonableness by substituting for the present language the accepted common law definition of the duty of a fiduciary.
> *Fletcher:* The term "fiduciary relationship" has been terrifyingly portrayed. The amendment substitutes for that language the accepted common law definition of the duty of a fiduciary.[52]

As enacted, the 1934 amendment to section 11(c) of the 1933 Act provided that the standard for determining what constitutes reasonable investigation and reasonable ground for belief "shall be that required of a prudent man in the management of his own property," rather than a standard defined as "that required of a person occupying a fiduciary relationship."[53]

The specific adoption of a "prudent man" test was foreshadowed by Rayburn the year before in explaining the Securities Act conference report to the House, when he said that a "fiduciary under the law is bound to exercise diligence of a type commensurate with the confidence, both as to integrity and competence, that is placed in him."[54] In specifically adopting the prudent man test, as both of the managers of the bill noted, Congress was accepting a basic common law concept. The standard of the prudent man was wholly a development of common-law trust law, later incorporated in various forms in statutes. In *Harvard College* v. *Amory*[55] (still the leading case after 150 years and generally identified as establishing the prudent man rule), the court prescribed as the test for a trustee's stewardship "how men of prudence, discretion and intelligence manage their own affairs. . .in regard to the permanent disposition of their funds."[56] *King* v. *Talbot*[57] states that "the trustee is bound to employ such diligence and such prudence. . .as in general, prudent men of discretion and intelligence in such matters employ in their own like affairs."[58]

According to Professor Austin W. Scott in his monumental treatise on trusts, the prudent man rule "involves three elements, namely care and skill and caution."[59] In the American Law Institute's 1959 summary of recommended trust law, the governing principle is what "a prudent man would make of his own property, having in view the preservation of the estate and the amount and regularity of the income to be derived."[60] In its 1958 summary of recommended agency law, the Institute refers to the responsibility required in securities matters from an agent as that of a "prudent investor for his own account, having in view both safety and income, in light of the principal's means and purposes."[61]

Scott and other authorities all draw essentially on the 1830 *Harvard College* case for their prudent man rationale, and subsequent judicial interpretations remain consistent with its holding. Accordingly, it appears reasonable to infer that the Securities Act provision of a prudent man test was similarly relying on *Harvard College*, first by requiring in 1933 that the standard of reasonableness be that which characterizes a fiduciary relationship, and then in the 1934 amendment by invoking the prudent man rule to define the fiduciary standard.

The prudent man test of section 11 of the Securities Act is not an isolated example of congressional reference where the Securities and Exchange Commission is involved. Section

315(c) of the Trust Indenture Act of 1939,[62] also administered by the commission, provided that the indenture must contain a provision requiring the indenture trustee in the event of a default "to use the same degree of care and skill in [his] exercise [of the trustee's rights and powers], as a prudent man would exercise or use under the circumstances in the conduct of his own affairs."[63] In explaining the bill to the Senate, Senator Alben W. Barkley noted that the "standard provided for is substantially the same as that which is applicable in the field of personal trusts."[64]

DISCLOSURE AND MARKETS EVALUATION

Together, the framers and their colleagues possessed a rich enough understanding of how the industry worked to know what the legislation must demand of it. And they also possessed a clear enough vision of where the industry seemed to be headed to know the likely side effects of those demands. They noted the tendency during the late 1920s to capitalize on the increased speed of syndicate operations in order to reduce the costs of flotation to issuers. And the primary documents associated with the 1933 Act—the private letters and papers of the framers, the legislative record of hearings and reports, the issues raised and debated in the press—all reaffirm the fear that the pursuit of efficiency would come at the expense of information. Efficiency-related issues surfaced most often in the worries of those opposed to the act, who feared—or at least purported to fear—the act's potentially depressing effect on the flow of new capital to industry.[65] As matters turned out, later amendments and a good record of performance by the SEC were required to overcome these fears and to stimulate the flow of capital. Even in hindsight, however, it is by no means clear whether the sharp drop in underwriting volume that followed the 1933 Act was a result of the generally depressed economic environment or of an intentional effort by many in the securities industry to boycott unwelcome legislation.

What is clear is that, fairly soon after the passage of the 1933 Act, the savings to issuers in underwriting and distribution costs outdistanced the higher costs associated with registration—that is, the expenses of gathering and presenting full information. As the senior financial economist of the SEC reported in 1937, "It is very likely that the publicity provisions of the Securities Act and the general influence of the work of the Commission have reduced the costs of underwriting and other forms of distribution to a degree more than sufficient to offset completely any additional expenditures caused through registration."[66] Underwriting spreads on bond flotations came down fairly steadily after the act went into effect.[67]

Of interest here, however, is not the possible inference that the framers were preoccupied with reducing the costs of flotation, that is, those expenses associated with an underwritten public offering of securities. There is nothing to indicate that they were seeking to boost efficiency in such offerings. To the contrary, as late as 1937, officials of the SEC still felt the need to argue publicly that the 1933 Act had not, as many critics had expected, *driven costs up*. No doubt it was a happy development that the new registration requirements did not in practice lead to the feared explosion of costs. It must also have pleased both framers and SEC officials alike to see how relatively painless it was for industry to absorb the expenses of disclosure. Similarly, the shifting of costs from high-powered salesmanship to careful presentation of information must also have struck them as a change for the better. Even so, it does not appear from the record that the calculation of costs or expenses took the attention of the framers of the 1933 Act, one way or the other. Important as they were pragmatically, such calculations or questions simply did not figure prominently in the public policy objectives behind the drafting of the act or in the congressional debate over its passage.

We have distinguished between interpretations based on efficiency and interpretations based on the restoration of legitimacy and public confidence for two particular reasons. First, it appears that the arguments based on efficiency as a historical foundation for the 1933 Act are in error. Second, such arguments necessarily overlook a most important part of the analysis on which the concept of the act rested. Given the historical experience of the securities industry during the 1920s and early 1930s, the growing speed and falling cost of flotations—the industry's efficiency—provided suggestive evidence to those who were looking for it, of an industry in the process of maturing. By the early 1930s, an ample body of antitrust sentiment existed, with which the framers of the 1933 Act were certainly familiar and presumably largely in sympathy, and it was out of this body of analysis and precedent—*not* out of the thought associated with laissez-faire capitalism—that the financial regulation of the New Deal emerged. The allegiances, intellectual and emotional, of the framers lay with those who questioned the value of bigness in corporate enterprise, who harbored suspicions of undue concentration of economic power, or who feared the ill effects of combination.

As previously pointed out, Alfred Chandler has described how genuinely large-scale enterprise in America grew, in the first instance, out of burgeoning market demand and the ability to serve that demand through coordinated systems of distribution.[68] Similarly, mastery of production at such levels of volume demanded, over time, an unprecedented ability to control in-house the regular flow of raw materials and goods at various stages of completion. The "rise of managerialism," as Chandler calls it, occurred in direct response to this dual need for coordination and control, much as business organizations themselves sought more effective modes of combination, first through horizontal integration and the trust structure, which the courts and Congress opposed, and then through tighter vertical integration in the chains of supply and distribution. Taken together, these developments in managerial systems and organizational structures were both the result of and a spur to the efficiency made possible by volume and large-scale operation.

It takes no great effort of imagination to recognize the applicability of this general pattern to the evolution of the securities industry. The changes in syndicate structure and operation during the late nineteenth century and the first three decades of the twentieth century, changes which came to a head in the remarkable explosion of demand and the equally remarkable acceleration in the speed of flotations in the years just before the crash, were every bit as much the embodiment of volume and efficiency as was Henry Ford's justly famous Rouge River complex.[69] And just as the Rouge was dedicated to the overriding proposition of "getting metal out the door," so the work of syndicates was dedicated ever more clearly to the production and distribution of corporate paper. Ford, however, had built his system to ensure quality as well as efficiency; the syndicates had not.

More to the point, Ford had also learned—and learned the hard way—that an organization designed to maximize scale economies and ride volume for all it was worth has distinctive vulnerabilities. As later research has shown, volume-driven operations inevitably push vertical integration to its limits, require the standardization of both product and process, and sacrifice flexibility for speed and efficiency.[70] Put another way, the tendency of an industry driven by considerations of volume is toward concentration, low margins, and the transformation of its product into a commodity. Especially during the feverish speculation of the 1920s, the pressure on the securities industry to maximize volume and to put new corporate paper quickly into distribution had much this kind of an effect. To meet the clamorous demand for product, industry leaders followed a course of action that tended to make their product more of a commodity and, at the same time, to extend their control over the vertical chain—in other words, to push their industry toward maturity.

Thus, one of the most significant results of the 1933 Act was the impact of its strategy of regulation by information on the impulse toward maturity. As is clearly apparent, by forcing a slowing down of the syndication process, and by requiring the disclosure of relevant information, the act worked directly to counter that impulse. Moreover, in terms of the industry's product, the act helped to reverse the movement toward commodity status by requiring, in effect, a kind of product diversification through information. No longer would the irresistible pressures of speed be allowed to blur the differences in the investment quality of various securities.

No longer would the need to keep the pipeline filled be allowed to turn the securities of American companies into simply a fungible commodity.

Those who have argued for the commoditylike status of security offerings ignore the act's true heritage and throw away the most valuable defense the industry has had over the years to charges of unfair monopolistic practice. Judge Harold Medina's decision in *U.S.* v. *Morgan*,[71] which dismissed the government's antitrust case against seventeen major investment banking firms, reasoned that because the flotation of a security issue was so complex, the process was not a standardized "it" that a few banking houses could monopolize. And because each issue was unique, bankers competed not by offering a commoditylike package of services at the lowest price, but instead by trying to "establish or continue a relationship with the issuer," based on past performance, current reputation, and faithful adherence to the industry's informal code of conduct.

As a result, when speaking of competitors, "nothing but confusion will follow unless we first determine what is the 'it' for which the competitors are supposed to be competing. Put simply, Medina saw the industry pyramid as embodying a considerable amount of competitive activity because the "single, entire, unitary transaction" involved in a major underwriting is really the sum of many different banking services.[72]

Competition that offered the consumer a choice among diverse products, not the production of indistinguishable if cheap commodities: This was the thrust of the 1933 Act. Volume and, along with it, some abstract measure of efficiency might be sacrificed, of course, but investor confidence would be restored. After all, to the framers of the act, legitimacy and not efficiency was what really mattered. Regulation by information in the securities sector works against commodity concepts and promotes confidence, and it has achieved that objective for half a century.

The real question left open by the objectives of the 1933 Act, therefore, is the broader issue raised in a different context in 1922 by Walter Lippmann. Is it possible, Lippmann wondered, in a modern democratic society for individuals to have enough facts and to know them well enough to make responsible decisions? "While men are willing to admit that there are two sides to a 'question,' " Lippmann noted, "they do not believe that there are two sides to what they regard as a 'fact.' "[73] On this proposition, the jury is still out.

NOTES

1. See generally, 77 *Cong. Rec.* 938, 1020–22 (1933) (statement of Sen. King).
2. Remarks to Boston Chamber of Commerce, November 15, 1934 (Washington, D.C.: Government Printing Office, 1934).
3. 77 *Cong. Rec.* 937 (1933) (message from President Franklin D. Roosevelt).
4. Ellis W. Hawley, *The New Deal and the Problem of Monopoly*, vol. 7 (Princeton, N.J.: Princeton University Press, 1966).
5. See note 3 above.
6. Michael E. Parrish, *Securities Regulation and the New Deal* (New Haven, Conn.: Yale University Press, 1970), p. 4.
7. Ibid., p. 2.
8. See, for example, Kan. Stat. Ann. §§17-1252 to -1284 (1982); original version at §§17-1223 to -1285 (1933).
9. Parrish, *Securities Regulation*, p. 12.
10. Ibid., p. 17.
11. Joseph W. Alsop and Robert E. Kintner, "The Battle of the Marketplace," *Saturday Evening Post*, 11 June 1938, p. 9.
12. William O. Douglas, *Democracy & Finance* (New Haven, Conn.: Yale University Press, 1940), p. 65, 70.
13. *Business Week*, 2 March 1932, p. 7.
14. Franklin D. Roosevelt, *Public Papers* (New York: Random House, 1938), vol. I, p. 653.
15. Ibid., p. 683.
16. Cited in Joel Seligman, *The Transformation of Wall Street* (Boston: Houghton Mifflin, 1982), p. 20.
17. Roosevelt, *Public Papers*, vol. I, p. 682.
18. The original bill was introduced in the Senate on March 29, 1933, through Senator H. Fountain Ashurst of Arizona, who was then chairman of the Judiciary Committee. The next day, referring to the bill as relating to the regulation of the sale of "investment securities" in interstate commerce, there was internal maneuvering in the Senate to change the committee assignment to the Banking and Currency Committee. Professing to be "indifferent as to the particular committee to which the bill may be sent," Senator Ashurst told the Senate that he had already told his committee concerning the bill that "There may be some opposition, but it will be secret, silent, subterranean opposition that will never come to the surface. If you explore the sources of opposition, you will probably find that the opposition comes from the or-

ganizations and promoters that have sold 'fake' securities throughout this country to the tune of billions of dollars; and have sunk their fangs into the pocket books of the innocent investors with greater rapacity than a school of sharks ever sank teeth into human flesh."

In debate on the change of committee referral, an interesting turn occurred when Senator Huey Long of Louisiana suggested, perhaps slyly, that the change should not be made because the Banking and Currency Committee was receiving help from S. Parker Gilbert, "one of J. P. Morgan's firm." Senator Long said that it might subsequently embarrass the Senate to have Gilbert "drafting the laws that they are proposing to the Senate for enactment and the same day be turning around to investigate the gentleman." Senator Duncan Fletcher of Florida, chairman of the Banking and Currency Committee, denied that the committee had had anything to do with Mr. Gilbert or J. P. Morgan & Co. The change in committee reference was in fact made. 77 *Cong. Rec.* 1018–22 (1933).

19. 15 U.S.C. §77k (1976). (Codifies the Securities Act of 1933 (15 U.S.C. §77a–bbbb) and the Securities Exchange Act of 1934 (15 U.S.C. §78a–kk). U.S.C. §77k (1976). Codifies 48 Stat. 82, ch. 38, title I, §11 (May 27, 1933) and 48 Stat. 907, ch. 404, title II, §206 (June 6, 1934).
20. See *Escott* v. *BarChris Const. Corp.*, 283 F.Supp. 643 (S.D.N.Y. Mar. 29, 1968). See also 15 U.S.C. §77k(b)(3) (1976).
21. See 15 U.S.C. §77k(b)(3)(i) (1976).
22. 77 *Cong. Rec.* 937 (1933) (message from President Franklin D. Roosevelt).
23. 15 U.S.C. §77h(a) (1976). (Codifies 48 Stat. 79, ch. 38, title I, §8 (May 27, 1933) and 54 Stat. 857, ch. 686, title III, §301 (Aug. 22, 1940).)
24. 15 U.S.C. §77h(a) (1976).
25. 86 *Cong. Rec.* 10250 (1940).
26. See generally 15 U.S.C. §77k (1976).
27. Ibid.
28. 15 U.S.C. §77m (1976). (Codifies 48 Stat. 84, ch. 38, title I, §13 (May 27, 1933) and 48 Stat. 908, ch. 404, title II, §207 (June 6, 1934).)
29. 15 U.S.C. §77m (1976).
30. *Webster's New International Dictionary* (Springfield, Mass: G. & C. Merriam Co., 1930), p. 624.
31. For a discussion of due diligence, see *National Steel and Shipbuilding Co.* v. *United States*, 419 F.2d 863, 875 (Ct. Cl., Dec. 12, 1969).
32. H.R. Rep. No. 85, 73d Cong., 1st sess. (1933).
33. Ibid., p. 3.
34. Ibid., p. 5.
35. Ibid., p. 6 (emphasis added).
36. Ibid., pp. 7–8 (emphasis added).
37. Ibid. (emphasis added).
38. 77 *Cong. Rec.* 2910, 2913 (1933).
39. Ibid.
40. 77 *Cong. Rec.* 2910, 2920 (1933).
41. Ibid., 2921 (emphasis added).
42. 77 *Cong. Rec.* 2910, 2934 (1933) (emphasis added).
43. H.R. Rep. No. 152, 73d Cong., 1st sess. 26 (1933) (emphasis added).

44. Ibid.
45. 77 *Cong. Rec.* 3891, 1901–3902 (1933).
46. Ibid.
47. 15 U.S.C. §77bbbb (1976). (Codifies 53 Stat. 1177, ch. 38, title III, §328 (May 27, 1933) and ch. 411 (Aug. 3, 1939).)
48. 78 *Cong. Rec.* 2264 (1934) (message from President Franklin D. Roosevelt).
49. 15 U.S.C. §77r. (Codifies 48 Stat. 84, ch. 38, title I, §13 (May 27, 1933) and 48 Stat. 908, ch. 404, title II, §207 (June 6, 1934).)
50. 78 *Cong. Rec.* 2264, 2268–2269 (1934) (statement of Sen. Fletcher).
51. 78 *Cong. Rec.* 8714, 8716 (1934).
52. H.R. Rep. No. 1838, 73d Cong., 2d sess. 41 (1934) (reported by Rep. Rayburn) 78 *Cong. Rec.* 8669 (1934) (statement of Sen. Fletcher).
53. 15 U.S.C. §77k(b)(3) (1976).
54. H.R. Rep. No. 152, 73d Cong., 1st sess. 26 (1933).
55. *Harvard College* v. *Amory*, 26 Mass. 446, 9 Pick. 454 (1830).
56. Ibid., p. 461.
57. *King* v. *Talbot*, 40 N.Y. 76 (1869).
58. Ibid., pp. 85–86.
59. Austin W. Scott, *The Law of Trusts* (Boston: Little, Brown, 3d ed. 1967), at 174.
60. *Restatement (Second) of Trusts* §227(a) (1959).
61. *Restatement (Second) of Agency* §425 (b) (1958).
62. 15 U.S.C. §§77ooo–bbbb (1976).
63. 15 U.S.C. §77ooo. (Codifies 53 Stat. 1171, ch. 38, title III, §315 (May 27, 1933) and ch. 411 (Aug. 3, 1939).)
64. S. Rep. No. 248, 76th Cong., 1st sess. 2 (1939).
65. Joel Seligman, *The Transformation of Wall Street*, pp. 113–114.
66. R. W. Goldschmidt, "Registration Under the Securities Act of 1933," 4 *Law and Contemporary Problems* 19, 27 (1937).
67. Paul P. Gourrich, "Investment Banking Methods Prior to and Since the Securities Act of 1933," 4 *Law and Contemporary Problems* 44, 69, 70 (1937).
68. Alfred D. Chandler, Jr., *The Visible Hand: The Managerial Revolution in American Business* (Cambridge, Mass.: Belknap Press of Harvard University Press, 1977), p. 347ff.
69. William J. Abernathy, Kim B. Clark, and Alan M. Kantrow, *Industrial Renaissance: Producing a Competitive Future for America* (New York: Basic Books, 1983), p. 39.
70. Ibid.
71. *United States* v. *Morgan*, 118 F.Supp. 621 (S.D.N.Y., Oct. 14, 1953) (Medina, J.).
72. Ibid., see also Samuel L. Hayes, III, Michael Spence and David Marks, *Competition in the Investment Banking Industry* (Cambridge, Mass.: Harvard University Press, 1983).
73. Walter Lippmann, *Public Opinion* (New York: The Macmillian Company, 1960), p. 126.

4

Registration and Diligent Investigation

What evolved from section 11 of the Securities Act of 1933, whether intended as a mandate or as a standard for defense in litigation, was a detailed procedure for reasonable investigation of negotiated securities offerings, whether of debt or of equity, which has been refined over the years since the act's passage. In this chapter, we shall show how the process of diligent investigation has evolved. The process addresses the question of the extent to which the Securities Act's directives have been regarded as imperatives and been carried out.

THE DILIGENCE OBJECTIVE

Diligence, as the 1933 Act envisions it, begins promptly once an agreement has been reached between a corporate issuer's representatives and a securities underwriter to proceed on a financing deal involving a public offering of securities. Each party selects its respective players for the team that will be assigned to prepare the registration statement. The opponent of the team is time itself. Everyone must gear to producing the product in the shortest time with the minimum of negative comment from the SEC on the content of the statement. "Winning" this contest means shortening the period of exposure between the time the preparation is undertaken and the date on which the public offering is made. Obviously the shorter the period, the less the market risk to the investment banker, although at risk is only a moral obligation, since the contract for the underwriting will not actually set a specific price until minutes before the public offering is made. In a practical sense, the investment banker takes on the obligation of carrying out the underwriting subject only to the condition that the SEC be satisfied with the registration statement. That, and not price, is the critical factor. Price will be determined by the market at the time of the offering. But whether there is to be an offering depends on the content of the registration statement.

However compelling the argument may be that reasonable investigation is not mandatory and is intended only to provide the underwriter with a statutory safe harbor against liability, the investment banker does not approach the transaction as an insurance carrier concerned with the possible costs of what may prove to be a risky underwriting. The degree of diligence is likened by the underwriters to that of the prudent person buying securities for himself. The objective of the underwriter is to eliminate all risks that could arise from a faulty registration statement, not to appraise the price to be charged for assuming a risk. The underwriter's representatives on the diligence team have only one task: to conduct every aspect of preparing the registration statement so as to carry out a reasonable investigation under the circumstances surrounding the issue. This process entails leaving no question unasked that experienced, sophisticated persons should ask, and leaving no answer intellectually unchallenged. Every answer must be tested to ascertain whether it, in turn, raises a pertinent question.

Because the success of the effort is measured by the time

required to complete the registration statement, and not by the complexity of the task, the history of prior public offerings of securities by the same issuer under the 1933 Act is of considerable importance. While a record of public trading and prior registration of securities under the 1934 Act may be helpful, this is a less relevant precedent than a prior public offering made under the 1933 Act, for only the latter carries with it the credibility that comes from a history of reasonable investigation by underwriters at arm's length. Issuers change their businesses, often radically, but the existence of a prior effective registration statement under the 1933 Act invariably shortens the amount of time necessary for preparing a subsequent one. It follows that the more such registrations have been filed, the shorter the time required for preparation of a new statement. This diminution may be taken to the point where no investigation is required at all. The preparation of the registration statement in those circumstances may take only a matter of hours. But even where an issuer has a long and frequent history of registrations under the 1933 Act, its business situation may have changed materially. It may recently have suffered an adverse antitrust action, or a plant or product calamity, or litigation which could materially affect a balance sheet or income statement.

Thus, even if the issuer is eligible to use the shelf procedure for registering the proposed securities under Rule 415 (discussed later in this book), the investment banker or the issuer itself may decide against using a shortened procedure. This decision would usually be related to the marketing and distribution aspects of the offering rather than the underwriting and pricing function, but it might also be related to material business facts. The prospectus included in the registration statement is intended by the law to be a sales piece, and it is the only one that can legally be used, except as otherwise permitted by SEC rules or administrative practice.[1] As such it can be discussed openly and distributed widely. But more exploration may be required in order to familiarize others with the issuer and its business. The issuer may have detailed discussions at meetings with potential members of an underwriting group, in an effort to achieve a reasonable investigation. Generally these meetings take the form of regional gatherings in American financial centers where the principal underwriter perceives a nascent interest in the issuer or where the issuer is considered already to have a following. Occasionally this "dog and pony" show may also travel to foreign capital centers or markets.

Stimulating distribution in this way through selling the merits of the issue may ultimately bring a higher price for the issuer and a lower spread, or mark-up, for the underwriters and dealers than a speedier offering. Thus, even where the issuer and its underwriter could take advantage of an accelerated offering date, speed might not provide the lowest transaction costs. Because of salesmanship, a conventional offering may, for example, produce a favorably longer maturity, or a higher future exercise price in a convertible bond, and thus a net lower overall cost for the issuer, notwithstanding the greater exposure to market risk from an additional expenditure of time.

The Diligence Team. Since no one person is likely to combine all the experience and sophistication which the task demands, the investment banker selects for its registration team players with a broad knowledge of the general kinds of questions likely to be raised. At a minimum these will cover all matters bearing on the issuer's organization and standing: its past financial affairs and predictions as to future ones; its operations, properties, and employee relations; its contracts, insurance, and patents; its litigation, contingent liabilities, and taxes; its debt obligations, guarantees, and lines of credit; its management; and the reasons for the issuance and intended use of the proceeds from the offering. These investigations will require in every case legal services, financial and securities expertise, general management background and talents, and familiarity with the industry. A reasonable investigation may require expert knowledge in a specific area, such as: genetics; space satellites and communications; nuclear energy; chemicals and product problems; environmental issues and problems; pipeline rights of way; petroleum reserves and marketing; mode, product, and "source competition"; relevant markets; and so on. Self-education by members of the team may become imperative but, because of the esoteric nature of the field, impossible to achieve quickly; in this case *ad hoc* experts may be added to the team.

At the first meeting of the team, the representatives of the issuer will invariably include counsel (these may be from inside or outside the issuer or both), financial and accounting staff, a corporate executive and, depending on the nature of the issuer's business, one or more production and operating personnel. The investment banker will also designate counsel and, to work with the partner or officer of the banker in charge of the transaction, one or more of the banker's staff personnel who are expert in the issuer's industry or generally experienced in underwriting public offerings.

The independent public accountants who have audited the issuer over the prior five years will join the group, not as members of the team but as experts who will be required to provide certified financial statements and to review various interim financial statements. They will also oversee presentation of statistical data, ensure compliance with accounting regulatory requirements, and render professional opinions of a financial or accounting nature. As part of the closing of the transaction—that is, the ultimate delivery of payment by the underwriters and of final certificates and documents by the issuer completing the deal—the accountants will be required to deliver a letter confirming that there have arisen no material changes in the financial matters they have reviewed. This letter is always regarded as an essential instrument for the completion of a reasonable investigation. Colloquially it is referred to as a "comfort" letter, and more frequently as "cold comfort."

This group—the team plus the independent accountants— will start to meet constantly, working typically without regard for traditional business hours in order to fulfill their responsibility for the content of the registration statement. The group may be supplemented from time to time by knowledgeable persons drawn from the issuer's staff or from the outside. The designated team typically numbers six or eight persons, and, with the addition of representatives of the independent accountants, becomes a working group of perhaps ten. Not uncommonly, roughly an equal number of additional persons may be called upon to participate before the final product is filed at the SEC.

The Calendar. The first task of the team is to prepare a calendar of events and critical dates and an agenda which sets forth work assignments, such as preparation of drafts. The critical dates are initially fixed at the advice of the investment banker as to a desirable time for public offering (days of the week, months of the year, and holidays are taken into consideration) and reflect such matters as the nature of the security being offered, the history of the issuer's prior offerings, any unique characteristics of the issuer's business, all relevant economic conditions, and the time required for producing the certified financial statements as required by SEC rules.

For illustration, let us assume a proposed public offering of securities by a hypothetical Delaware corporation, Youngcorp. Youngcorp wants to sell a million shares of its common stock for its own account and also to register 150,000 shares of its common stock to be sold by certain of its controlling stockholders. Youngcorp has also agreed with the banker with whom it has been negotiating to grant an option to the underwriters to purchase up to an additional 100,000 shares to cover overallocations of the stock being sold that were made by the underwriters to the dealers selling the securities. Youngcorp's common stock, it is here assumed, is now traded over the counter with relatively small volume and activity.

The calendar of events and critical dates might take the following weekly form in its initial structure, to be refined and finalized on a daily basis in about the third week of the team's work. Assignments to individuals would necessarily be general in the first schedule but would soon become specific. While flexibility of calendar would be available to some degree in the early weeks, everyone would be concerned about creating a time cushion to absorb the inevitable unanticipated delays or to avoid extraordinary expense such as overtime printing costs.

YOUNGCORP COMMON STOCK
CALENDAR OF EVENTS

DATE	*DESCRIPTION*	*ASSIGNMENT*
Week 1	1. Meeting at company to plan schedule and re-sponsibilities.	The group.[2]
	2. Program for preparation of financial statements; selection of printers.	Company and under-writer's counsel; inde-pendent accountants.
	3. Officers' and directors' questionnaires mailed.	Company officers and counsel.
	4. Meetings to analyze in-tended use of proceeds and arrange visitations necessary for preliminary diligence.	The team, but with specific delegation of various diligence tasks.
	5. Commencement of cor-porate check.	Underwriter's counsel and representatives.
Week 2	Assign initial drafting of:	
	6. Registration statement.	Company officers and counsel.
	7. Underwriting agreement.	Underwriter's counsel.
	8. Agreement among underwriters.	" "
	9. Selected dealer agree-ment.	" "
	10. Blue sky memorandum.	" "
	11. Completion of initial cut-and-paste draft.	Company counsel.
Week 3	12. Initial distribution, and review, of registration statement.	The group.
Weeks 4 and 5	13. Completion of diligence investigation, and meet-ings with counsel for selling stockholders.	Underwriter's counsel, company counsel, sell-ing stockholders and their counsel.
	14. Commence redraft of the registration statement.	The group.
Week 6 and 7	15. Complete revised draft of registration statement.	The group.
	16. Draft of registration statement to printer.	Company counsel.
	17. Printer's proof of regis-	The group.

tration statement is re-
viewed.

	18. Commence preparation of SEC required exhibits to registration statement, including material regarding selling stockholders.	Company counsel and underwriter's counsel.
	19. Complete drafting of registration statement and compilation of exhibits.	The group.
	20. Registration statement, including exhibits, delivered to printer.	Company counsel.
	21. Filing with SEC and NASD.	Company counsel and underwriter's counsel.
	22. Press release.	Company counsel and underwriter's counsel.
	23. Underwriting group formed definitively.	Underwriter.
	24. Check of officers' and directors' questionnaire responses.	The team.
Weeks 8 and 9	25. "Dog and pony show" in selected cities.	Underwriter and company officers.
Week 10	26. SEC comments on registration statement received and reviewed.	The group.
	27. Amendment to registration statement prepared and filed with SEC.	The group.
Week 11	28. Meeting to determine price and spread.	Underwriter and company officers.
	29. Price amendment to registration statement filed with SEC.	Company counsel and underwriter's counsel.
	30. Registration statement becomes effective.	SEC order.
	31. Public offering commences.	Underwriter.
Week 12	32. Closing, at which Youngcorp and selling stockholders receive payment for the shares sold in the offering.	The group, and selling stockholders and their counsel.

During the ten weeks which will have elapsed on this calendar from the first meeting until the filing of the first amendment (the deficiency amendment; that is, the response to the SEC comments on the registration statement) the process of investigation by the underwriters will not have ceased. The representatives of the underwriter will constantly question and probe until it is clear to them that they need no longer ascertain what may require disclosure but must, instead, determine the actual materiality of the facts now known and decide what to disclose about them.

The Corporate Check.   As they move into the area of due diligence—usually in the second week, though earlier if manpower permits—the team must promptly pursue two areas of reasonable investigation: The underwriter's counsel must conduct a "corporate check," and its financial personnel must begin a historical (at least five years) and predictive earnings analysis.

The corporate check involves a review of the validity, in form and substance, of Youngcorp's articles of organization and all amendments in order to provide the underwriters with a written legal opinion that Youngcorp was duly incorporated and is now a corporation in good standing in Delaware and has full authority to conduct its business wherever it is doing so. Counsel will also have to review the bylaws and all minutes of meetings of directors, shareholders, or committees of the board in order to determine whether they were conducted in accordance with all applicable requirements. Where the minutes refer to documents, counsel will have to secure and review them and prepare an analysis of their bearing on the proposed offering. Depending on the nature of Youngcorp's business and operations, counsel may have to review franchises, leases, licensing agreements, qualifications to do business, registrations of various kinds, and records of public authorities relating to them.

Counsel will also have to review all books, records, agreements, and instruments affecting ownership, voting, or control of Youngcorp's common stock in order to advise as to the authorized, issued, and outstanding common stock, the authorization for the stock to be issued by the company, including the option to the underwriters, preemptive rights, cumulative voting, the forms of the stock certificates, the stock of subsidiaries, and the title and rights of selling shareholders.

The Financial Check. The "financial check," which is carried on concurrently with the corporate check, usually entails a review of all financial statements over a period of years. Any change in auditors or accounting methods during the period raises a myriad of questions which must be answered. The financial check also requires a consideration of the issuer's tax status. In addition, sales projections, operating and capital budgets, and statements of sources and applications of funds are reviewed with company financial officers. The nature of the business determines the specific diligence required by the registration statement.

All issuers are analyzed by expert business personnel, usually a partner or principal of the underwriter, as to the quality of the business and of its management. Determining the nature and prospects of an offering and justification for the underwriter to put its name on it involve a subjective diligence. The general development of the business; its domestic and world competition; the political, governmental, and public policy factors which may affect it; its important customers or suppliers; and the state of the art and possible changes in it must be pondered by the underwriter. After closely questioning the issuer, the underwriter may turn to outside public and private sources of information or even personal, intuitive reactions. The people in management must then be investigated—their demonstrated talent, reputation both personal and professional, age, wealth, personality, education, acceptance by subordinates—as well as composition of the management team and relationships among key management personnel.

Selecting Material Information. The underwriter now knows whether it wants to do the deal. From the mass of knowledge accumulated by the underwriter, the registration statement must include all material facts, omitting nothing essential to making the registration statement not misleading. Since the prospectus, which is part of the registration statement, is the only permitted general public sales piece, there are also strong pressures to make it readable and persuasive. Throwing in all possible material data, in an excess of caution, can destroy the usefulness of the prospectus, as well as the underwriter's reputation for acumen. Thus, the underwriter next tests everything in the registration statement from the standpoint of its materiality. Some matters are required by law to be disclosed, but for the most part, the underwriter must use his own judgment on what to include.

Once the question of materiality is answered, issues of quality and quantity enter into the process. As a rule, there is a tendency to err on the side of amplification rather than abridgment. Since the disclosure may be judged by a third person, or a series of them culminating with the federal courts, or even the Supreme Court, experience suggests that there is some degree of comfort to be derived from an inclusive approach to the subject matter.

The many official notions of materiality range from the subjective to a supposedly objective test of what a reasonable and prudent individual would be likely to regard as important in making a decision to invest. The underwriter's representatives cannot assume either investment sophistication or the lack of it, or qualitative or quantitative requirements. For example, in the years preceding the enactment of the Foreign Corrupt Practices Act of 1977, the SEC made it clear that it regarded as material any "questionable payment," without reference to amount or to the financial stature of the operation making the payment. Such a payment was deemed material simply because it had a bearing on the standards and practices of the management. Auditors constantly review questions from the standpoint of financial materiality, and they may employ a quantitative rule of thumb. But even minor matters must be examined for significance or uniqueness and may be considered material under the circumstances.

The drafters of the registration statement thus employ their own unofficial test of materiality. The subject matter included must relate to facts established by their diligence. Rarely do opinions or beliefs not demonstrable through facts qualify as material. The facts are then turned over and bounced off everyone concerned. If the facts were disclosed, would they be likely to influence investment? If so, who would be influenced? If a reasonable person, a kind of investment Everyman, would consider the facts important, the team must disclose them.

Overhanging all subjective determinations are two SEC rules under the 1933 Act: Rule 176 (which we shall discuss in some detail in subsequent chapters) specifies circumstances that the commission considers would affect the determination of what constitutes a reasonable investigation, and Rule 405 defines a material fact as one to which there is a "substantial likelihood that a reasonable investor would attach importance" in deciding whether to buy the security.

Because of this subjective-objective diligence process, the cases that emerge publicly under the 1933 Act dealing with the adequacy of materiality disclosure are far outnumbered by those litigated under the 1934 Act. Essentially the same materiality standard applies to proxy materials under the latter act; and to the periodic reports required to be filed, and various voluntary public releases of information (or failure to make such releases). But the process under the 1934 Act is unilateral, lacking the give-and-take of two sides having different concerns. For the most part, cases brought by private parties under the 1934 Act have involved SEC Rule 10b-5, promulgated under section 10 of the 1934 Act, in which an issuer may not even be involved. The legal issue, however, may involve the same questions as in a 1933 Act case since Rule 10b-5 in part specifically makes it unlawful "to make any untrue statement of a material fact or to omit to state a material fact necessary in order to make the statements made, in the light of the circumstances under which they were made not misleading."[3]

THE STOP ORDER

Under the 1933 Act, the SEC is itself concerned with materiality in carrying out its regulatory responsibility. Section 8(d) of the act provides the commission with its principal weapon against an offerer—the "stop order" proceeding. When the commission considers that a registration statement includes "any untrue statement of a material fact or omits to state any material fact required to be stated therein or necessary to make the statements therein not misleading," it may at any time, both before or after a public offering has commenced, stop all proceedings.[4] The "stop" may be called simply because the registrant failed to meet what the SEC unilaterally considers to be the full requirement of the materiality standard. A hearing by the SEC must follow within fifteen days, at which the materiality issue is tested. Any SEC findings as to failure of material disclosure are then subject to judicial review.

During the early years under the 1933 Act, the commission used the stop order weapon frequently. Between 1934 and 1936, 127 stop order proceedings were instituted. Only 124, however, occurred over the next thirty-five years—a historical average of less than four such cases annually.[5] Recently, from August 1983 through September 1984, the commission instituted seven such proceedings.[6] Since all of these cases involved initial public offerings of securities, a significant conclusion that may fairly be drawn from these data is that the investment bankers' investigation is an extraordinarily effective method of achieving disclosure of material facts. Similarly, from the paucity of SEC generated proceedings, conclusions may be drawn on the issue of whether the banker regards the investigation as mandatory under the law or only a method of achieving a litigation shield.

Conceptually, and as a matter of law, the commission is not required to tell the registrant what it conceives to be the deficiencies in the registration statement. The administrative practice, however, is for the SEC staff to advise the registrant through a letter of comment, known colloquially as the "deficiency letter," of the questions which have emerged from a staff reading of the statement. The questions may involve such various problems as questions of materiality, compliance with substantive rules, or failure to observe matters of prescribed form. Occasionally the registrant or the underwriter will disagree with the comments and attempt to negotiate a mutually agreeable result with the SEC staff, which historically has tried to accommodate such negotiations.

The determination of what will be involved in the staff examination process is somewhat reminiscent of the secret guidelines used by the Internal Revenue Service to decide whether to audit particular tax returns or groups of returns. In describing its examination procedures publicly, the SEC uses terms with specific in-house meanings, such as "review," "screen," and "monitor." The actual nature of the examination is not made public, although the clear indication is that the initial securities registration of any offerer under the 1933 Act is subject to a review. This, again by analogy to taxes, is a full audit, or "an in-depth examination of the accounting, financial, and legal aspects of a filing."[7] The screen is a process for determining whether a registration statement requires a review, and appears to take into account the nature and extent of prior registrations that became effective under the 1933 Act. The monitoring examination is, in effect, a limited review for a specific purpose not requiring a screen examination.[8] Rule 415 shelf registrations would fall into the monitoring category, if indeed they are examined at all.

The staff assigned by the commission to 1933 Act examination functions consists of personnel of various talents and disciplines. Staff review is an informal procedure in which thousands of registration statements are examined annually. In the vast majority of cases a deficiency letter is almost certain but, as the statistical stop order results establish, only rarely does the staff find a violation of the SEC's guidance rule forbidding "careless disregard of the statutes and rules or a deliberate attempt to conceal or mislead."[9]

The significant degree of compliance by issuers and underwriters with the intent of the 1933 Act, and the even more significant absence of private law suits against underwriters and issuers under section 11, are certainly a result of the diligence process employed by the underwriter, coupled with an objective approach on its part to determinations of materiality.

In the fiscal year ending September 30, 1983, a record 6,100 registration statements were filed with the SEC. The securities involved accounted for a money volume of $243 billion.[10] While the number of full reviews by the SEC staff is not publicly known, some two thousand statements were first offerings by a registrant, and may fairly be assumed to have had a full review.[11] In the remainder of cases, it seems likely that a screening or monitoring was all that the SEC staff considered necessary. Since only seven stop orders were issued in approximately the same period, the odds in favor of achieving effectiveness were nearly one thousand to one. In terms of value, the average of the two thousand initial offerings was about $27 million, and the average value of the remaining offerings was about $45 million. The underwriters in a sense have become the regulators, replacing the SEC staff as reviewers of material deficiencies. As an SEC staff officer put it, "Perhaps equally significant in a regulatory scheme that depends to a great extent on the fundamental concept of full disclosure, the Commission's return to a more frequent use of its stop order authority may well be the best means of impressing upon those seeking access to public financing that anything less than full and accurate disclosure, as mandated by the securities laws, will be dealt with firmly and quickly by the Commission."[12]

THE PRICE AMENDMENT AND ACCELERATION

After the underwriter has made all substantive deficiency changes, and these changes have been vetted by the SEC staff, the next point of pressure in the registration process is the filing of the document known as the price amendment. In it the underwriter states the price of the offering and the compensation to be paid the underwriters and dealers.

Finally, the underwriter requests acceleration—that is, the immediate granting of effectiveness of the registration statement by the SEC. Members of the team or their assistants stand by in Washington, often with an open telephone line, waiting to get the offering price and spread data then being negotiated at the issuer's or underwriter's office. When the figures have finally been inserted in the blanks, and the issuer and the underwriter have signed the underwriting agreement in its complete form and delivered copies to each other, the word is given concurrently to the stand-by personnel in Washington. Within a few minutes, they file conforming copies with the SEC. Once the amendment containing the pricing data has been filed, the registration statement is complete. Since the filing of the price amendment serves, however, to commence another twenty-day incubation period, the SEC is routinely asked to accelerate the effectiveness of the registration to that date, which it does by an order. The underwriter may then proceed with the distribution of the securities.

Acceleration need have little relationship to the statutory twenty-day period required for the incubation of a registration statement. The SEC may shorten the period either on an *ad hoc* basis or by announcing administratively a procedure (as in the case of Rule 415) requiring only a monitoring of certain offerings. Or the SEC review may result in the registration statement becoming effective weeks or even months after the twenty-day period has elapsed, if indicated deficiencies remain unresolved.

UNDERWRITING DOCUMENTATION

The underwriting papers generally consist of three documents, as shown in Appendix I. One of these is the *underwriting agreement*, which is executed and delivered between the underwriter and the issuer. It generally appears as an exhibit in the *agreement among underwriters*, in which the principal underwriter agrees with the underwriting group as to the terms, conditions, and provisions of the deal with the issuer. A second exhibit to this agreement is the *selected dealer agreement*, which is necessary where a wide distribution is contemplated among securities dealers who are not underwriters.

The underwriting agreement is the key instrument for the issuer. When the issuer signs it, every eye is on the officer authorized to do so in its behalf. In the representations and warranties contained in the agreement, the issuer becomes responsible for what the underwriter has hoped to have discovered by its diligent investigation.

In section 2 of the underwriting agreement that appears as Exhibit A to Appendix I, the issuer asserts to each of the listed underwriters that neither the preliminary prospectus nor the effective registration filed with the SEC contains an untrue statement of a material fact or an omission of a material fact necessary to make a statement in it not misleading; that the financial statements are complete and accurate; that the issuer is duly incorporated in good standing; that the issuer's outstanding common stock has been duly authorized, and the new stock will be validly issued, fully paid, and nonassessable, and will conform to the registration statement, with no need for further approval of shareholders or directors; that since providing information for the registration statement, the issuer has incurred no obligations or liabilities not in the ordinary course of business; that there has not been any significant adverse change in the condition of the issuer's operation or any material loss; that no material legal or governmental proceeding has been instituted or threatened; and that there is no pending or threatened suit which might result in an adverse change. If the issuer cannot make a particular representation, then the underwriter must determine whether the requirement should be waived by the underwriters.

In section 3 of the form, the underwriters agree to buy the stock at a specified purchase price per share. Price is the key variable in the deal. There is no deal until the issue is ready to be sold by the underwriters, after all diligence has been performed, the SEC has signed off, and the issuer has reaffirmed at the moment of signing that disclosure of all material facts has been made.

THE CLOSING

Subsequent sections of the underwriting agreement lay out the mechanics for carrying out the sale. Then the concept of diligence reemerges in section 6 of the form, which sets forth the conditions of the closing, at which time the underwriters will pay for the shares they have underwritten. The closing generally occurs five business days after the registration statement becomes effective. Thus, the diligence pattern which began with the underwriter's counsel and staff independently examining corporate, financial, operating, and administrative data of every sort and progresses through representations and warranties by the issuer in the underwriting agreement confirming full disclosure, is finally completed at the closing by reaffirmation of the full disclosure by the issuer, accompanied by a legal opinion to the same effect from its counsel and a comfort letter from the independent public accountants asserting that the financial statements remain accurate.

THE UNDERWRITER'S APPROACH TO INVESTIGATION

Some critics of the investigatory procedure have suggested that the underwriter's diligence is nonchalant, perfunctory, or indifferent, and that there is room for doubt as to the degree of reasonable investigation which has been conducted. This is rarely so. No aspect of the diligence process is perfunctory. A failure to comply completely with the conditions of closing can result in the underwriter terminating the transaction. At every point in the process the issuer (and at closing the issuer's counsel) must reaffirm that the registration statement and related investments do not contain an untrue statement or a material omission of fact.

Of course, what is clearly reasonable investigation in one set of circumstances may be unnecessary in another. Size, nature of the business, industry standing, reputation among investment bankers, frequency of prior and current public offerings, and respect for integrity and acumen of management are among the factors that enter into what one may call the virtuousness test of reasonableness. By that test, even in the case of an offerer with no public track record at all, past private offerings may indicate experience, prior success, irreproachable reasons for the offering, and will engender the faith of experienced persons in the adequacy of the disclosures being made.

The underwriter must nevertheless, constantly remain alert for problems that can strike even the most virtuous offerers. An underwriter must be skeptical when an issuer gives strong assurance that a particular event was "extraordinary," since the extraordinary event can be more telling than recurring events. What, for example, is suggested about the company by a calamitous explosion in an important plant? How must the underwriter respond to an announcement that the board of directors has created a reserve for a write-off of a valuable asset whose nature is at the heart of the business? Or to an announcement that the corporation is consenting to a finding of violation of criminal law and a punishment for it? Or that certain senior officers have resigned, by request, from management? Or that a new product hailed two years ago as a breakthrough is now beset by manufacturing problems, or unable to secure regulatory approval, or being attacked on patent infringement grounds, or uneconomical to produce? These examples do not begin to address the effect on specific operations of such matters of general applicability as changes in the tax laws, significance of currency exchange factors, or government trade policies. Even if the underwriter sincerely believes that a particular event is unlikely to recur, it must nevertheless question how and why it did occur and appraise its effects.

In addition to the virtuousness factor, the investment banker may also apply the incredulousness factor. That is not to say that the investment banker must disbelieve everything the offerer has said. No investment banker would ever consider underwriting any offering of securities by an offerer it cannot trust. The incredulousness factor means only that the banker must view with deliberate skepticism every presumed fact and question whether other facts have been omitted. The skepticism is that of the scientific approach, which holds that no fact can be accepted without examination or testing. Simply put, no issuer's judgment or knowledge can be assumed to be perfect.

The virtuousness and incredulousness factors determine not only what constitutes a reasonable investigation but also who will conduct it. David Henkel, an experienced counsel for underwriters, has asserted that "the lawyer's function in the investigation process is circumscribed. Both the lawyer and the underwriter should recognize the limitations on the lawyer's skill as an investigator." He distinguishes between those areas in which he considers the lawyer to be the logical investigator and those where he is not, noting that as "to the matters for which the lawyer may be competent as an investigator, there should be careful delineation between lawyer and client of the precise aspects which he shall investigate."[13]

When the investigation turns to determinations of materiality, Henkel stresses again the underwriter's function: "Counsel is called upon, and I think properly, to assist in the decisional process of materiality. . . .The client should be made well aware of the limited function that by the nature of things counsel can play in this area and that the sole decision should not be left to counsel. . .[and] while the lawyer can help. . .the investment banker is in as good or better position to know what enters into customers' decisions to buy or sell securities."[14]

THE ABSENCE OF FRAUD

The incredulousness factor is designed to assist in the determination of materiality. It is not specifically aimed at discovering fraud or chicanery, though it certainly offers that possible result. That the phrase "Ponzi scheme" is part of American financial language is a reflection of the prevalence of fraud based on misuse of securities proceeds.[15] More complicated frauds than such simple stealing have occurred in such areas as banking, insurance, mortgages, nursing homes, tax shelters, and oil and gas exploration in spite of the diligence requirements of the 1933 Act.[16]

Although some cases of fraud have eluded the diligence process, they amount to a mere handful among the thousands of effective registration statements filed annually since the law took effect over fifty years ago. Even the number of stop order proceedings, as we have noted, has been statistically low. What do these happy regulatory consequences indicate? It seems fair to conclude that the success of the process of regulation by information is due almost wholly to the conduct of the investment banker in an enlightened regulatory atmosphere. The SEC has not been obliged to employ its sanctions under the 1933 Act to any significant extent.[17] Its administrative process has been at the heart of achieving relatively fast effectiveness of registration statements. Without this approach to self-regulation by the SEC, the statutory objective of not discouraging essential financing might have failed. But the successful implementation of the intent of the statute could not have been achieved without the investment bankers' recognizing their responsibility to conduct a reasonable investigation.

The argument that the banker's reasonable investigation is only diligent enough to entitle him to the statutory defense against a lawsuit is not supported by established practice. The investment banker has made the 1933 Act a very effective method of self-regulation. This is due in significant part to pride of reputation, skill, and responsibility, rather than a self-serving desire to avoid liability. This pride and the reasons for it are constantly being demonstrated. When the business world accepts that the pride is warranted, it beats a path to the door of the banker. The law properly recognizes that there are different degrees of reasonable investigation. But for the system to work as it has since 1933, the investment banker knows that there must always be due diligence.

NOTES

1. "The purpose of [the prospectus] is to secure for potential buyers the means of understanding the intricacies of the transaction into which they are invited. This requirement will undoubtedly limit the selling arguments hitherto employed. *That is its purpose.* . . . Any objection that the compulsory incorporation in selling literature and sales argument of substantially all information concerning the issue will frighten the buyer. . .states one of the best arguments for the provision." H.R. Rep. No. 85, 73rd Cong., 1st sess. (1933) (emphasis added).
2. The "group" includes the team and the independent public accountants. The team is made up of counsel to the company and to the underwriter and their respective representatives.
3. SEC, "Employment of manipulative and deceptive devices," 17 C.F.R. §240 10b-5.5 (1980).
4. 15 U.S.C. §77h(b)(d).
5. William McLucas, "Stop Order Proceedings Under the Securities Act of 1933: A Current Assessment," 40 *The Business Lawyer* 515, 516 (1985), citing J. Seligman, "The Historical Need for a Mandatory Corporate Disclosure System," 516 n.7 40 *The Business Lawyer* 515.

6. Ibid., pp. 534–535.
7. Ibid., p. 521 and note 31.
8. Ibid., p. 521.
9. Ibid., pp. 521–522.
10. Ibid., p. 515.
11. Of the balance, Rule 415 statements (with some exceptions) received at most a monitoring process, leaving some 3500 registration statements which were screened or partially reviewed. Ibid., p. 515 and note 3.
12. Ibid., p. 536.
13. David Henkel, "Liability of Counsel for Underwriter," 27 *The Business Lawyer* 641, 642 (1969).
14. Ibid., p. 643.
15. The president of the North American Securities Administrators Associations, the state regulators and administrators of Blue Sky laws, has said: "Deregulation 'for the sake of deregulation,' together with the absence of federal enforcement efforts in this area [has proven to be] a marriage made in heaven for the promoters of Ponzi schemes." 17 *Securities Regulation and Law Report* (31 May 1985), p. 967.

 Charles Ponzi some fifty years ago promised persons who advanced cash to him a high rate of earnings on their "investment." For a time he carried out his promise by using subsequent receipts to make the promised payments. Borrowing from Peter, a new investor, to pay a current investor, Paul, had its inevitable ending—the last investor had no source of reimbursement.
16. In *Don Quixote*, Cervantes says "Diligence is the mother of good fortune." Bad fortune may not be due solely to lack of diligence, but it can certainly be offset to a degree, as the French government learned to its discomfort. *The Economist* (7 January 1984, p. 35) reported that [then] President Giscard of France witnessed secretly in 1978 an oil firm's experiment involving equipment later called the "sniffer plane," which employed a process "designed to show that France possessed a revolutionary key to oil wealth and military security." A project was subsequently "developed in the utmost secrecy" between 1976 and 1981. At that time, some five years later, "the industry minister took an initiative which the Elysée Palace or the [government-owned] oil firm [Elf-Aquitaine] might have thought of back in 1976." An independent expert was called in. With relatively simple tests, he demonstrated that the "two boxes filled with electronic equipment code-named 'Delta' and 'Omega' " were a hoax. According to *The Economist*, the cast of persons involved or deceived in Elf-Aquitaine's expenditure of 790 million francs included the prime minister at the time, two former heads of Elf-Aquitaine, a former head of the state audit court, an international lawyer, a disappearing Italian inventor, a Belgian count, and the dean of French conservatives. The board of directors of Erap, the holding company of Elf-Aquitaine, was apparently unaware of the project, "which, it was said, was dangerously radioactive." Secret clearance was given for the transfer of funds to the promoters in Switzerland, who were "said to enjoy the backing of highly placed European and American investors."

 The history of the project became publicly known in 1983, and *The*

Economist reported on 29 September 1984 (p. 43), that "Mr. Mitterrand used his influence to prevent a parliamentary commission questioning Mr. Giscard d'Estaing about the affair of the 'sniffer aeroplane.' "

17. The originally proposed stop order provisions of the 1933 Act were, perhaps second only to section 11, among the most controversial issues debated in the legislative process. A host of objectors testified that such a provision would frustrate business and would, in effect, make the government a guarantor. Hearings before the Sen. Comm. on Banking and Currency, 73rd Congress, 1st sess., March 31-April 8, 1933.

5

Evolution of the Securities Industry Since 1933

Just as procedures evolved for dealing with the underwriter's investigation in the wake of the 1933 Act, so too did the securities industry change form following the enactment of the Glass-Steagall Act in 1933 and other reform legislation during the 1930s. The Glass-Steagall Act, in effect, erected a Chinese Wall between the functions of investment and commercial banking. Where formerly all banking firms were unrestrained in the types of banking they might wish to conduct, they were now compelled to elect either to be in the business of underwriting securities or making loans. Many investment bankers, such as First Boston Corporation, formerly the investment operation of The First National Bank of Boston and others, came into being as independent firms at that time. The evolution within the securities industry of new forms, new relationships, and new regulation eventually led to the circumstances which prompted the initiation of integrated disclosure and the subsequent introduction of shelf registration.

Immediately after passage of the reform legislation, the securities industry assumed a new, although still relatively uncomplicated structure in comparison to its predepression forms. The investment banking community became enlarged to include a number of former securities affiliates of leading predepression banking houses, which, electing to retain their commercial banking activities, were required to limit themselves to those securities-related activities, such as general obligations of states and other political body issuers, not otherwise barred under the Glass-Steagall Act. The investment firms thus spun-off initially had small capital bases and only a handful of employees, but they retained client bases drawn from long, traditional relationships built up over many years by their former parent banks.

There was only a limited, traditional range of financing instruments and arrangements by which corporate issuers could expect to raise outside capital. As discussed in Chapter 2, individual investors provided the bulk of this capital, although the trauma accompanying the collapse of the securities markets after 1929 had significantly shrunk the size of that market. For many years this relative paucity of business, coupled with the restrictions imposed by the Glass-Steagall Act, had the practical effect of discouraging potential new entrants into the securities banking business.

As Figure 5-1 demonstrates, the volume of financings did increase at points during the 1930s, but renewed economic malaise in 1937 depressed underwriting volume until the approach of World War II spurred a modest revival. The war years, however, were ones of such complete disruption to the securities markets that they have to be considered an aberration in any historical perspective.

POSTWAR DEVELOPMENTS

The late 1940s were also abnormal times because of the spurt of inflation that occurred in response to the lifting of wartime price controls, the catch-up in war-postponed spending, and

Figure 5-1 **Corporate Security Issues**
Annually

**Billions of
Dollars**

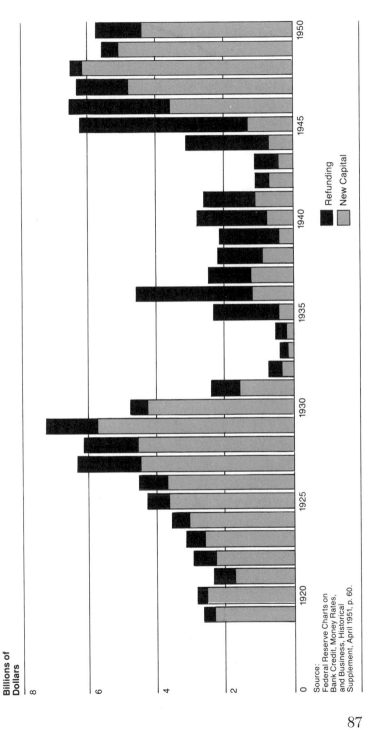

Source:
Federal Reserve Charts on
Bank Credit, Money Rates,
and Business, Historical
Supplement, April 1951, p. 60.

87

the strong fears in some business circles of another serious recession or even depression once that pent-up demand for goods and services had been satisfied.[1] In addition, the securities banking industry was thrown on the defensive when the Justice Department launched an ultimately unsuccessful antitrust action against seventeen underwriting firms, charging conspiracy and the exercise of monopoly power.[2]

The 1950s saw the beginning of the real postwar economic expansion, which was to have a profound impact on developments within the securities industry, including patterns of underwriting new securities. This decade was characterized by robust secular growth, low inflation, a strong dollar, and a favorable American balance of payments position. Securities firms as a group enjoyed relatively high prosperity during this period, particularly because of tight cost controls inherited from the earlier lean years. Part of that cost control had made itself felt in a general hiatus on hiring new employees during the 1930s and 1940s. Although active hiring was resumed in a more substantial way as the U.S. economy gathered further momentum during the 1950s, the leadership that had been in place at the time of the 1930s legislation was in large part still in command at the beginning of the 1960s.[3]

For the most part, underwriting and other corporate business was closely controlled by a relatively small number of securities firms, successors to the powerful banking houses that had dominated the business before the depression. By controlling the flow of new securities, these firms were able to exercise substantial influence over the smaller and more fragmented retail distribution firms, whose heavier overhead costs made them more dependent on the selling commissions emanating from that flow of new product.[4]

Leadership Challenges in the 1960s. Consolidations, however, were constantly taking place among the largely retail-oriented securities firms.[5] And, during a decade of uninterrupted economic expansion in the 1960s, the operating profits of a wide variety of firms in the securities industry reached new postdepression heights.[6] Concurrently, a new, relatively young group of investment bankers began moving into senior partner positions during this period. The new leadership of some of the aspiring retail firms used this sustained period of prosperity to challenge the securities-originating firms which had occupied the apex positions in the industry structure since the banking reorganization of the 1930s.[7] This effort coincided with the emergence of the institutional investor as a powerful new marketing focus for a number of securities firms.

It was during the 1960s that several of these aspiring firms made some headway in challenging that traditional leadership structure. Merrill Lynch did it by creating an internally efficient organization to service the needs of individual investors profitably. Salomon Brothers did it via an early recognition that institutional investors would require an effective marketing supplement to the New York Stock Exchange specialists if purchases and sales of securities were to be effected without seriously disrupting the market. Donaldson, Lufkin and Jenrette, initially organized in 1959, built a major position by pursuing their strategic determination that these emerging institutional investors would require a more sophisticated research product than had routinely been produced for the individual investor constituency.

The first major postwar shakeout and realignment of securities firms came at the end of the long economic expansion of the 1960s. In 1969–70, a number of firms were overwhelmed by the large increase in trading volume experienced during the last heady months of the 1960s bull market, and some disappeared as independent entities when their back offices proved incapable of handling the volume.[8] Others sought to strengthen their competitive positions by going public, raising capital by selling their own equity securities to the public, and thus breaking the prohibition in the rules of the New York Stock Exchange that had previously barred Exchange member firms from being publicly owned.[9] This move to raise public capital was justified by the desire of the firms to lock in funds to service better the growing institutional sector and to cushion the firms from the consequences of volatile swings in operating results. Other observers, however, saw this public financing move as a convenient "bailout" opportunity for aging senior partners with substantial equity investments in their firms, who were alarmed by what they viewed as adverse market and industry developments. The younger partners, however, welcomed the removal of a threatened reduction in the firm's capital whenever a retiring or deceased partner's capital had to be redeemed from the firm's assets.[10]

A pullback by institutional investors from the markets in 1970–71 temporarily increased the competitive leverage of the retail brokerage firms that could deliver their individual investor customers to corporate issuers eager to convert volatile short-term bank financing into longer-term fixed rate debt arrangements. Nevertheless, by the early 1970s there was enough continuing evidence of the growing importance of institutional investors to the marketing of securities that leading wholesale firms made impressive new commitments of capital and personnel to the areas of trading and institutional services. Morgan Stanley's decision to realign itself in that direction was viewed by many as a watershed in the postwar evolution of Wall Street and a favorable reflection of the capacity and willingness of leading securities firms, when sensing change, to move aggressively to accommodate and exploit it. Such a competitive response had been successfully made by European investment and merchant banks over a period of several centuries.[11]

The Turbulent 1970s. Although the securities markets enjoyed a revival in 1971 and 1972, economic and organizational pressures which had begun to assert themselves at the end of the 1960s reappeared and worked in combination to push the fortunes of the securities industry to one of their lowest points since World War II.[12]

At the root of many of these problems was the rising level of inflation. Purchasing-power erosion had been nominal during much of the postwar period, although it had gradually gathered force during the last half of the 1960s, as the United States pursued a dual course of making massive defense expenditures while also sustaining a high level of civilian consumption. The consequent demand-pull inflation caused labor compensation to fall further and further behind in real purchasing power and thus, even after the economic expansion stopped during the first quarter of 1969, pressures for wage increases continued unabated. This led to a new wave of cost-push inflation. By the summer of 1971, the dollar was under substantial pressure, and with a growing trade deficit, President Nixon floated the dollar in August of that year. This move gave additional impetus to the growth of the Euro-markets and set the stage for larger volume sales of securities of U.S. issuers in those markets in the decade ahead.

A simultaneous expansion phase for the United States and other industrialized Western nations during 1972 and 1973 created shortages in a number of raw materials sufficient to set off a new round of commodity-based inflation. Consumers were most aware of this phenomenon because of the skyrocketing prices of such staples as sugar, wheat, and coffee, but manufacturers and processors were also experiencing sharp price increases in a number of basic raw materials. The impact of this development was exacerbated by the 1973 Arab-Israeli war and the decision of the major OPEC countries to impose a fourfold increase in the price of oil in the winter of 1973–74. This pushed the inflation rate even higher in Western industrialized countries, including the United States.

Interest rates soared in the United States, thus causing both bond and stock prices to fall precipitously. As both institutional and individual investors withdrew from the market in disarray, trading and underwriting volume dried up, while the costs of doing business in the personnel- and systems-intensive securities business rose sharply, particularly for the retail-oriented firms.[13] The stock market's disillusionment with publicly owned securities firms reached such proportions that the shares of one major retail brokerage house, E. F. Hutton & Co., were selling for $4 per share in November 1974—less than either the sum of the cash it then had on hand or its projected earnings for one year of good trading volumes.[14]

The wholesale securities firms fared much better during this lean period, both because of their relatively lower overhead and because of the persistence of some lucrative corporate fee-based activities.[15] Still, their business was negatively affected by the SEC's decision to disallow fixed brokerage commissions as of "May Day," May 1, 1975. Although volume discounts for large (mainly institutional) traders had been in effect for a number of years, the presence of fixed commissions had kept total transaction fees at an artificially high level, thereby acting as a protective umbrella for less efficient brokers. Immediately after May Day, commissions fell to between 40 and 50 percent of the earlier fixed rate levels.[16] Soon thereafter, firms specializing in security analyses (so-called research boutique firms) that had depended largely on soft commission dollars from institutional investors to pay their overhead were put under severe pressure. There followed another wave of consolidations as a number of firms, like Mitchell Hutchins and H. W. Wainwright, were either liquidated or absorbed through merger.

Parallel developments were taking place in the corporate services sector. Higher levels of sophistication among corporate finance officers and other top level managers were forcing an acceleration in the rate of new product innovation and the broadening of proffered services in the investment banking community.[17] Corporate clients continually sought more efficient and less costly ways to obtain Wall Street services, and in certain areas brought financing-related activities in-house rather than relying on securities firm vendors to provide them.[18] While there was a solid front of resistance among securities-originating firms to any compromise on the traditional seven-eighths of one percent gross spread on investment-grade public bond issues, de facto price cutting was already taking place through various indirect means, including overtrading on swaps of old bonds for new ones.[19] In this sense, the underwriting market was experiencing pressures for margin reduction not dissimilar from those that had hit the institutional brokerage businesses prior to May 1975.

Meanwhile, on the retail side, the rise in interest rates which accompanied the acceleration in inflation in 1973–74 had spawned an important new phenomenon: the money market mutual fund. Whereas during the earlier period of high interest rates in 1970, retail brokerage firms had often been able to channel their customers' cash balances into long-term, fixed-rate debt instruments of corporate clients, that was no longer the case. The declines in securities values and the losses thus sustained by investors made them much less willing to make longer-term, fixed-rate bond investments. They sought instead short-term debt arrangements that offered more than the rates banks were permitted to pay under Federal Reserve regulations, but still gave them a measure of protection against capital loss.

The money market mutual funds established to respond to this need were subject to regulation under the Investment Company Act of 1940 administered by the SEC. Commonplace portfolios of stocks and bonds are generally associated in the public mind with mutual funds. The money market mutual funds, however, are confined by their managers to investments solely in short-term corporate and governmental notes and other borrowing instruments. The new approach is also open-end in its rights, that is, it permits an investor to invest or redeem at will, and in the case of the new funds, at a fixed price of one dollar per share. The fund investment fluctuates only in terms of the yield, like a conventional bank savings account, and not in terms of changes in asset value.

These funds quickly gained phenomenal acceptance because they respond directly to the public desire in a high interest rate era to earn more on savings than banks were permitted to pay, while essentially preserving the liquidity of a savings bank account. By the early 1980s they had grown to more than $200 billion.[20] Implicit in their growth was a fundamental shift in consumer savings habits which was to have a large impact on most of the financial services sector, including commercial banks, savings and loans associations, credit unions, and insurance companies operating primarily on the deposit-taking side of the Glass-Steagall "Chinese Wall." Retail securities firms on the securities dealing side of that wall moved to protect what had historically been lucrative free credit balances by offering, at first, interest on selective customer cash deposits, and then later their own captive money market mutual funds available to all their customers. Merrill Lynch's introduction of the "cash management account" in 1977 was a landmark event which was to change permanently the options available to, and the patterns of savings utilized by, investors.[21]

This pattern of inflation-induced responses to the financial markets had a profound effect on the informal live-and-let-live compact within the industry that had evolved as an implementation of—and a complement to—the reform legislation of the 1930s. In the expanding postwar U.S. economy, financial institutions on both sides of the Glass-Steagall wall were largely content to pursue business that, while overlapping in some instances, generally minimized head-to-head competition. Now the slowdown in economic growth and the rapidly changing savings and investing patterns of investors were putting that informal pact under strain.[22]

In the immediate wake of the unfixing of securities commissions in 1975, a relatively few discount brokerage houses sprang up to service individual investors, but their share of the market was small, and they were not then seen as a significant threat to the full-service retail brokerage firms. However, as commercial banks and insurance companies watched new investment instruments such as money market mutual funds erode their savings bases, and cheaper alternative financing arrangements such as commercial paper erode their long time relationships with blue chip clients, they began to take actions that would further alter the competitive relationships in the financial services sector. This process helped push the marketplace toward the sort of competitive environment in which price competition to obtain corporate borrowing business would more readily accommodate the shelf registration phenomenon.[23]

CONTEMPORARY INDUSTRY STRUCTURE

By the mid-1980s the U.S. securities business had evolved into a vastly larger and more complex entity than could realistically have been envisioned at the time of the framing of the reform legislation in the 1930s. These changes had been shaped largely by the dramatic alterations in the economic climate in which the business operated. The securities industry's range of activities and servicing requirements were much more diverse than they had been fifty years earlier, and the competitive forces at work in the contemporary environment were exerting pressure in a number of quarters, including the securities underwriting area. To understand these influences on underwriting, however, it is important to review each of these major competitive forces.

Corporate Capital Users. The private sector had, of course, undergone enormous growth and development in the years since the passage of the 1933 Act. Private sector corporate assets totaled $8.5 trillion at the end of 1981, compared with $268 billion in 1933. Total corporate sales had reached $6.2 trillion at the end of 1981, compared with $103 billion in 1933; and corporate profits after tax were $140 billion in 1981, compared to $4.8 billion in 1933.[24] Even on an inflation-adjusted basis these size comparisons would offer dramatic contrasts.

The total number of publicly owned business firms in the United States stood at 2.8 million at the end of 1981, compared with 470,000 in 1939, the earliest statistics available. By 1984, there were some ten thousand companies with publicly traded securities, 1,543 of which (with a total of more than 50 billion shares) were listed on the New York Stock Exchange, compared to eight hundred on the Big Board at the end of 1935. Daily share transactions in all established securities markets generally aggregated more than 200 million in 1985.[25]

Private sector financing activity reflected the enormously expanded size and geographic reach of these businesses. Whereas the annual volume of gross new U.S. financings was $397 million in 1934, by 1983 it had reached $100.5 billion.[26] Furthermore, Euromarket activity on behalf of U.S. issuers accounted for an additional $21 billion of debt securities in 1984.[27]

State and Local Capital Users. Municipal and nonprofit sector capital raisers had also emerged by the mid-1980s as an important force in the capital markets. In the 1930s this activity had been submerged within the general "buying" (corporate services) departments of most investment banking firms. But in the decades after World War II increasing numbers of both the wholesale and retail securities firms set up separate public finance departments and assumed more visible positions in this market. This was spurred by the growing popularity in the 1960s and 1970s of bonds backed by specific revenue streams as a relatively cheap and flexible financing vehicle for a variety of capital users. Profit-making corporations, in particular, discovered that, with the cooperation of public agency issuers, they could finance facilities with tax-exempt public credit. While the commercial banks competed aggressively for general obligation municipal financings, that is, bonds which were based on the overall taxing power of the public issuer, they were barred by the Glass-Steagall Act from underwriting or trading revenue-backed securities. This protected market niche grew into a particularly active and lucrative business for securities underwriters, much to the frustration of the commercial banks.[28]

Retail Investors. Whereas until the 1930s the retail investor group constituted the great bulk of potential securities customers (particularly for equities), that market share steadily declined in the post-World War II years. For instance, in March 1953 individuals still did 75 percent of the "public" volume on the New York Stock Exchange (i.e. the volume other than the trades initiated by member firms for their own account). By the end of 1980, that share of public volume had shrunk to 35 percent.[29] Nonetheless, the absolute size of the retail investor presence still remained very large in absolute terms.

The New York Stock Exchange reported that at the end of 1983 there were approximately 26 million individual shareholders, an increase of 19 million from the earliest comprehensive figures (6.9 million) compiled in 1956 and 16 million more than an estimated 10 million at the end of the 1920s.[30] Moreover, if one added the number of individuals directly holding mutual fund shares (as distinct from employer-managed pension funds, insurance company capital pools, and other institutional activities involving individual equity investment positions), the total grew to over 42 million individual shareholders.[31]

A breakdown of individual holdings of corporate and foreign debt securities in 1980 indicates that, since the 1930s, the participation of individual investors in corporate debt issues has shrunk substantially from its former 50 percent share to only 17 percent in 1980 ($83 billion out of $490 billion), while institutional holdings expanded to more than an 80 percent share by 1980. Individuals, however, still account for a significant proportion of direct holdings of equity securities, particularly in certain industry sectors such as utilities.[32]

Institutional Investors. From a relatively modest position as capital supplier to the markets in the 1930s, the institutional investor sector had grown enormously in the post-World War II period. In March 1953 it accounted for only 25 percent of the "public" share volume on the New York Stock Exchange but by the end of 1980 that figure had grown to 65 percent.[33] Moreover, because that percentage has continued to grow, there is the prospect that the dominance of institutional investors in the markets will become even more pronounced in the years ahead. It was estimated in 1985 that pension funds subject to federal regulation held $1 trillion of all types of investment securities and could be expected to have a position of that amount in equity securities alone by the end of the century.[34]

A breakdown of institutional-owned New York Stock Exchange-listed equity assets at the end of 1980 showed that approximately 15 percent were held by insurance companies, 50 percent by noninsured corporate pension funds, 10 percent by investment companies, another 10 percent by nonprofit institutions, and 13 percent by foreign institutions.[35]

Product and Investment Channels. The contrast between the financing options available to capital raisers in the 1930s and those available in the 1980s is striking. In the period before World War II, financing instruments were essentially limited to distinctions among maturities and seniority classifications of debt, preferred stock, and common equity. Convertible securities and warrants had been recurringly used at certain points in the market cycle but not with much innovation in their terms.[36]

After World War II, a growing variety of instruments was employed, particularly as the sophistication of both investors and issuers increased. The characteristics of these investment vehicles were bounded only by the ingenuity of the investment bankers and the drafting talent of their lawyers. Corporate finance officers and their investment banking advisers became increasingly adept at structuring instruments to optimize the specific needs of both investor and issuer. This could be seen in the proliferation of variations on preferred stock alone employed during the merger wave of the late 1960s, and even more dramatically in the late 1970s and the 1980s as competing investment banks jousted to come forth with new financing innovations as a means of attracting—and holding—corporate and municipal clients.

Alternative channels of financing have also added to the contemporary securities markets' complexity. The immediate postwar period saw the rise of the corporations' private capital placements with large institutional investors and the 1960s saw the formation and rapid development of the supranational Euromarket. The establishment of the "fourth market," a computer-assisted medium by which institutions could eliminate the investment banks' traders and deal directly among themselves, took place in the early 1970s. The proliferating uses of commercial paper, commercial paper puts, letters of credit, and interest rate and currency swaps commencing in the 1970s, as well as the securitization of assets as a financing technique employing such devices as leases, limited partnership interests, and specialized certificates, are other examples of new or reconstituted unconventional financing alternatives that have continued to surface at an accelerating rate.

There are no foreseeable limits to the types of corporate securities that may be engendered. Legal requirements tolerate not only all kinds of debt instruments but also equity securities. While all state corporate laws contemplate shares as evidencing ownership rights,[37] there is now an established view that historical concepts of common and preferred securities are anachronistic.[38] Ingenuity alone will determine the tailoring of securities by issuers and bankers to style, tastes, needs, and deals. From a public interest standpoint, the only restriction on such ingenuity is that a public offering of securities must comply with the Securities Act of 1933.

New Entrants. As we mentioned earlier, during much of the postwar period in the United States, the various groups of financial institutions on either side of the Glass-Steagall wall were largely content to follow their own courses without a great deal of encroachment on one another's territories. As the primary, secondary, and even tertiary effects of the inflation surge of the 1970s made an impact in the United States and abroad, however, that tacit non-encroachment agreement dissolved. Each institution began to beggar its neighbors in an effort to recapture lost volume, or to seize profits and growth momentum. These actions had the effect of seriously trespassing on the areas of business previously considered the private preserves of other financial organizations. The securities industry, having been much affected by these developments, pursued a course of litigation to test the barriers which it considered to have been originally intended by Congress.[39]

Commercial banks were particularly caught up in this competition. Mention has already been made of their loss of important aspects of their relationships with corporate clients, many of whom were substituting commercial paper underwritten or marketed by investment bankers as well as other lower-cost accommodations in the place of traditional bank lines of credit. Commercial banks were moving with increasing aggressiveness to reinvigorate those relationships (and their associated revenue streams) by pushing into areas some of which, such as the marketing of industrial commercial paper, were once thought to be precluded by the Glass-Steagall Act. Where possible, they sought fee-based revenues to augment the traditional asset-based revenues. Not surprisingly, these new initiatives prominently included the underwriting of commercial paper sales, private placements, and a variety of off-shore financing activities opened up by the impressive growth of the Euromarkets and not barred by Glass-Steagall.[40] The banks sought to increase their interstate banking reach by pursuing the concept of a bank which, by performing only one of either the deposit or loan functions, would legally be regarded as a nonbank, while seeking legislation to permit interstate chain banking of a traditional kind. These extensions of activities were sought in part to strengthen the banks' position against other institutions, such as retail brokers and mass merchandisers like Sears, that already were operating nationwide branch networks.

The banks were also pushing aggressively in the public financing sector. Because they were deemed to be barred under the Glass-Steagall Act from the large and lucrative revenue bond financing area, they lobbied strenuously in Washington during the 1980s to effect a change in the law.[41] Such an amendment would not only give an immediate access to the gross profit margin from revenue bond underwriting (which constituted more than 75 percent of contemporary municipal financing volume),[42] but it would also provide a larger underwriting and trading base with which to develop both the in-house competence and the "culture" adaptation needed for the ultimate legislative assault to gain the authority to underwrite and trade corporate securities generally.[43]

Insurance companies were making a similar bid for corporate financing business,[44] as well as for a renewal of their historical role as savings repositories for individual investors. They were escalating the competition for corporate private placements and searching out other investment vehicles and revenue-generating activities which would enhance the earning power of their asset bases, thus boosting their competitive edge in competing for the savings dollars of both individuals and groups. In the course of this campaign, they were entering new market niches where permitted, and in a number of prominent cases were purchasing securities firms to gain a foothold in a wide range of financing, trading, and other securities market activities.[45] Conversely, investment banking firms were moving into the insurance business, thus challenging these interlopers on their own turf.

Virtually all of the institutions operating on the deposit-taking side of the Glass-Steagall wall were moving with an increasing sense of urgency to shore up their deposit bases. As we noted earlier, the inflationary 1970s saw the uprooting of entrenched, individual savings patterns, and those changes appeared to be permanent. As part of their effort to hold onto the individual savings dollar, commercial banks, savings and loans, insurance companies, and other institutions were significantly expanding their product lines. Discount securities brokerage, limited to execution of customers' retail orders, was one of the more important initiatives of this sort. From virtually a standing start in 1975, when fixed commissions on securities transactions were abolished, discount brokers had gained a 14 percent share of the retail equity business on the New York Stock Exchange by the beginning of 1984.[46] At that point, some 1,500 commercial banks had set up or affiliated with such brokerage operations, a course followed as well by a number of savings and loans, life insurance companies, and investment company management organizations.[47]

The growth in mutual fund management and sales was another development with important implications for traditional securities firms. We have noted the direct negative impact which money market mutual funds had on traditional deposit-taking institutions during the 1970s. By 1985, revised interpretations of the relevant statutes were permitting commercial banks, savings and loans, and others to offer vehicles fully competitive with those sponsored by both brokerage firms and conventional investment management groups. For some time commercial banks and others had sought permission to manage and distribute conventional stock and fixed income pooled funds to the general public. Notwithstanding repeated rebuffs, they continued to make headway in entering this field.[48]

Securities firms with a substantial retail presence have shown increasing concern about the inroads being made by these new competitors. These retail firms have acquired a large, semifixed overhead cost base that is viable only with sufficient and sustained volume, which becomes more uncertain. This is true in part because of the heightened volatility of the markets since the 1979 change in Federal Reserve monetary policy recognizing that various measures of money supply were significant determinants of inflation and economic growth. In addition, it has become difficult for these securities firms to compete against outside financial service firms whose overhead for branch and other deposit-collection networks may already be covered by other activities. Thus, the retail-oriented securities firms have become increasingly apprehensive of the move toward nationwide branch banking, in which competitors can utilize such devices as automatic teller machines, credit cards, and computer-based home banking services to extend their reach into securities-related activities.

In the area of conventional corporate finance counseling, as well as merger and acquisition services, commercial banks and other deposit-taking institutions have made only modest progress.[49] However, a number of money center commercial banks have made substantial gains in devising and promoting such transactions as interest rate and currency swaps, and several of these large banks have been able to establish significant underwriting and trading positions in the Euromarkets, thus competitively confronting head-on some of the leading U.S. wholesale securities firms.

INVESTMENT BANKING RESPONSE

Until events of the late 1960s and 1970s unleashed responses which they could no longer fully control, the traditionally dominant wholesale investment banks were able to maintain their leading positions, in substantial part, as mentioned earlier, through the intertwined protection of client lists, control of the securities syndication and distribution process, and the workings of reciprocity among the underwriting firms.[50] When the extended economic expansion during the 1960s loosened the disciplinary hold of these securities wholesalers over the traditional distribution firms, they found the latter accelerating their drive for a share of the very profitable corporate origination business. Rather than see their position erode, however, the wholesalers, buttressed by several recently elevated compatriots to the top underwriting bracket, responded to this new competitive threat by increasing their own corporate and institutional service capabilities, including in some cases massive new capital and human resource commitments to the trading area. This was necessary to ensure continuous pricing intelligence and to establish a reliable outlet among institutional investors for their corporate clients' securities.[51]

The dimensions of this response were truly impressive. There has been an enormous increase in both the wholesalers' and aspiring retailers' corporate finance staffs since the beginning of the 1970s.[52] The firms' competitive strategies have led them into fielding a much broader array of services in diverse areas of interest to both their current and potential clients. At the same time, these firms have increased the depth of their skills in each of these areas, in the process creating narrower and more intense specialization among their corporate finance personnel.

The sheer size of the securities firms has grown commensurate with their depth and scope of activities. Total assets of New York Stock Exchange member firms rose from $22 billion in 1974 to $275 billion in 1984. Securities and commodity inventories accounted for much of the increased asset base, growing from $10 billion in 1974 to $205 billion in 1984. Equity capital plus subordinated debt increased from $3.4 billion to $16.8 billion over the same period.[53] The introduction of such a greater potential risk of swings in inventory values has been offset by the application of sophisticated hedging strategies in securities transactions.[54]

The superior returns accruing to the wholesale as compared to the retail securities sector are obvious (see Figure 5-2). Furthermore, it is probable that even these returns understate the true productivity of the invested capital because of a suspected tendency of the private firms to state their profitability conservatively in order to deflect attention from the wealth of their individual members.

The impressive growth and profit record of the wholesale firms in recent years has been matched by market share information. While there have been more instances in recent years of corporate clients switching investment bankers or fragmenting the traditional banker's influence by establishing multiple relationships, a recent study showed that this switching and fragmentation have occurred largely among a group of five or six leading originating firms and have not resulted in a significant broadening of the competitor group.[55]

Thus, in the wholesale securities sector, neither the efforts of other aspiring securities firms nor attempted inroads by

Figure 5-2   **Investment Banks' After Tax Return on Equity**
1975–1985

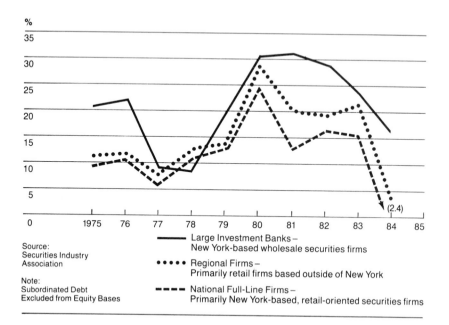

Source:
Securities Industry
Association

Note:
Subordinated Debt
Excluded from Equity Bases

——— Large Investment Banks –
New York-based wholesale securities firms

•••• Regional Firms –
Primarily retail firms based outside of New York

■■■■ National Full-Line Firms –
Primarily New York-based, retail-oriented securities firms

commercial banks and other financial institutions from the other side of the Glass-Steagall wall have thus far been able to dislodge the incumbent group of wholesale firms. They have responded vigorously to each new challenge for an extension of service or the adoption of a financing innovation. And as we shall see in Chapter 6, that philosophy was sustained in their response to the introduction of shelf registration. It was not surprising that, as corporate issuers pushed toward lower cost and greater flexibility and efficiency in new securities offerings, securities underwriters responded to meet this challenge. A de facto form of bidding for certain types of public financings had developed in which the leading securities underwriters competed vigorously. When under Rule 415 the SEC proposed the experimentation with a new instant securities offering procedure designed to enhance competitive efficiency and thereby drive down issuer costs still further, the underwriters, although loudly protesting the new proposal, nonetheless resolutely geared themselves up to compete.

But before looking at how this new shelf underwriting phenomenon unfolded, it is important to look at certain regulatory and information-disseminating developments that were also moving in the same direction and were indeed engendered, at least in part, by SEC determination to create a foundation for the shelf approach to the public offering of securities under the 1933 Act.

NOTES

1. In one well-known example, Montgomery-Ward, under the leadership of CEO Sewell Avery, was so convinced that just such a repeat of the economic depression of the 1930s was in the offing that the firm retrenched during the late 1940s in order to build a giant hoard of cash to tide it over the expected depression. Sears, Roebuck, meanwhile, having a contrary opinion, was busy expanding both its mail order and branch store network in the expectation of a continuing boom in postwar consumer spending.
2. *United States* v. *Morgan*, 118 F.Supp. 621 (S.D.N.Y., Oct. 14, 1953).
3. Samuel L. Hayes, III, Michael Spence, and David Marks, *Competition in the Investment Banking Industry* (Cambridge, Mass.: Harvard University Press, 1983), chap. 1.
4. Samuel L. Hayes, III, "Investment Banking: Power Structure in Flux," *Harvard Business Review* (March-April 1971), p. 138ff.
5. Ibid.
6. See various issues during the 1960s of *Fact Book* of The New York Stock Exchange.
7. Hayes, 1971, p. 142.
8. "Funds Set Aside by Hayden Stone," *New York Times*, 15 January 1969, p. 59.
9. "Big Board Defied by Member Firm," *New York Times*, 23 May 1969, p. 1.
10. "Bache & Co. Posts a Three Month Profit," *New York Times*, 18 December 1970, p. 59.
11. "The New Style at Morgan Stanley," *Business Week*, 19 January 1974, p. 47ff.
12. See particularly, *Fact Book* of The New York Stock Exchange for 1975 and 1976 as well as various editions for prior years.
13. Hayes, 1971, p. 137.
14. E. F. Hutton & Co., *Annual Report* (1974).
15. Samuel L. Hayes, III, "The Transformation of Investment Banking," *Harvard Business Review* (January-February 1979), p. 154.
16. *The Securities Industry in 1979*, Securities and Exchange Commission, Directorate of Economic and Policy Analysis, September 1980.
17. Hayes (1979), pp. 155–156.

18. See, for example, "The Exxon Corporation—Dutch Auction," (Boston: Harvard Business School, Case 1-278-070, 1977).
19. *Papilsky* v. *Berndt*, 333 F.Supp. 1084 (D.C.N.Y., 1971), *aff'd* 466 F.2d 251 (2d Cir. 1972), *cert. denied*, 93 S.Ct. 689 (1972).
20. *Savings and Loan News*, U.S. League of Savings Associations (Chicago: April 1981), p. 6.
21. *Banking*, Journal of the American Bankers Association (Washington, D.C.: July 1977), pp. 78, 80.
22. Samuel L. Hayes, III, "Investment Banking: Commercial Banks' Inroads," *Economic Review*, Federal Reserve Bank of Atlanta (May 1984): 52, 53.
23. Mard D. Coler and E. M. Ratner, *Seventy Percent Off*, Facts on File, Inc. 1983, p. 41ff.
24. U.S. Bureau of the Census, *Historical Statistics of the United States: Colonial Times to 1970*, pt. 2, series V 108–150, p. 925; U.S. Bureau of the Census, *Statistical Abstract of the United States*, 1985, no. 890, pp. 523, 532, 533.
25. U.S. Bureau of the Census, *Historical Statistics of the United States: Colonial Times to 1970*, pt. 2, series V-12, p. 911; U.S. Bureau of the Census, *Statistical Abstract of the United States*, 1985, table 868, p. 516; NASDAQ 1984 Fact Book, Published by the National Association of Securities Dealers (New York: 1985), p. 12; *Fact Book*, The New York Stock Exhange (1972), p. 79; *Fact Book*, The New York Stock Exchange (1985), p. 79.
26. U.S. Bureau of the Census, *Historical Statistics of the United States: Colonial Times to 1970*, series X 499–509, p. 1005; U.S. Bureau of the Census, *Statistical Abstract of the United States.*, 1985, no. 852, p. 506.
27. Statistics provided by *Euromoney* magazine, as quoted in the *New York Times*, 31 December 1985.
28. Douglas M. Bailey, "Industrial Revenue Bonds: The Controversy Continues," *New England Business*, 20 September 1982, p. 16ff.
29. *Fact Book*, The New York Stock Exchange (1985), p. 56.
30. Ibid., p. 52; *Fact Book*, The New York Stock Exchange (1972), p. 46.
31. *Fact Book*, The New York Stock Exchange (1985), p. 52.
32. "Flow of Funds, Accounts, Assets and Liabilities Outstanding, 1969–1980," Board of Governors of the Federal Reserve System (February 1981).
33. *Fact Book*, The New York Stock Exchange (1985), p. 56.
34. Diane Harris, "The Rise of Pension Funds," *Financial World*, 15 June 1982, pp. 47–51.
35. *Fact Book*, The New York Stock Exchange (1985), p. 55.
36. Arthur Stone Dewing, *A Study of Corporate Securities* (New York: Ronald Press, 1934), pp. 376–415; see also Arthur Stone Dewing, *The Financial Policy of Corporations*, 5th Ed., vol. 1, (New York: Ronald Press, 1953), pp. 256–273.
37. See, for example, *Revised Model Business Corporation Act*, Law & Business, Inc. (New York: Harcourt Brace Jovanovich, 1983). The word *share* is defined as meaning "the units into which the proprietary interests in a corporation is divided." Model Business Corp. Act §1.40(21) (1983).

38. Ibid., pp. 86–87. "The revised Model Act breaks away from the inherited concepts to reflect the actual flexibility in the creation of classes of shares that exists in modern corporate practice."

39. "ICI, SIA Seen Near Decision to Appeal Case Against FDIC," *Wall Street Letter*, 17 June 1985, p. 4.

40. Hayes, "Investment Banking: Commercial Banks' Inroads," p. 50ff.

41. Raoul Edwards and Watson Fenmore, "Breaching Glass-Steagall: A Status Report," *United States Banker*, September 1982, pp. 18–20.

42. Ibid., p. 19.

43. Hayes, "Investment Banking: Commercial Banks' Inroads," p. 58.

44. "Equitable to Lump Corp. Finance, Portfolio Management in One Subsidiary," *Corporate Financing Week*, 25 March 1985, p. 3.

45. In 1981 Prudential Insurance purchased Bache & Co. and American Express purchased Shearson Loeb Rhoades. Equitable Life Assurance announced the purchase of Donaldson, Lufkin & Jenrette in late 1984 and other insurance companies have been buying up leading regional securities firms; see, for instance, "Boettcher Executives Considering Buyout Offer from Kemper," *Wall Street Letter*, 4 February 1985, p. 2.

46. William B. Hummer, "Bankers March on Discount Brokerage," *Bankers Monthly Magazine*, 15 January 1985, p. 27.

47. Ibid., p. 26.

48. "Several Banks Plan Stock Mutual Funds as Industry Pushes to Enter Business," *The Wall Street Journal*, 22 January 1985, p. 5.

49. Hayes, "Investment Banking: Commercial Banks' Inroads," p. 54ff.

50. Hayes, "Investment Banking: Power Structure in Flux," p. 145ff.

51. Hayes, "The Transformation of Investment Banking," p. 161ff.

52. Ibid.

53. *Fact Book*, The New York Stock Exchange (1976), p. 64; *Fact Book*, The New York Stock Exchange (1985), p. 60.

54. Barbara Donnelly, "The Academic Invasion of Wall Street," *Institutional Investor* (December 1984): 73.

55. Hayes, Spence, and Marks, *Competition in the Investment Banking Industry*, p. 55ff.

6
Integrated Disclosure

The developments chronicled in Chapter 5 led not surprisingly to a conviction on the part of many observers that the disclosure requirements set up in the 1930s needed to be reassessed and possibly modified. In this chapter we shall discuss the changing attitudes toward disclosure requirements as an integral part of the philosophy of regulation by information. Ultimately, these new attitudes paved the way for the introduction of shelf offerings.

INTERRELATIONSHIP OF 1933 AND 1934 ACTS

In his message to Congress of February 9, 1934, President Roosevelt referred back to the 1933 Act, saying that it was "but one step in our broad purpose of protecting investors and depositors."[1] He then recommended the enactment of additional legislation providing for the federal regulation of the operations of securities exchanges.

Four months later the 1934 Act was passed, creating the Securities and Exchange Commission. The law made it clear that securities transactions, whether on exchanges or over the counter, affect the public interest. Thus the 1934 Act regulates and controls pertinent trading practices, including transactions by insiders, requires the filing of appropriate reports, and ensures "fair and honest markets." This congressional declaration of purpose is followed by a statement of the reasons for enacting the law: securities transactions involve interstate commerce by way of the issuance of securities, the use of particular financing credit, and the national credit; the prices involved in securities transactions are disseminated widely in the United States and abroad, and constitute a basis for determining federal taxes and establishing the value of securities as collateral for bank loans; the prices at which securities transactions are conducted "are susceptible to manipulation and control," and the dissemination of the prices in turn gives rise to "excessive speculation" which itself affects the volume of available national credit, the proper appraisal of values for tax and collateral purposes, and thus the effective operation of the national banking and Federal Reserve systems; and finally, national emergencies are precipitated, intensified, and prolonged by manipulation of securities prices and by excessive speculation on exchanges and markets, thus putting the government to such great expense "as to burden the national credit" in meeting such national emergencies.[2]

This statement appears to suggest that the Great Depression was caused solely by the sins of the securities trade.[3] But this hyperbole may be excused as understandable in the circumstances. As it turned out, the remedies prescribed by the act were much less draconian than the fears expressed by the opposition.[4]

So far as expressed purpose and legislative intent are concerned, the substantive distinction between the 1933 Act and the 1934 Act is not apparent from the statutes themselves, since the earlier act contains no declaration of policy objectives parallel to that specifically set forth in section 2 of the later act. The closest thing to an expression of intent for the

1933 Act appears in President Roosevelt's message of March 29, 1933. That makes it clear, as we noted in Chapter 2, that his recommendation for what finally emerged as the 1933 Act was based on the concept that "*every issue of new securities* to be sold in interstate commerce shall be accompanied by full publicity and information, and that *no essentially important element* attending the issue *shall be concealed* from the buying public."[5]

It seems reasonable to conclude, therefore, that, at least when the two statutes were enacted, their respective disclosure requirements were not contemplated to be functionally related.[6] The disclosure requirement of the 1933 Act was designed only to prevent fraud in the sale of new securities in a public offering—a transactional concept—while in the 1934 Act, the disclosure concept suggests a broad attack on securities fraud, "excessive speculation," and "manipulation and control." The 1934 statute was clearly designed to set a comprehensive policy permanently establishing caution flags for trading markets in interstate commerce. The act's regulatory pattern, while also relying on information as the medium, was to ensure through required periodic and episodic reporting that material information would enter the public domain under a system of penalties and sanctions. Thus a buyer or seller of securities would have ready access to pertinent information, enabling him to reach an informed opinion regarding the value of those securities either directly or through the advice of others.

This requirement, unlike those of the 1933 Act, is not based on the idea of the fulfillment of fiduciary responsibilities between buyer and seller—or between a securities dealer and either of them—short of fraud. Indeed, the reporting requirements of the 1934 Act form an implicit foundation for the current-day efficient market concept. While the 1934 Act, apart from instances of fraud, does not change the common law concept of *caveat emptor,* the 1933 Act did in fact reverse that common law concept. The 1933 Act's *caveat vendor* approach in the public offering of new securities has no real counterpart under the 1934 Act. While the administration of the 1934 Act necessarily involves concepts of efficient markets, the 1933 Act assumes that an efficient market for the securities in question exists only at that brief moment in time when the diligence investigation has been completed, the securities have been priced, and the offering has commenced.

The two statutes were proposed during a twelve-month period by the president as two steps in a program necessary to protect investors, and they were seemingly so regarded by Congress. For this reason the lack of integration between the two acts in disclosure requirements is curious, particularly since a disclosure nostrum is at the heart of both statutes. Milton Cohen, a prominent observer and participant in securities matters, suggested in a seminal 1966 article that had the two laws "been enacted in opposite order, or together," the disclosure scheme would have been better designed.[7] Certainly a single statute dealing with the two disclosure concepts would have eliminated the overlapping of identical requirements embodied in them separately. But since the two concepts are being separately enforced in their schemes of public and private sanctions, the suggestion that a change in the order of statutory enactment would have produced a difference in the thrust of the 1933 Act's design of informational disclosure seems overly speculative.

THE MANDATES REVISITED

Some thirty years after each of the statutes went its own way in Congress, the SEC set about exploring whether the broad reporting requirements of the 1934 Act could subsume some of the *ad hoc* requirements of the 1933 Act. The desire to eliminate overlaps in disclosure requirements did not arise out of any failure on the part of the statutes to achieve their recognized objectives. The SEC merely sought to establish greater efficiency through what ultimately became known as "integrated disclosure." The findings reported in the Integrated Disclosure Release of March 2, 1982, had as their goal "to revise or eliminate overlapping or unnecessary disclosure and dissemination requirements wherever possible, thereby reducing burdens on registrants while at the same time ensuring that security holders, investors, and the marketplace have been provided with meaningful, nonduplicative information upon which to base their investment decisions."[8] Whether or not the process was actually triggered by Cohen's 1966 article, it was certainly stimulated by his having pointed out the duplication inherent in certain requirements of the two statutes and his recommendations concerning the integration of the two disclosure systems.

In 1967 the SEC took its first formal step in that direction.[9] It adopted a simplified registration form under the 1933 Act (Form S-7) for securities offered for cash by companies having long records of earnings and stability of management, and subject to the reporting requirements of the 1934 Act. The shortened form was designed to simplify the task of preparation for the registrant and to simplify the SEC's processing of the registration.[10]

The Wheat Report.   Concurrently, the SEC appointed an internal study group to examine in detail the respective disclosure systems. The resulting 1969 report, "Disclosure to Investors: Reappraisal of Administrative Policies Under the 1933 and 1934 Acts," known as the Wheat Report, made extensive recommendations.[11] These aimed at conceptually strengthening and improving reporting under the 1934 Act (for example, through more comprehensive forms), administration and enforcement of preparation and filing, and dissemination of the information being reported. Contingent upon such improvements, the Wheat Report concluded that disclosures under the 1934 Act could be substituted for disclosures otherwise required by the 1933 Act.[12]

Consistent with the Wheat Report, the SEC supplemented its initial move by adopting Form S-16 in 1970.[13] This permitted issuers qualified to use Form S-7, when registering securities to be sold in certain secondary distributions, to incorporate by reference information in this kind of 1933 Act registration information already filed in 1934 Act reports. This broadening of the nature of disclosure necessarily assumed that, since the issuer had similar securities currently outstanding, the market price already reflected the information upon which a secondary distribution would necessarily be based. Eligibility to use Form S-7, encompassing a relatively small group of issuers, remained the test of this significant step toward integration of disclosure.[14]

Significance of an Efficient Market. The SEC's decision to proceed in this fashion was almost certainly influenced by the rapidly accumulating academic research and literature on the empirical evidence of the financial markets' efficient valuation of securities. The efficient market concept became both the reason for requiring broadened disclosures under the 1934 Act and the justification for considering those disclosures sufficient to meet the requirements of the 1933 Act.[15]

In essence, the efficient market hypothesis states that, at any point in time, the market price of a security fully reflects all available information about that security.[16] The average investor need not, therefore, be aware of any particular piece of information in order to be able to participate in the market on a fair basis with other investors—even those with greater sophistication and/or better means of collecting and analyzing data about individual companies. At any particular time the true value of a security is as likely to be above the actual market price as below it. Therefore, every buyer or seller of that security (other than one possessing inside information) is in exactly the same position. The strongest adherents of the theory would maintain that not even an investor with specific undisclosed information about a company could identify an undervalued security or an overpriced one, because the implications of that information would already be reflected in the security's market price.[17]

Adherents of the efficient market hypothesis are not all of the same mind as to the spontaneous power of market forces to draw in relevant information about a company and incorporate it into its securities' prices. These adherents are divided into three camps: those who subscribe to the strong form of the theory, those who embrace the semistrong form, and those who subscribe only to the weak form of the hypothesis.

Adherents of the strong form take the position that all information relevant to a corporate issuer, even that which would initially be known only to a company insider, is drawn into the marketplace by a variety of means and relatively quickly incorporated (or discounted) in the securities' prices.

The semistrong theory rejects the market's capability to ferret out and incorporate insider information,[18] but cites evidence that it is effective in quickly incorporating publicly disseminated information of the type required to be filed under the 1934 Act.

Adherents of the weak form do not even accept the market's ability to incorporate publicly issued information efficiently but, instead, maintain that day-to-day price movements in a company's securities are randomly determined, and therefore technical analysis of price movement patterns is futile and misleading.

The empirical evidence buttressing the claims of each of these positions is mixed. Although some studies suggest that the market does have the capacity to penetrate all of the supposedly secret recesses of issuer information, the greater weight of evidence seems to reject that suggestion of market x-ray vision.[19] Even the semistrong form of the hypothesis has its detractors, moreover. Some studies have questioned the efficiency with which the markets incorporate information that is readily available in the public domain.[20] This somewhat ambiguous status for the market efficiency hypothesis as it relates to both publicly released information and to information and insights about a securities issuer which are not publicly released obviously bears importantly on the feasibility of the SEC's position with respect to the significance of market efficiency as a foundation for shelf registrations.

INITIATION OF FILING RELATIONSHIPS

In 1976, satisfied that improvement had been realized in the quality, scope, and dissemination of 1934 Act reports upon which the Wheat Report recommendations had been premised, the SEC broadened the availability of Form S-7 to primary securities—that is, truly new securities—issuers. The range of both eligible issuers and the transactions for which it was available was enlarged.[21]

The Advisory Committee Report. An Advisory Committee on Corporate Disclosure was appointed by the SEC to study the issues further. In 1977 it recommended a complete integration of the two disclosure systems. Reports under the 1934 Act could be incorporated in registration statements under the 1933 Act merely by a reference to the 1934 Act filing. But the committee recognized that this liberalization could not be made universally applicable. It suggested that issuers be classified in three categories, for which different forms (and hence different degrees of eligibility for integration of disclosure) would be available. The committee said, "The necessity of providing information to offerees should vary with the type of company and the type of security involved, and the amount of information already available."[22]

The advisory committee's report led the SEC in 1978 to enlarge the availability of its registration form that previously was confined only to secondary offerings of outstanding securities, to include primary offerings as well. The commission, however, envisioned this liberalization only in the case of primary offerings for "a small top tier of companies which usually provide high quality corporate communication documents, including 1934 Act reports, and whose corporate information is widely disseminated."[23] Thus the SEC was increasing its reliance on the efficient market as a proxy for 1933 Act disclosures. The commission required that "members of this class [the 'small top tier'] of registrants [be] widely followed by debt and equity analysts."[24]

The recommendations of the advisory committee became a full reality in March 1982, when the SEC adopted an integrated disclosure system which comprehensively restructured the reporting requirements under both the 1933 and 1934 Acts. A three-tier registration structure involving Forms S-1, S-2, and S-3 was adopted under the 1933 Act, with issuer eligibility dependent upon the presumed degree of availability of information about the registrant in the public domain. The basis of classification was to be the registrant's participation in the disclosure and reporting system under the 1934 Act.[25]

Regulations S-K and S-X. At the same time, the SEC adopted an expanded and revised Regulation S-K, which contains its standard instructions for filing forms under the 1933 Act and 1934 Act. Together with the commission's separate general rules and regulations under the 1933 and 1934 Acts, as well as separate interpretative releases under these acts and the content of the forms themselves, Regulation S-K provides the detailed disclosure requirements for the *non-financial* portions both of registration statements offering securities for sale under the 1933 Act and for the various statements, reports, and proxy materials required by the 1934 Act. The principal sections of Regulation S-K give instructions regarding presentation and content of required information concerning the registrant's business, securities, financial information, its management and ownership, the prospectus under the 1933 Act, and the necessary exhibits to the registration statement.

The required form and content of *financial* statements are set forth separately in Regulation S-X, which, together with the commission's accounting series releases, establishes the requirements applicable both to registration statements under the 1933 Act and to the various statements, reports, and proxy materials under the 1934 Act. Specific separate instructions covering unique industry financial data requirements supplement the general instructions.

Having adopted its integrated disclosure system, the commission was now receptive to the implementation of a rule designed to accelerate to the ultimate—a matter of hours or even minutes—the incubation period in eligible cases between the registration of a new security and its public offering. The regulatory stage was thus set for the introduction of shelf registration.

BACKGROUND OF SHELF REGISTRATION

In 1967 and 1968, concurrently with the quickening of its interest in establishing integration of disclosure provisions under the 1933 Act and 1934 Act, the commission established guidelines for the initiation of a pragmatic form of shelf registration. For the nearly thirty-five years since passage of the 1933 Act, the SEC had held that a conventional underwritten public offering of securities could not be registered for sale at an indefinite future time; it could not be put "on the shelf" for subsequent use. Because of the legal need for full disclosure and the commission's view that this entailed a prospectus currently effective under the 1933 Act, if an issuer failed to proceed with an offering immediately after the registration statement became effective, the issuer had to file either a delaying amendment acceptable to the commission or an actual withdrawal—that is, a deregistration. For some years, however, the commission had realistically recognized that there were securities whose future rather than present issuance was specifically contemplated by the terms of the securities currently being registered. For example, the securities being offered could subsequently be converted into a different security, or have rights subsequently to be exercised, without requiring further registration procedures.

The Conceptual Predecessor. In 1968 the commission addressed this problem and moved to adopt what was the conceptual forerunner of Rule 415 shelf registration. It permitted the continuous or delayed future offering of securities to be issued in acquisition programs or securities expected to be issued on exercise of other securities such as options, warrants, and rights.[26] It also accepted as administratively appropriate for future issuance under the 1933 Act such shelf offerings as limited partnership tax shelters, employee benefit plans, and mortgage-backed pass-through certificates.[27] Recognizing that its earlier interpretation of the intent of the 1933 Act now created huge obstacles to issuing of securities not designed for immediate offering, the commission noted that "these types of shelf offerings may only be feasible on a traditional shelf basis."[28]

Whether the 1968 guidelines and subsequent administrative practices which sanctioned these traditional shelf offerings were consistent with the intent of the 1933 Act—at least as it had been applied by the commission for some thirty-five years—was never a burning issue. The commission had required issuers to agree that they would constantly update the shelf registration statements by so-called posteffective amendments to ensure subsequent necessary disclosures. The pragmatism of this approach and its results permitted the commission to note, when subsequently adopting Rule 415, that it was "not aware of any disclosure, due diligence or other concerns having been raised" about the registration of these traditional offerings on a continuous or delayed basis.[29]

Relationship of Due Diligence to Efficient Markets.   In adopting integrated disclosure, the commission specifically recognized its essential presence in a system of accelerated securities issuance from which Rule 415 was fashioned. Integrated disclosure in the commission's view is a particularly valuable ingredient in achieving market efficiency. It said that in connection with its adoption of Rule 415, companies for which Form S-3 is available[30] "provide a steady stream of high quality information to the marketplace [which] is constantly digested and synthesized by financial analysts, who act as essential conduits and is broadly disseminated on a timely basis."[31] A key question, however, is whether the information thus generated and incorporated into the prices of already outstanding securities is likely to be exhaustive and sufficiently specific from an investment banker's standpoint under the 1933 Act. Can that kind of quality be obtained in an investigation which is not goaded by the legal responsibility of the person making the investigation? Contemporary rules which aim to speed up the process of securities issuance thus run head-long into the requirements for achieving due diligence—that is, an adequate opportunity to pursue this unique investigatory function.

Need For a Definition of Diligence.   This concern produced a dilemma. The commission cannot make rules to protect the underwriter from liability under section 11, and only Congress can amend the law. Accordingly, if the underwriter has failed to conduct a reasonable investigation of the issuer, whether the process is interpreted as a mandatory requirement of the 1933 Act or merely an effective shield in litigation for persons other than the issuer, the commission has no power to absolve this failure. Thus, having enacted Rule 415 on a temporary basis on March 3, 1982, the commission also adopted Rule 176 (discussed in Chapter 8) as part of its integrated disclosure system.[32] Its intention was to address this dilemma by providing some degree of comfort, if not absolute protection to investment bankers and their financial intermediaries, but not to the issuer.

The commission's reliance upon market efficiency reached a predictable culmination in 1984, when it brought integrated disclosure into the state of the art for investment communication by adopting a computerized electronic filing system—acronym EDGAR—which would perform electronic data-base gathering, permit retrieval, and establish the source of integrated disclosure data. The SEC believed that the system could ultimately replace paper documents such as proxy statements and even permit shareholder voting by computer. The commission then anticipated that as many as one thousand registrants might be incorporated in the system by the end of 1985, with the system wholly operational by the end of 1986.[33] It obviously hoped that this would enhance the speed and efficiency by which publicly issued information would work its way into the market prices of securities.

In retrospect, during the fifteen years from 1967 to 1982 when the commission worked directly and through committees on the establishment of the system integrating disclosures under the 1933 and 1934 Acts, its preoccupation with the latter act emerges strongly. In contrast with a high of only 6,100 registration statements under the 1933 Act during calendar 1983, there are many times that number of *daily* trading transactions to which the 1934 Act applies. The commission appears to be influenced by this volume distinction. By emphasizing market efficiency and the relation of integrated disclosure to achieving that, it seems reasonable to infer that the commission considers the pricing process in trading markets to be a more important goal than the assurance of diligence in public offerings under the 1933 Act. While its adoption of shelf registration for 1933 Act purposes fits neatly into its efforts to bring the two laws into one, does it create problems? Compliance with a public policy of 1933 Act diligence which has held sway for more than a half century is the focus of our consideration in the chapters which follow.

NOTES

1. 78 *Cong. Rec.* 2264 (1934) (message from President Franklin D. Roosevelt).
2. 15 U.S.C. §78b (1976). Although enacted in 1934, the reference to codification of the 1934 Act (as well as the 1933 Act) is 1976.

3. Representative Wadsworth of New York, a member of the committee on the bill, expressed his perturbation in the debate with the expressed congressional declaration of purpose, as follows:

"There is a long argument in the first two pages of the bill. In fact section 2 is a speech, and I would advise you all to read it. I have never seen anything quite like it proposed in legislation. It starts by stating that certain things are important and certain things are evil, and then goes on to say that the important things should be handled and the evil things should be prevented, and it ends up with an exhortation that the whole thing is the right thing to do and is well within the provisions of the Constitution, or words to that effect. That, of course, is designed to control the Supreme Court. If I had my way, as a matter of bill drafting, I would strike it out. It has no place in a statute of the United States. You do not put your arguments in statutes; you put your arguments in the reports of the committee or you make them on the floor of the House or the Senate." 78 *Cong. Rec.* 7715 (1934).

4. Representative Merritt of Connecticut addressed the House at length to stress that opponents of the bill were motivated by a legitimate desire "to protect their own property against undue depreciation." He said that he had never "heard any objection to the farmers getting together to protect their own interests," and added: "You doubtless appreciate that in the past 50 years the amount of liquid personal property in stocks and bonds in this country has increased tremendously, and very much to the advantage of the people of this country. You will agree, I think, also, that while the so-called 'panic of 1929' was largely connected with this personal property, and that while the blow-up was more evident on the stock exchange than anywhere else, the stock exchange was not primarily to blame. . . .

"I am not saying that there have not been abuses that should be corrected. What I am pleading for here is that in considering this legislation it should not be undertaken in any vindictive spirit. It should not be conducted with a notion that anybody who has made or may make a suggestion concerning the bill has been actuated by anything but an honest motive, and not by any propaganda." 78 *Cong. Rec.* 7710 (1934).

5. 77 *Cong. Rec.* 937 (1933) (emphasis added).

6. The legislative history is barren of any attempt to reconcile the disclosure requirements of the two acts. See, for example, 78 *Cong. Rec.* 2264, 2269–2271 (1934), in which Senator Fletcher introduces what became the 1934 Act and gives a statement and digest of it. He made no reference to existing 1933 Act disclosure concepts. Specifically with regard to proposed 1934 Act disclosure, he said:

"The evidence before the Senate Banking and Currency committee has demonstrated that those in charge of stock exchanges in the past have not required adequate disclosure by persons and concerns listing or maintaining the listing of securities on the exchanges. At times the excuse has been advanced that exchange officials have not had sufficient power. There can be no question that the American public is entitled to have the fullest disclosure, as a condition to the listing of securities and as a condition to maintaining such listing on the public exchanges. The federal government has the power to require this full disclosure, and the bill is so written that the disclosure may now become assured to the great body of our investors" (p. 2271).

7. Milton H. Cohen, "Truth in Securities Revisited," 79 *Harvard Law Review* 1340 (1966).
8. Sec. Act Rel. 6383 (March 2, 1982) [47 Fed. Reg. 11380 (1982)], hereinafter cited as Integrated Disclosure Release.
9. Sec. Act Rel. 4886 (November 29, 1967) [32 Fed. Reg. 17934 (1967)].
10. Ibid. The simplification evidenced by Form S-7 [17 C.F.R. §239.33] included the permitted omission of such Form S-1 disclosure requirements as: parents of registrant; description of property; pending legal proceedings; directors and executive officers and their remuneration; options to purchase securities; principal holders of securities; and interest of management and others in certain transactions. In large part, these data would have been replicated by required proxy statement disclosures under Section 14 of the 1934 Act.
11. Securities and Exchange Commission, "Disclosure to Investors: A Reappraisal of Administrative Policies Under the 1933 and 1934 Acts" (1969), hereinafter cited as Wheat Report.
12. A series of proposals were published in 1969 to implement the Wheat Report's recommendations for improvements in administering the 1934 Act. See, for example, Sec. Exchange Act Rel. 8680, 8681, 8682, 8683 (September 15, 1969) [34 Fed. Reg. 15235 (1969)].
13. Sec. Act Rel. 5117 (December 23, 1970) [36 Fed. Reg. 777 (1970)].
14. Ibid. In 1970 the SEC also expanded the reporting requirement of the 1934 Act by adopting Form 10-Q for quarterly reports. Sec. Exchange Act Rel. 9004 (November 14, 1970) [35 Fed. Reg. 17537 (1970)].
15. Integrated Disclosure Release (see note 8).
16. Eugene Fama, "Efficient Capital Markets: A Review of Theory and Empirical Work," 25 *Journal of Finance* 383 (1970).
17. Apart from disclosures of material fact emanating from issuers or disclosures by acquirers or statutory insiders whose purchases or sales may require public disclosure, there is always the likelihood of significant trading transactions not requiring disclosure. As long as such transactions are deemed not to be deceptive or manipulative, their impact on market prices can be known only, if at all, after they have affected market prices, possibly in a material manner. For example, the concept of arbitrage in its pure form can thrive only on differences in prices in two or more markets simultaneously which permit riskless trading profit, an operation which, therefore, relies on the absence of market efficiency. As market index and related futures contracts trading has developed—in itself a market function not inconsistent with the concept of an efficient market—it has engendered a related inconsistent trading impact of considerable effect, particularly on individual investors. This impact, called program trading, has no necessary relationship to individual securities, although it affects their prices. A typical program may involve, for example, an institution's instructions to its broker to buy or sell a list of securities of one hundred companies that are considered to represent fairly the prospects, up or down, of Standard & Poor's or any other broad index being traded by the institution through index futures contracts. The program list has analytical significance only for its function as a proxy for the index, and execution of the program may strongly influence the market prices of the securities involved, which by hypothesis are market leaders other-

wise deemed efficiently priced. As one market observer notes, "You push a button [to put the program into effect] and, bam, it goes. There's absolutely no regard for values, just strategy." See *New York Times*, 30 August 1985, p. D1.

18. Jeffrey F. Jaffee, "Special Information and Insider Trading," 47 *Journal of Business* 410 (1974).

19. Joseph E. Finnerty, "Insiders and Market Efficiency," 31 *Journal of Finance* 1141 (1976); K. Paul Asquith and David Mullins, "Signalling with Dividends, Stock Repurchases and Equity Issues," Harvard Business School Paper for 75th Anniversary Colloquium on New Perspectives on Corporate Finance Decisions (1984).

20. William W. Jahnke, "The Growth Stock Mania," 29 *Financial Analysts Journal* 65 (1973); William W. Jahnke, "The Growth Stock Mania Revisited," 31 *Financial Analysts Journal* 42 (1975).

21. Sec. Act Rel. 5791 (December 20, 1976) [41 Fed. Reg. 56304 (1976)]. See also, Sec. Act Rel. 6235 (September 2, 1980) [45 Fed. Reg. 63693 (1980)].

22. Report of the Advisory Committee on Corporate Disclosure to the Securities and Exchange Commission, 95th Congress, 1st sess. (Comm. Print 1977), p. 432.

23. Sec. Act Rel. 5923 (April 11, 1978) [43 Fed. Reg. 16677 (1978)] (quoting Advisory Committee Report, pp. 433–434).

24. Ibid.

25. Integrated Disclosure Release (see note 8). Under this framework, registrants under the 1933 Act would be classified into three categories: (1) companies that are widely followed by professional analysts; (2) companies that have been subject to the periodic reporting system of the 1934 Act for three or more years but are not widely followed; and (3) companies that have been in the 1934 Act reporting system for less than three years. The first category would be eligible to use Form S-3, which relies upon incorporation by reference of 1934 Act reports and requires minimal disclosure in the prospectus.

26. Sec. Act Rel. 4936 (December 9, 1968) [33 Fed. Reg. 18617 (1968)].

27. Sec. Act Rel. 6369 (March 12, 1982) [47 Fed. Reg. 11701 (1982)].

28. Ibid., p. 11705.

29. Sec. Act Rel. 6499 (November 17, 1983) [48 Fed. Reg. 52889 (1983)].

30. For an example of a Form S-3 [17 C.F.R. 239.13] registration involving significant incorporation by reference, see Appendix II. The right under the commission's rules not to repeat information already disclosed in a public filing, but simply to refer to that filing as a source is the basic approach to integrated disclosures under the two acts. Since the 1934 Act requires periodic and extraordinary reporting, while in the 1933 Act reporting becomes pertinent only upon a public offering of securities, the integration is essentially a one-way street, with incorporation by reference to 1934 Act public reports being used in 1933 Act prospectuses without providing the information specifically.

31. Sec. Act Rel. 6499, p. 12.

32. Integrated Disclosure Release (see note 8).

33. *Securities Regulation and Law Report* (December 21, 1984), pp. 1990–1991.

7
Introduction of Shelf Registration

Viewed in the context of developments in the securities and financial service markets discussed in Chapter 5 and the modifications and alterations in disclosure procedures discussed in Chapter 6, the forces pushing toward the introduction of shelf registration and the securities firms' response to the new procedure are not difficult to understand.

PRESSURES FOR SIMPLIFICATION

Developments within the market for the growing number of securities offerings in recent years has put greater pressure on spreads, that is, the difference between the underwriter's cost for a security and its publicly announced selling price. Financial officers of corporate issuers appear to be moving toward the same periodic auditing with their investment bankers of fees paid versus services received that they have applied to commercial banking relationships for some years.

We have mentioned that institutional investors were already being granted discounts on new offerings, often by "overtrading," that is, receiving artificially high prices on a yield basis for portfolio holdings in swap for new securities.

It was also noted earlier that corporate clients have viewed commercial bank term loans, Euromarket financings made outside the United States in either dollar or foreign currency, and interest rate and currency swaps as trade-offs for conventional U.S. debt placements. They have increasingly opted for these offshore and swap arrangements, not only for the realization of a lower average net cost of funds, but also because the speedier execution of private or offshore transactions outside the requirements of the 1933 Act has enabled them to make use of perceived temporary windows of opportunity in the world's capital markets.

A conviction was developing within the issuer and regulatory communities in the United States that the procedures for issuing securities should be streamlined, particularly for the large, well-known, and frequent capital raisers. It was hoped that moves in this direction would reduce bureaucratic delays and, overall, lower the issuance costs to corporate capital raisers. Many observers expected that throwing open the capital raising activity to de facto competitive bidding would increase the number of underwriting competitors. It was also hoped that such steps would enhance the attraction of domestic financings vis-à-vis alternative accommodations available in the Euromarkets where many of the advantages referred to above were already obtained.

Under the shelf registration procedure, as we will see, an eligible issuer is permitted to file registration documents specifying that it intends to sell a certain maximum amount of a particular class of securities at one or more unspecified points within the succeeding two years. Detailed offering terms are, of course, delayed until the actual time of sale to investors. One or more qualifying underwriters may also be listed. Within the two-year time limit subsequent to the registration, when the issuer and its advisers see a favorable opportunity in the marketplace, they can quickly effect a sale of some or all of the securities specified in the registration statement. In all likelihood, once the registration statement has been filed, they will from time to time receive calls from a variety of investment banking firms offering to buy the securities at a given set of terms and price. Similar acquisition procedures were commonly used in the late nineteenth and early twentieth centuries, although in the environment of the 1980s, because of the contemporary higher risks from potential price volatility, underwriters are loath to accept the gradual liquidation of their acquired inventory of securities typical in earlier times. They would rather sell (or, even better, presell) all or most of the offering within a few hours or a day.

As already indicated, because the acquisition procedures adopted for shelf registration were formulated so as to create as level a playing field as possible for prospective underwriters (regardless of any historical or traditional association with the issuer), observers expected that the competitive vigor surrounding these offerings would be enhanced. The number of investment bankers vying to underwrite such issues was expected to be broadened, and the cost to the issuer of the distribution was therefore expected to be reduced to the minimum.

RULE 415 AND SUBSEQUENT SHELF ACTIVITY

Rule 415 emerged in proposed form seeking public comment through notices on December 23, 1980,[1] and on August 6, 1981.[2] It was adopted by the SEC in a temporary—that is, experimental—form on March 3, 1982,[3] and was extended in the same temporary form to December 31, 1983.[4] At the beginning of 1984, shelf registration became a permanent option.[5]

In the period since shelf registration was first introduced on a trial basis, this financing technique has made impressive inroads in the U.S. capital markets. To provide a before-and-after perspective, Figure 7-1 shows total annual public financing data for the period since January 1, 1979. It should be noted that the three years of shelf experience has coincided with a record level of public corporate financings.

Figure 7-1   **Public Financing Volume: 1979–1984**
Shelf vs. Nonshelf

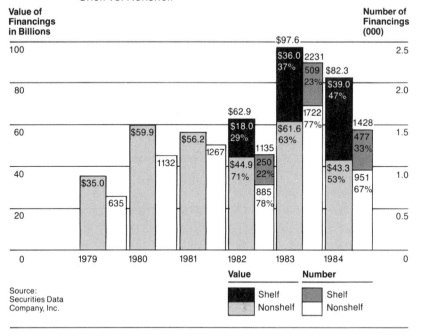

Source:
Securities Data
Company, Inc.

The shelf method got off to a fast start in 1982, when, in only nine months of authorized use, the technique captured 29 percent of the total volume of issues marketed during the year. In 1983, a year of record public financing volume, shelfs captured 37 percent of the total volume. By 1984, with a continuing high level of financing activity and with Rule 415 permanently in effect from the beginning of the year, shelfs captured almost half (47 percent) of the year's total financing volume.

Figure 7-1 also shows that the proportion of total issuers using the shelf technique grew substantially between 1982 and 1984, from 22 percent to 33 percent of issues. Not only was a larger proportion of issuers utilizing shelf registrations during this period, but as Table 7-1 shows, the shelf financings were, on the average, substantially larger than the nonshelfs, primarily because equity shelf offerings were very much larger than nonshelf equity financings. It should be noted that an investment banker's perspective of the nature of an equity shelf offering does not permit any precise formulation. When the syndicate managers of several large investment banking houses were asked to describe a true equity shelf offering, their definitions included some or all of the following possibly inconsistent factors: (1) the fact that securities are taken off the shelf from time to time; (2) the speed with which the offering is brought to market; (3) an absence of orchestrated offering procedures; (4) a minimal marketing effort; (5) a nonfixed price offering; (6) the presence of competitive bidding in industrial offerings; (7) block-type transactions; and (8) the possible initiation of the transaction after registration by the unsolicited bid of an investment banker.

Negotiated Debt Offerings. Among negotiated publicly offered debt issues, the size differential between shelfs and nonshelfs was not large, as Figure 7-2 shows. Nonetheless, experience in the negotiated debt market from 1982 to 1984 is a key to understanding the dimensions of the shelf phenomenon, since this is where the bulk of Rule 415 activity has taken place.

Figure 7-2 shows that debt shelfs got off to an impressively fast start in 1982, capturing 38 percent of the $41 billion of volume in just nine months' time. The following year, with total debt volume up by 21 percent over the previous year, shelfs captured almost 50 percent of the market. In 1984 the volume of negotiated debt financing continued to climb, with shelf registration garnering 52 percent of the $65 billion of debt financings during that year.

As these exhibits show, the proportionate number of debt issuers utilizing shelf registration paralleled their volume share of the market fairly closely. Thus, the size differential between shelfs and nonshelfs remained fairly constant, although widening somewhat in 1984.

Negotiated Equity Offerings. Figure 7-3 shows that negotiated equity financings were essentially flat (averaging $15 billion) during four of the five years from 1979 to 1984, the exception being 1983, which enjoyed an extraordinary volume of $44 billion. Shelf registrations captured 9 percent

Figure 7-2 **Negotiated Debt Financing Volume: 1979–1984**
Shelf vs. Nonshelf

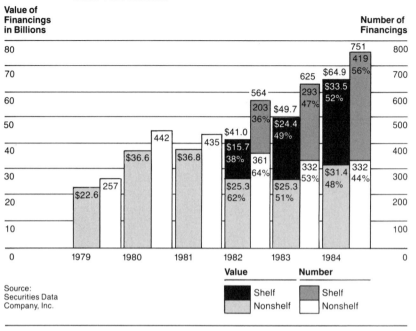

Figure 7-3 **Negotiated Equity Financing Volume: 1979–1984**
Shelf vs. Nonshelf

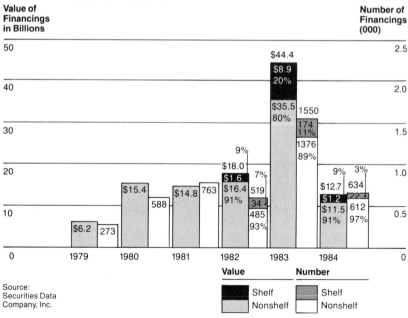

Table 7-1

Average Size of Financings (*In Millions of Dollars*)

	1979	1980	1981	1982	1983	1984
Total Financings						
Total financings	$55	$51	$44	$55	$44	$58
Shelf financings	—	—	—	72	70	82
Nonshelf financings	—	—	—	50	36	46
Negotiated Debt Financings						
Total debt financings	$88	$83	$85	$73	$80	$86
Shelf debt financings	—	—	—	77	83	80
Nonshelf debt financings	—	—	—	70	76	94
Negotiated Equity Financings						
Total equity financings	$22	$26	$19	$35	$29	$20
Shelf equity financings	—	—	—	47	51	55
Nonshelf equity financings	—	—	—	34	26	19

Source: Securities Data Company, Inc.

of the negotiated equity volume in both 1982 and 1984 and an impressive 20 percent during high-volume 1983.

Figure 7-3 also shows that 7 percent of the issuers sold 9 percent of the volume in 1982, 11 percent sold 20 percent of the volume in 1983, and 3 percent of the issuers sold 9 percent of the volume in 1984.

Table 7-1 shows that the average size of equity shelf deals was growing modestly during this period, and that the size differential between shelf and conventional equity financings was growing larger in each succeeding year.

Cost Savings. The popularity of the shelf registration form of financings is better understood if one can point to tangible benefits accruing to the issuer and motivation for the underwriting competitors to pursue the business vigorously. The SEC had hoped that significant cost savings would be achieved as a result of more favorable timing and flexibility, as well as the opportunity for more vigorous competition among securities underwriters for each piece of business. Several studies of comparative all-inclusive (all-in) costs were undertaken by academic researchers under SEC sponsorship to test out that hypothesis, and the results did indeed point in the direction of such cost savings.[6]

Specifically, the studies suggest that industrial bond issues sold by shelf registration incur an all-in cost of funds between twenty and thirty basis points (that is, portions of one percent, which is one hundred basis points) lower than the all-in cost of funds for comparable nonshelf offerings. The cost savings are apparently achieved because of the more intense bidding by competing underwriters for the bond issues. The studies also tested to determine whether and to what extent savings could be effected by astute timing of new issues. They found some statistical support for that hypothesis, at least during periods when the markets were relatively stable.

It is noteworthy that the great bulk of the shelf underwriting volume has been in the debt area, where cost savings are most readily demonstrated. Both issuers and investment bankers maintain that, in the equity sector, the negative impact of the public knowledge of an impending stock sale serves as a depressant on share price and therefore makes the shelf procedure relatively less attractive than would be true of debt financings.

Competition for Shelf Business. As we noted earlier, substituting the shelf format for a conventional negotiated underwriting (utilizing one of the issuer's traditional investment bankers) was expected to enhance competition. The evidence of significant average cost savings for the shelf financings—at least among debt issues—would seem to confirm that this has in fact happened.

A closer scrutiny of the actual experience with shelfs indicates, however, that the altered competitive picture is not so simply summarized. There appears to be little doubt that there has been vigorous competition for much of the shelf business. This is not surprising, in view of the opportunities and benefits which would be expected to accrue to banking firms that were ultimately successful in purchasing the securities for resale. They would have such prospects as (1) direct profit contributions from the activity; (2) an increased supply of securities marketable through their sales networks; (3) the possibility of blocking another securities firm from gaining a foothold with a traditional client; and (4) the benefits of initiating a business relationship with a desirable corporate issuer.

Although the successful underwriters' spreads on Rule 415 issues have indeed been thin, the use of a comparatively small underwriting syndicate (or the absence of one altogether in the case of a "bought" deal where one underwriter contracts to buy from the issuer the entire proposed issue) can preserve for the participating securities dealers a potentially substantial dollar profit, assuming that the securities are sold quickly to avoid or minimize the risk of inventory losses. Because most of the sales of shelf-registered securities have been to institutional investors, where selling costs are largely fixed, most of the spread (however thin) can be brought down to the profit line on the underwriter's earning statement.

A securities firm is also mindful of the desired balance between the capacity, appetite, and morale of its distribution network on the one hand and the ebbs and flows in the supply of appropriate product on the other. Continuing a dialogue between salesmen and the nationwide network of securities buyers represented by portfolio managers is a constant preoccupation. Even the largest and most diversified securities firms are unable to achieve continuing self-sufficiency in generating new in-house product.[7] Thus, salable securities obtained in successful competition for Rule 415 offerings can be a valuable support to a firm's marketing effort and momentum, and the aggregate volume thus achieved is a *sine qua non* for good industry standing. The ability to advertise one's industry standing in relative underwriting volumes is itself productive of various types of banking business.[8]

As the discussion in Chapter 5 demonstrated, it could be reasonably assumed that when a traditional investment banking client is involved, underwriters would be motivated to bid on shelf securities even in the face of difficult market conditions or inadequate time to make a sufficient investigation to avoid due diligence liabilities.[9] If a valued client passes up the conventional advance negotiated financing route and files instead for debt or equity securities to be offered under Rule 415 without naming a banker, its traditional investment bankers would be loath to risk their future banking relationship by adopting a cautious or time-consuming investigative stance on the offering. They would more likely feel compelled to bid aggressively on these securities, whether or not the timing, price range, or issuer's terms were particularly attractive. The prospect of another investment banker's buying the securities for resale and thereby possibly establishing the beginnings of a relationship with the client is usually unpalatable.[10] Corporate clients, and particularly their chief financial officers, value such personal access to their investment bankers in order to keep fully informed about securities markets. In turn, informal communications and social relations are welcomed by the bankers since they often yield intelligence that later generates new revenues.

Advice to a potential issuer on capital structure and financing strategies can produce such additional revenues for the banker and demonstrate its awareness of the state of the art and its ability to devise even further innovation. Also, there are the variations and permutations of the investment banker's role in mergers and acquisitions, including the issuer as an aggressor seeking to take over another company; the issuer as the target of an acquirer; the issuer as friendly partner in a merger; the issuer's management as an interested party in structuring and financing a leveraged buyout; and the issuer as needing an opinion as to the fairness of the value and terms implementing the purchase or sale of a company or division. In each of these merger and acquisition roles, the investment banker's fees can be lucrative (there are examples of such fees exceeding $30 million).[11] As indicated, gaining access to that business is often a function of a prior relationship, public standing achieved through an aggressive underwriting, or well-publicized acquisition involvement which prompts the issuer to call the investment banker for assistance.

Among other possible benefits flowing from a successful Rule 415 bid is obtaining the personal accounts of key officers of the issuer company. These not only create fees and commissions but build an individual's loyalty to the banking firm that can tip the balance on future contested pieces of business. Still another important new business benefit to a securities firm from an ongoing relationship with an issuer is the opportunity to appear at the issuer's board meetings to make presentations and be available for questions from members of the board. This serves both as a showcase for the investment banker's talents to outside directors whose own companies could be potential clients, and as a means of protecting against the potential inroads of other investment banks directly or indirectly affiliated with members of the board.

The competition for new client relationships is therefore intense. Some investment bankers will not hesitate to pursue aggressive pricing offers to pry another banker's client loose from that firm. Thus it is understood that certain securities firms have formulated a conscious policy to "buy" an introduction to targeted potential corporate clients via a successful bid on that issuer's shelf securities.[12]

The foregoing further advances our hypothesis, discussed in Chapter 5, that investment banking activities related to corporate and municipal issuers and to institutional investors are an integrated process rather than separate lines of commerce, as they are often assumed to be by economists.[13] Each activity supports other activities within the cluster; one part typically cannot be pursued efficiently in the absence of the others. Pursuing Rule 415 distributions thus feeds into and supports a securities firm's system of interrelated investment banking activities.

UNDERWRITING RANKINGS

The data in Figure 7-4 demonstrate that the same group of leading underwriting originators that dominated their markets before the introduction of shelf registration also dominated them afterwards.

Thus, the jousting for position in the post-Rule 415 era has been confined to a relatively small number of firms at the apex of the competitive hierarchy rather than among the broader competitive group that had been anticipated. Essentially, the group encompasses the five so-called "special bracket" firms, Salomon Brothers, Morgan Stanley, Merrill Lynch, First Boston, and Goldman Sachs, plus Lehman (now Shearson Lehman).

134

Figure 7-4   **Public Financing Volume: 1979–1984**
Market Shares of Top Six Firms

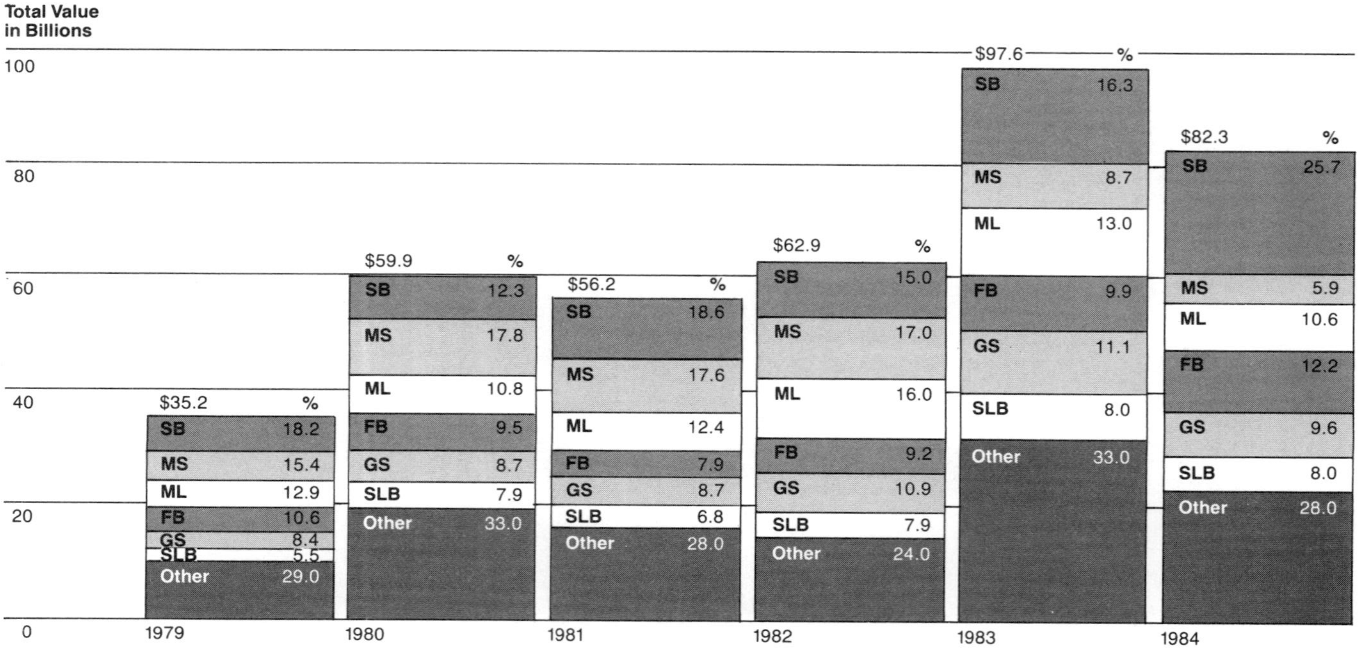

**Total Value
in Billions**

					$82.3

1979   1980   1981   1982   1983   1984

SB Salomon Bros.
MS Morgan Stanley
ML Merrill Lynch

FB First Boston
GS Goldman Sachs
SLB Shearson Lehman Bros.

1984 ($82.3)
SB 25.7%
MS 5.9
ML 10.6
FB 12.2
GS 9.6
SLB 8.0
Other 28.0

1983 ($97.6)
SB 16.3%
MS 8.7
ML 13.0
FB 9.9
GS 11.1
SLB 8.0
Other 33.0

1982 ($62.9)
SB 15.0%
MS 17.0
ML 16.0
FB 9.2
GS 10.9
SLB 7.9
Other 24.0

1981 ($56.2)
SB 18.6%
MS 17.6
ML 12.4
FB 7.9
GS 8.7
SLB 6.8
Other 28.0

1980 ($59.9)
SB 12.3%
MS 17.8
ML 10.8
FB 9.5
GS 8.7
SLB 7.9
Other 33.0

1979 ($35.2)
SB 18.2%
MS 15.4
ML 12.9
FB 10.6
GS 8.4
SLB 5.5
Other 29.0

Source:
Securities Data
Company, Inc.

These data also indicate, however, that during the period some important shifts have taken place in the relative standing of firms within this group of leading underwriting competitors. Figure 7-4 shows that, over the entire period, Salomon Brothers was the biggest gainer, with an increase in market share from 18 percent in 1979 to 26 percent in 1984. Morgan Stanley was the most prominent loser, falling from a 15 percent market share in 1979 to a 7 percent share in 1984. The relative positions of other securities firms are tempered by the impact of using alternative base years and the interpretation of the history of 1983 and 1984, since several of the underwriters suffered diminished market shares in 1984 as compared to 1983.

Figure 7-5 examines the relative rankings in the area of negotiated public offerings of debt securities. Here, Salomon's rise and Morgan's decline essentially parallel the data in Figure 7-4 for all securities underwriting. But in this segment Goldman Sachs's position also shows significant erosion since the advent of Rule 415.

By contrast, Table 7-2, examining equity negotiated underwritings, shows Salomon Brothers with a much more modest (7 percent) share of the market, which, admittedly, was considerably less important in 1984 than the debt market. Morgan Stanley also presents a different—and stronger—picture in the negotiated equity market. Merrill Lynch suffered some erosion in 1983 and 1984 compared to earlier years, but Shearson Lehman's and Goldman's equity market shares were up markedly in 1984 although the total volume for the year was $13 billion compared with $44 billion in financings experienced in 1983. The significant differences among the top six houses in relative shares of debt compared with equity public financings involve a number of factors: reputation for expertise in a particular mode; traditional banking relationships; degree of due diligence considered essential; interest in the larger spreads in equity offerings; and in-house characteristics of sales and distribution staffs.

Shelf Underwriting Rankings. Not surprisingly, these six firms' performance in the shelf sector of the securities markets had a lot to do with the overall standings in U.S. under-

Figure 7-5   **Negotiated Debt Financing Volume: 1979–1984**
Market Shares of Top Six Firms

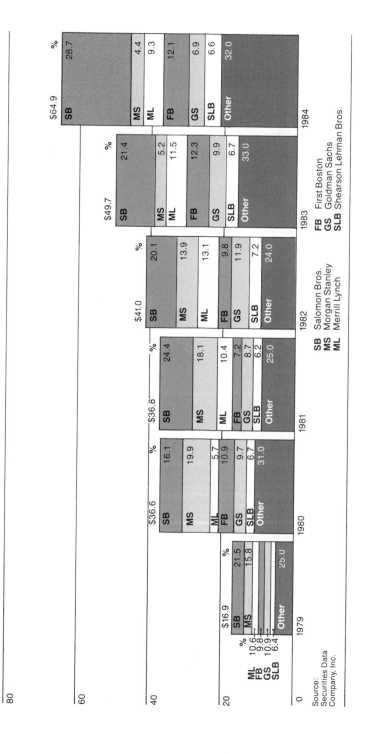

Total
Dollar Value
in Billions

Source:
Securities Data
Company, Inc.

SB Salomon Bros.
MS Morgan Stanley
ML Merrill Lynch

FB First Boston
GS Goldman Sachs
SLB Shearson Lehman Bros.

136

Table 7-2

Total Equity Negotiated Underwritings (Common/Preferred): 1979–1984 with Top Six Firm Comparisons
(*In Billions of Dollars*)

	1979		1980		1981		1982		1983		1984	
	Volume	%	Volume	%	Volume	%	Volume	%	Volume	%	Volume	%
First Boston	.35	5.6	.80	5.2	.33	2.2	.95	5.3	2.09	4.7	.72	5.7
Goldman Sachs	.34	5.5	.97	6.3	.96	6.5	1.62	9.0	4.62	10.4	1.89	14.9
Merrill Lynch	.95	15.3	2.42	15.7	1.81	12.2	3.80	21.1	4.75	10.7	1.14	9.0
Morgan Stanley	.94	15.2	1.83	11.9	2.04	13.8	3.65	20.3	4.92	11.1	1.46	11.5
Salomon Bros.	.03	0.4	.37	2.4	.60	4.1	1.03	5.7	4.31	9.7	.89	7.0
Shearson/Lehman	—	—	.85	5.5	1.21	8.2	.83	4.6	2.84	6.4	1.26	9.9
Sub Total	2.61	42.0	7.24	47.0	6.95	47.0	11.88	66.0	23.53	53.0	7.36	58.0
Other	3.59	58.0	8.16	53.0	7.85	53.0	6.12	34.0	20.87	47.0	5.34	42.0
Grand Total	$6.2	100.0	$15.4	100.0	$14.8	100.0	$18.0	100.0	$44.4	100.0	$12.7	100.0

Source: Securities Data Company, Inc.

137

Figure 7-6   **Shelf Financing: 1982–1984**
Market Shares of Top Six Firms

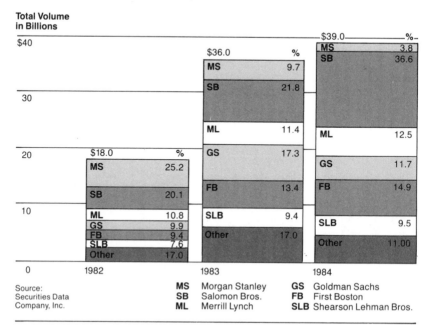

Source:
Securities Data
Company, Inc.

MS Morgan Stanley   **GS** Goldman Sachs
SB Salomon Bros.   **FB** First Boston
ML Merrill Lynch   **SLB** Shearson Lehman Bros.

writing activities. Figure 7-6 confirms the impressive market share of total shelf financings taken by Salomon Brothers alone in 1984 (37 percent) compared with 20 percent in 1982. Equally significant is the decline in market share of underwritings by Morgan Stanley from 25 percent in 1982 to 4 percent in 1984.

Because the debt securities have loomed so large in recent years, the combined debt and equity shelf results set forth in Table 7-3 are closely mirrored in the data on debt shelf financings in Figure 7-7. The relative performances of Salomon and Morgan in this sector are quite similar to their standings in other sectors, but one can note a significant decline in market share for Goldman Sachs in 1984 as compared to 1983.

In the negotiated equity subsector of the financing markets, shelf offerings practically disappeared altogether in 1984 after having had a relatively banner year in 1983. Even in 1983, however, as Table 7-2 shows, the top six underwrit-

Table 7-3

Negotiated Equity Shelf Security Underwritings: 1982–1984 with Top Six Firm Comparisons
(In Billions of Dollars)

	1982		1983		1984	
	Volume	% of Total	Volume	% of Total	Volume	% of Total
First Boston	—	—	.61	6.9	.08	6.3
Goldman Sachs	.120	7.5	1.68	18.9	.22	18.7
Merrill Lynch	—	—	1.05	11.8	—	—
Morgan Stanley	.700	43.5	.76	8.5	—	—
Salomon Bros.	.160	9.9	.53	5.9	—	—
Shearson/Lehman	.030	2.1	—	—	—	—
Sub Total	1.010	63.0	4.63	52.0	.30	25.0
Other	.590	37.0	4.27	48.0	.90	75.0
Grand Total	$1.600	100.0	$8.90	100.0	$1.20	100.0

Source: Securities Data Company, Inc.

139

Figure 7-7   **Negotiated Debt Shelf Financing: 1982–1984**
Market Shares of Top Six Firms

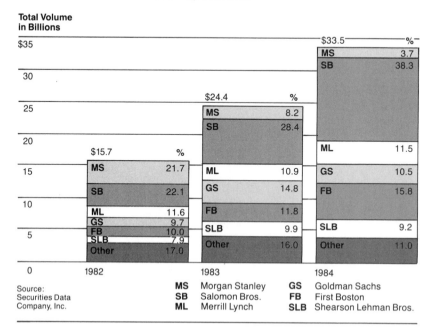

Source:
Securities Data
Company, Inc.

MS	Morgan Stanley	**GS**	Goldman Sachs
SB	Salomon Bros.	**FB**	First Boston
ML	Merrill Lynch	**SLB**	Shearson Lehman Bros.

ing firms accounted for only about half of the negotiated shelf equity financings, indicating that market shares of these shelf offerings were quite dispersed. But if one had thought to find Morgan Stanley continuing in a leading position in negoti- ated shelf equity financings during the three years of shelf experience, the data suggest otherwise. While Morgan had the largest individual share of the minuscule $1.6 billion in shelf equity financings during 1982, shown in Table 7-3, its share fell to only 8.5 percent of the $8.9 billion offered in 1983. The 1984 volume of $1.2 billion is too small to be meaningful for purposes of comparison.

Finally, Figure 7-8 presents a quarter-by-quarter plot dur- ing the years 1982–1984 of the dollar volumes of all public securities financings, showing all shelf securities financings, as well as shelf debt and shelf equity financings. Note that the shelf activity tracks fairly consistently with the overall trend in public financing activity. As we saw earlier, the shelf

Figure 7-8 **Shelf Portions of Public Financings 1982–1984**
by Quarters

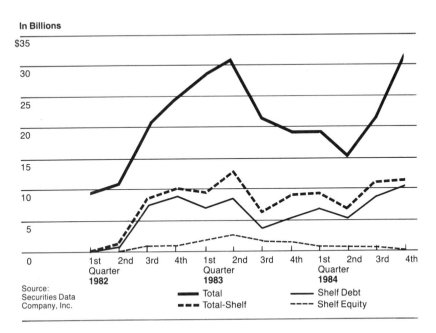

figures are dominated by the activity in debt financings, with equity shelf financings having been significant only in 1983.

Concentration Trends. While the preceding data suggest that recent realignments in competitive position have been confined to firms at the apex of securities underwriting competitors, there is still the question of whether the introduction of shelf underwriting has made a discernible difference in the degree of concentration within the securities underwriting sector as a whole.

Statistics indicate that there is no dramatic trend in overall industry concentration as a result of the shelf phenomenon.

Table 7-4 shows some evidence of modest increased concentration since 1979 for all securities as a single group. The top fifteen investment banking firms underwrote 93 percent of all public offerings of new securities in 1981, the last full year before the shelf experiment. During 1982, the first year of the shelf experiment they underwrote 95 percent, in 1983

Table 7-4

Dollar Volume Concentration on Selected New Issues: 1979–1984
(*Individual Categories as Percentage of Overall Grand Total*)

		1979	1980	1981	1982	1983	1984
All Securities							
Top 4	$	20.2	30.2	32.1	36.8	39.2	50.4
	%	57	50	57	59	40	61
Top 8	$	30.0	46.8	46.1	52.7	66.3	71.9
	%	85	78	82	84	68	87
Top 15	$	34.0	54.8	52.1	59.8	79.6	78.9
	%	97	92	93	95	82	96
Negotiated Debt							
Top 4	$	13.3	20.8	22.6	24.2	27.4	42.3
	%	59	57	61	59	55	65
Top 8	$	20.0	28.6	29.6	33.9	39.6	55.4
	%	88	78	80	83	80	85
Top 15	$	21.4	31.8	31.7	36.7	42.4	59.8
	%	95	87	86	90	85	92
Negotiated Equity							
Top 4	$	2.6	5.8	5.8	7.8	15.5	3.6
	%	42	38	39	43	35	28
Top 8	$	3.7	8.7	8.8	10.2	23.7	5.7
	%	60	57	60	57	53	45
Top 15	$	4.3	10.5	10.7	11.8	30.1	6.8
	%	69	68	72	66	68	54

Source: Securities Data Company, Inc.
All securities refers basically to Top 15 firm volume.
All dollar figures are in billions

82 percent, an aberrational year in volume, and in 1984, 96 percent under the permanent rule. The results before and after Rule 415, comparing 1979–1982 with 1984, show little variance in the totals or when broken down to analyze the top four and top eight houses. The same modest increase in concentration can be noted in the negotiated debt sector. In the negotiated equity sector, however, concentration appears to have declined significantly during the six-year period. The median share for the top fifteen houses of about 70 percent in the 1979–1981 period declined during the beginning of the shelf era to a low of 54 percent (a decline of 30 percent) in 1984. This result is heavily influenced by the 43 percent decline in share of the top four firms from about 40 percent to 28 percent, whereas the top eight firms paralleled the whole group of fifteen with a 31 percent decline of market share from 59 percent to 45 percent.

In summary, the basic competitive structure of the underwriting industry has not been fundamentally altered by the introduction of shelf registrations. Cost savings accruing to issuers choosing the shelf route have come as a consequence of more intensive competition among the firms at the top of the underwriting hierarchy. Given the shifts in market shares among this apex group, there have clearly been some gains and losses in client relationships as a consequence. Notable shifts in market shares—and consequent gains and losses in client relationships—have been largely confined to this apex group.

NOTES

1. Sec. Act Rel. 6276 (December 23, 1980) [46 Fed. Reg. 78 (1980)].
2. Sec. Act Rel. 6334 (August 6, 1981) [46 Fed. Reg. 42001 (1981)].
3. Integrated Disclosure Release, Sec. Act Rel. 33-6383 (March 3, 1982) [47 Fed. Reg. 11380 (1982)].
4. Sec. Act Rel. 6423 (September 2, 1982) [47 Fed. Reg. 39799 (1982)]; 6470 (June 9, 1983) [47 Fed. Reg. 27768 (1983)].
5. Sec. Act Rel. 6499 (November 17, 1983) [48 Fed. Reg. 52889 (1983)].
6. David Kidwell, M. Wayne Marr, and G. Rodney Thompson: "Shelf Registration: Competition and Market Timing," Working Paper No. 192, College of Business Administration, University of Tennessee, Knoxville, July 1984; Kidwell, Marr, and Thompson, "SEC Rule 415—

The Ultimate Competitive Bid," *Journal of Financial and Quantitative Analysis* (June 1984); Rogowski and Sorensen, "Shelf Registrations and the Cost of Capital: A Test of Market Efficiency," Washington State University and the University of Arizona Working Paper, 1983.

7. Samuel L. Hayes, III, "The Transformation of Investment Banking," *Harvard Business Review* (January-February 1979), p. 155.
8. Ibid.
9. Lenny Glynn, "Morgan Stanley Faces Its Mid-Life Crisis," *Institutional Investor* (June 1984).
10. Ibid.
11. Peter Petre, "Merger Fees that Bend the Mind," *Fortune*, 20 January 1986, p. 18 ff.
12. "Life with Rule 415," *Institutional Investor—International Edition* (February 1983), p. 199ff.
13. Samuel L. Hayes, III, "Investment Banking: Commercial Banks' Inroads," *Economic Review*, Federal Reserve Bank of Atlanta (May 1984) p. 56.

8

Corporate Profiles of Shelf Registrants

In the previous chapter we placed the shelf underwriting phenomenon within the context of competitive developments in the securities markets and suggested that, rather than being a radical departure, it was a logical consequence in a chain of industry developments. Later in this book we shall consider the degree to which shelf registration is congruent with the objectives of the 1933 Act and the ground rules it sanctions for raising new public capital. The object of those ground rules, as we have noted, is to ensure that full and complete material information about the issuer is available for the investor to make an informed judgment at the time of purchase. Shelf issues pose a special challenge for meeting this requirement because of the speed with which they are typically undertaken. In order to assess the extent to which these financings might present a problem in this respect, we need to know more about the issuers who would qualify for the shelf procedure.

In this chapter, therefore, we shall explore the characteristics of the companies that have utilized the shelf registration procedure and of those that are empowered to do so under the permanent form of Rule 415.

CORPORATE SHELF FILERS DURING TRIAL PERIOD

As a basis for making Rule 415 permanent the commission relied substantially on its experience with the application of the rule during the trial period from March 1982 until September 1983. During this period, it reported that 369 debt shelf filings were made, representing 53 percent of the $133 billion of total debt issues filed.[1]

The commission also reported 195 equity shelf filings representing about 6 percent of the $212 billion in total equity securities registered. Over half of these were fixed-price, syndicated offerings filed under Rule 415 largely for the procedural convenience the rule afforded. Approximately 70 percent were for common stock and 30 percent for preferred stock.[2]

By contrast with the commission's figures, an analysis of the characteristics of companies specifically identified from a private data-gathering agency as having made shelf filings from March 1982 to August 1983 reveals 234 debt filers and 283 equity filers.[3] Several differences in assumptions would account for the discrepancies in numbers.[4] We believe the list employed here accounts for the bulk of shelf registrations undertaken during the sample period. In order to discover what types of companies took advantage of temporary Rule 415, we collected data bearing on the breadth and quality of each filing company's corporate and operating profile. These items (based on 1982 information) included (1) Standard Industry Code (SIC) classification; (2) size of the issuer's business, as measured by both sales and assets; (3) growth of sales and profits over a recent three-year period; (4) return on equity capital; (5) capital structure as measured by long-term debt as a percentage of long-term capital; (6) comprehensive financial risk measured by total liabilities as a percentage of total assets; (7) presence or absence of a bond rating by Standard & Poor's and, where rated, the bond rating designation[5] (8) presence or absence of a stock rating by Standard & Poor's and, where rated, the stock rating designation; (9) the percentage of the firm's equity held by institutional investors; and (10) the firm's market price-to-earnings (P-E) ratio.

Debt Filers. During the initial seventeen months of shelf registration, the most frequent debt filers were banking (36 percent of filers) public utility (19 percent) and communication (4 percent) firms. These organizations typically have such a large need for capital that they are relatively frequent participants in the financial marketplace. Thus they were considered especially likely to appreciate the flexibility provided by Rule 415's two-year "open window" period, permitting the issuing of new securities without concern for the delay in the 1933 Act's registration process. A variety of manufacturing and electronic firms also used the rule's registration procedure. Most (85 percent) of these debt filers were well-known business organizations with assets of $1 billion or more (Figure 8-1).

The bonds of all but thirty of the group were rated by Standard & Poor's (Figure 8-2), and the great bulk of the ratings were in the investment grade classification (Figure 8-3). There was, moreover, evidence of wide institutional investor interest in many of these large companies, lending credence to the notion that many issuers are actively monitored by sophisticated investors. This would make it more likely that up-to-date information about their operations would be disseminated periodically and frequently through the many conventional financial data services.

There was, however, a subgroup of the Rule 415 debt filing group with less robust characteristics. These generally smaller debt filers were less likely to be rated by Standard & Poor's (that was the case with seventeen of fifty-nine companies in the lowest sales quartile, and they tended to have a relatively small institutional following (about half the companies in the lowest quartile had institutional ownership of less than 20 percent; see Figure 8-4). While neither the absence of a bond rating or an observed low level of institutional interest necessarily indicates an inferior credit standing, they would suggest that the dissemination of material information to the markets about this class of issuer might have been less complete or timely than for other groups of shelf registrants, and certainly compared to those issued in the conventional manner with time allotted for due diligence efforts. Moreover, these smaller debt filers were substantial users of debt, and they appear to have relied more heavily on short-term credit sources (Figure 8-5) than on traditional long-term debt funds (Figure 8-6). Hence, the potential for financial risks associated with their capital structures could be relatively greater.

The smaller debt filers tended to grow at a faster pace than their larger counterparts, whether measured by sales growth (Figure 8-7) or growth in profits (Figure 8-8). Nonetheless, these smaller debt filing companies did not earn substantially higher returns on their shareholders' equity than did larger firms (Figure 8-9). This, combined with the potentially greater volatility in their operating results and levered capital structure, helps account for lower P-E ratios relative to their larger counterparts among Rule 415 debt filers (Figure 8-10) and lower quality ratings on their equity securities (Figure 8-11).

Equity Filers.   The companies filing shelf registrations for equity securities were drawn from approximately the same industry classifications as debt filers. Public utilities were the most frequent equity filers and were followed by banking, and miscellaneous business service companies. In a number of other respects, however, they present quite a different picture.

There was a much larger proportion of relatively small equity filers than was true in the case of debt filers. Figure 8-12 shows that all but twenty companies in the lowest quartile of equity filers had less than $300 million in assets, and only about half of the total equity filing group had as much as $1 billion in assets. Not surprisingly, therefore, there were many more equity filing companies without a Standard & Poor's bond rating. For instance, Figure 8-13 shows that most of the

Figure 8-1 **Reported Assets of 234 Shelf Debt Registrants**
(by Volume of Sales)

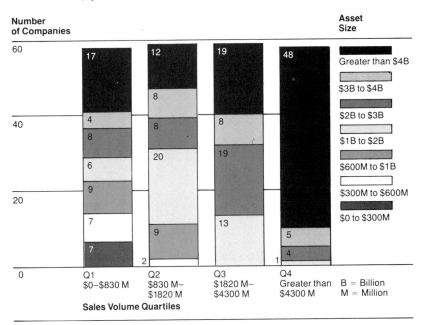

Figure 8-2 **Rated Debt Among 234 Shelf Debt Registrants**
(by Volume of Sales)

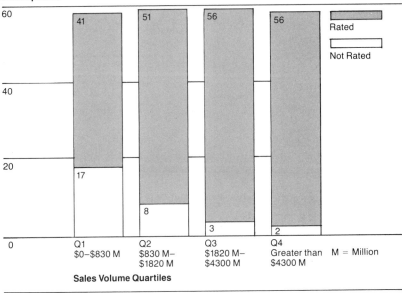

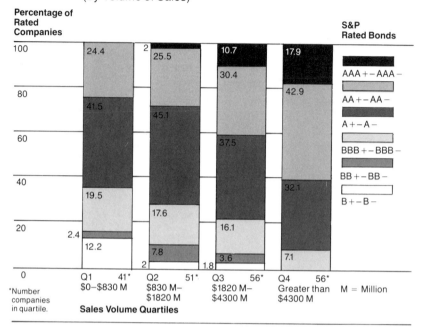

Figure 8-3 **Bond Ratings Among 234 Shelf Debt Registrants**
(by Volume of Sales)

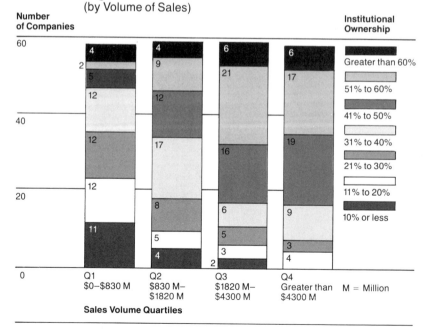

Figure 8-4 **Institutional Stock Ownership Among 234 Shelf Debt Registrants**
(by Volume of Sales)

Figure 8-5
Liabilities as Percent of Total Assets of 234 Shelf Debt Registrants
(by Volume of Sales)

Number of
Companies

Total
Liabilities/
Total Assets

Greater than 85%

76% to 85%

66% to 75%

56% to 65%

46% to 55%

36% to 45%

35% or less

Q1
$0–$830 M

Q2
$830 M–
$1820 M

Q3
$1820 M–
$4300 M

Q4
Greater than
$4300 M

M = Million

Sales Volume Quartiles

Figure 8-6 **Debt as Percent of Total Capitalization of 234 Shelf Debt Registrants**
(by Volume of Sales)

Number
of Companies

Debt/
Debt + Equity

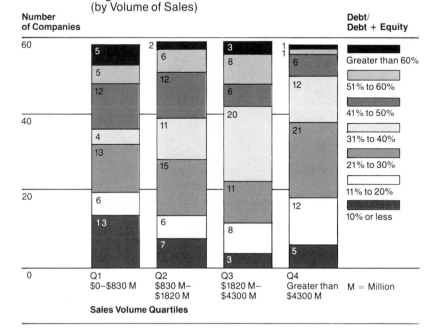

Greater than 60%

51% to 60%

41% to 50%

31% to 40%

21% to 30%

11% to 20%

10% or less

Q1
$0–$830 M

Q2
$830 M–
$1820 M

Q3
$1820 M–
$4300 M

Q4
Greater than
$4300 M

M = Million

Sales Volume Quartiles

151

Figure 8-7 **Sales Growth of 234 Shelf Debt Registrants**
(by Volume of Sales)

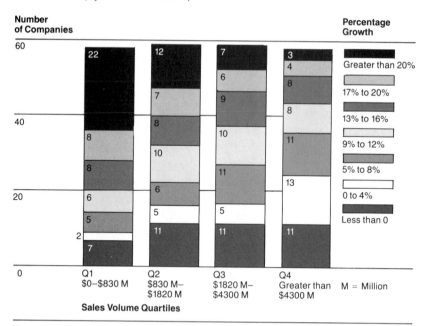

Figure 8-8 **Income Growth of 234 Shelf Debt Registrants**
(by Volume of Sales)

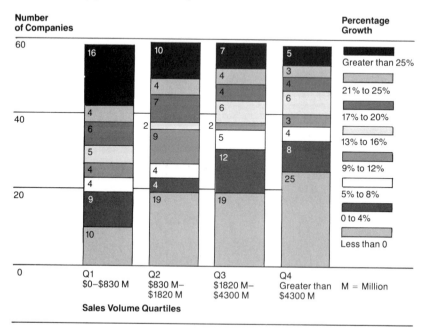

Figure 8-9   **Return on Equity of 234 Shelf Debt Registrants**
(by Volume of Sales)

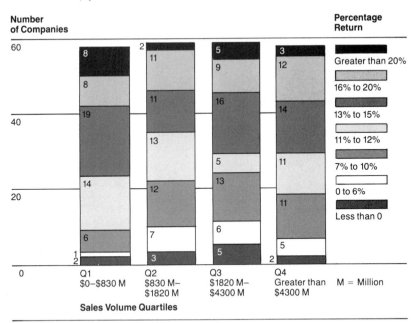

Figure 8-10   **Ratio of Market Price to Earnings of 234 Shelf Debt Registrants**
(by Volume of Sales)

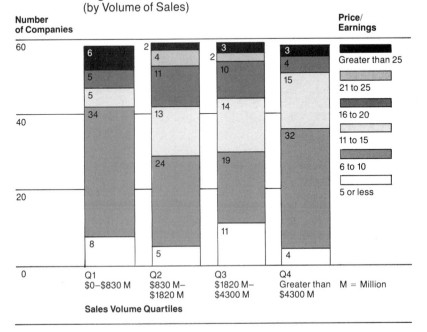

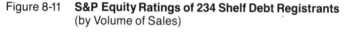

Figure 8-11   **S&P Equity Ratings of 234 Shelf Debt Registrants**
(by Volume of Sales)

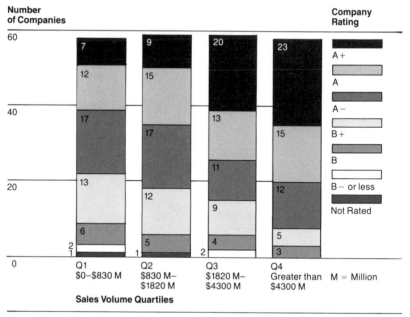

companies in the lowest size quartile were not bond rated. Sixty percent of the companies in the bottom half of the equity filing group were not bond rated by Standard & Poor's.

Among the Standard & Poor's rated equity filers, there appears to have been a correlation between credit quality and issuer size. Figure 8-14 shows that eight of the fourteen rated companies in the lowest quartile had a single B bond rating, a category the credit agency defines as "containing considerable speculative elements."[6] All the rest were unrated. In the highest size quartile (where almost all the companies were rated), only four of sixty-two rated companies had a rating as low as B. More than a quarter of the lowest quartile of equity filers had less than 20 percent institutional ownership of their common shares. In fact, excepting the highest quartile, each of the groups contained filing companies with either modest or nominal institutional ownership (Figure 8-15).

In contrast to debt filers, smaller equity filers tended to rely

less on borrowed funds. This tendency is noted in the calculation of debt as a percentage of long-term capital (Figure 8-
16) and in the measure of total liabilities as a percentage of
total assets (Figure 8-17). Thus, one could surmise that risks
emanating from their capital structures per se would be more
modest than would be true for large firms in the group, allow-
ing for industry and operating idiosyncrasies which would
have a bearing on the capacity to carry the burdens of
financial leverage.

As with smaller debt filers, smaller equity filers exhibited
significantly faster sales growth than their larger counterparts
over the three-year period 1980–82 (Figure 8-18). Growth
in profit was also inversely correlated with size (Figure 8-
19). The smaller equity filers exhibited a clearly superior return on equity performance compared with their larger
counterparts (Figure 8-20). The price-to-earnings ratios of
these smaller equity filers rewarded that financial performance: thirty companies in the lowest quartile had P-E ratios
of over twenty-five times earnings, whereas only six in the
top size category fell into that high P-E category (Figure 8-
21). The potential volatility implicit in this higher growth may
help account for the fact that the smaller equity filers' equity
ratings were lower than their larger counterparts' (Figure 8-
22).

In sum, the financial data suggest that the profile of the
large majority of the companies that filed debt shelf registrations over the trial period was that of a large public company
with characteristics suggesting both a certain stability in its
business operations and a broad dissemination of information
about those operations. A substantial subgroup of the equity
filers, however, did not fit that reassuring profile.

Given the differences in the numbers included in the list
as compared to the total reported by the commission, the
profiles of the equity filers in particular have to be treated
with caution. As the commission noted in its release adopting
Rule 415 in its final form, the equity shelf filers during the
trial period represented a very small part of total equity
filings; accordingly, such offerings may not be considered
representative of companies that might make use of this technique in the future.[7]

Figure 8-12 **Reported Assets of 283 Shelf Equity Registrants**
(by Volume of Sales)

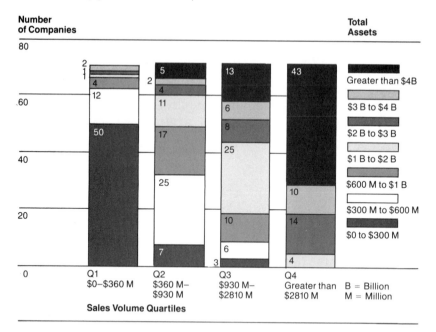

Figure 8-13 **Rated Debt of 283 Shelf Equity Registrants**
(by Volume of Sales)

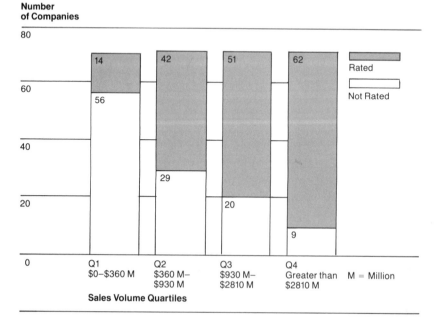

Figure 8-14   **Bond Ratings Among 283 Shelf Equity Registrants**
(by Volume of Sales)

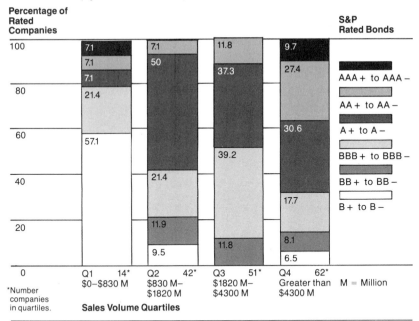

Figure 8-15   **Institutional Stock Ownership of 283 Shelf Equity Registrants**
(by Volume of Sales)

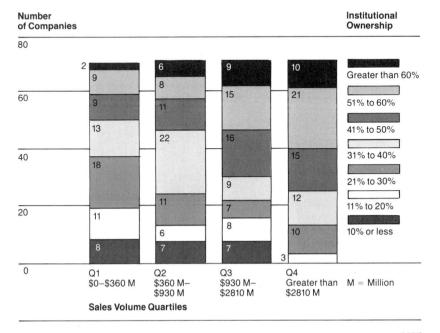

157

Figure 8-16   **Debt as Percent of Total Capitalization of 283 Shelf Equity
Registrants**
(by Volume of Sales)

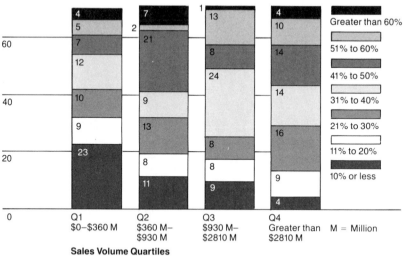

Figure 8-17   **Liabilities as Percent of Total Assets of 283 Shelf Equity
Registrants**
(by Volume of Sales)

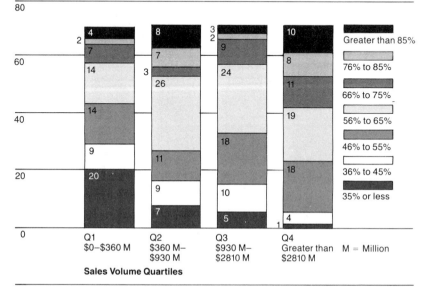

Figure 8-18   **Sales Growth of 283 Shelf Equity Registrants**
(by Volume of Sales)

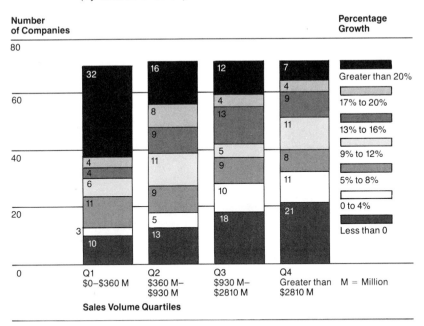

Figure 8-19   **Income Growth of 283 Shelf Equity Registrants**
(by Volume of Sales)

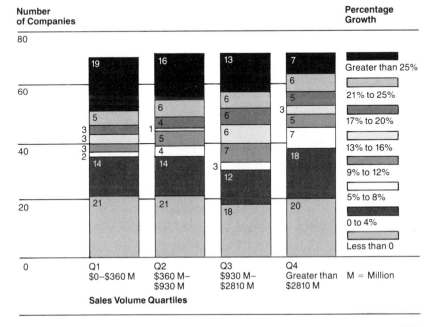

159

Figure 8-20 **Return on Equity of 283 Shelf Equity Registrants**
(by Volume of Sales)

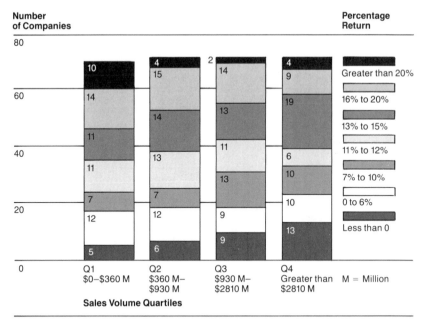

Figure 8-21 **Ratio of Market Price to Earnings of 283 Shelf Equity Registrants**
(by Volume of Sales)

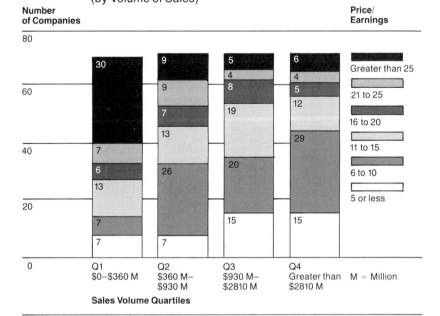

160

Figure 8-22 **S&P Ratings of 283 Shelf Equity Registrants**
(by Volume of Sales)

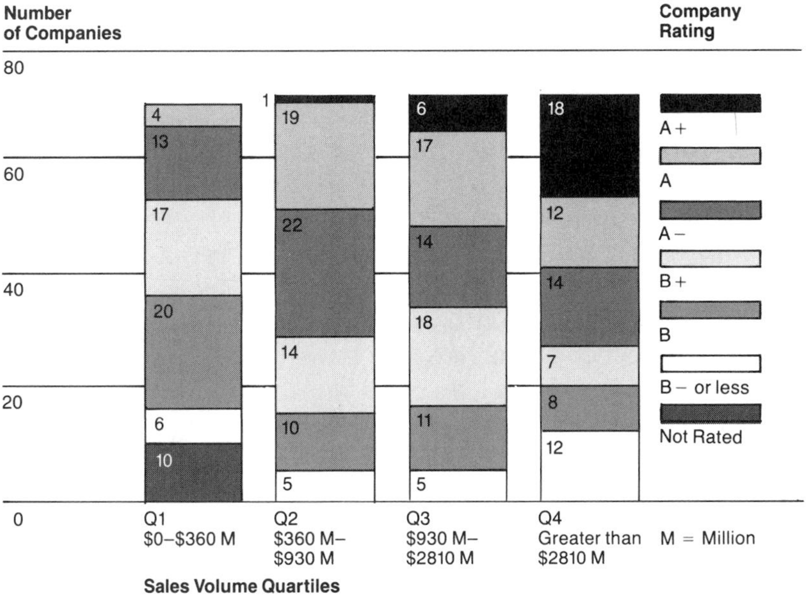

ADOPTION OF THE PERMANENT RULE

When, after a year and a half of experience with the temporary form, the commission revised the availability of shelf registrations and adopted Rule 415 in its permanent form, the decision was not unanimous. Adoption was passed by a vote of four to one, the chairman concurring in the result in a separate opinion, and one commissioner concurring in the decision as it related to debt securities but dissenting as it related to equity securities. Rule 415 became effective December 31, 1983.

Issues Presented and Resolved. Under the temporary rule, the concept of shelf registration was as broad as seemed possible. It had been extended widely to primary offerings of both debt and equity securities, in effect making the shelf technique available for most offerings of debt securities. As the commission moved toward adoption of the permanent rule, they found that this general availability of shelf registration evoked concerns, particularly among professionals in the securities industry, about the quality and timing of adequate disclosure and the conduct of due diligence under the 1933 Act.[8]

Investment bankers and broker-dealers were also concerned that the temporary rule might result in an increase in the rate of institutionalization of securities markets,[9] and in the further concentration of underwriting power in the securities industry, and that it might have deleterious effects on the retail distribution of securities and on secondary securities markets. The commission did not agree that these concerns were directly related to the issue of shelf registration. It considered Rule 415 to be a procedural rule designed to provide an optional method of compliance with the 1933 Act, and did not regard the rule as relating to any particular form or method of securities distribution.

The commission, however, did regard the questions of adequacy of disclosure and due diligence as important issues, bearing directly on the statutory intent of the nature and quality of information that investors should receive in a public offering of securities. It concluded that the broad availability of shelf registration existing under temporary Rule 415 should be limited on a permanent basis to only those issuers eligible to use the short-form registration of securities under the 1933 Act (Form S-3, and Form F-3 for foreign issuers). The commission further decided to continue the rule's availability for "traditional" shelf offerings. The rationale underlying the selection of Form S-3 as a basis for eligibility was that the integrated disclosure system coupling the 1933 Act and the 1934 Act effectively addressed the concerns that had been expressed about the quality and timeliness of disclosure. As for concerns about the nature of the diligence required to ensure appropriate disclosure, the commission pointed to "evolving continuous due diligence by enhancing the ability of underwriters to conduct due diligence investigations of widely followed registrants."[10] In effect, the commission felt that all important concerns regarding permanent shelf registration were resolved by the existence of an efficient market engendered by the integrated disclosure system.

Reach of the Permanent Rule.   In its textual form and detail, the permanent form of Rule 415 permits continuous and delayed offerings of traditional shelf offerings and other securities that may be registered on Form S-3 (and Form F-3). Form S-3, in summary, requires that the issuer must (1) have voting stock held by nonaffiliates with a market value of at least $150 million; or (2) have voting stock held by nonaffiliates with a market value of at least $100 million and a trading volume of at least 3 million shares annually; or (3) be selling investment-grade debt securities or preferred stock.[11]

The securities eligible for shelf registration on Form S-3 (or Form F-3) may be offered and sold only by or on behalf of the registrant, or its subsidiary or parent. The securities also may be registered only in an amount that is reasonably expected to be offered and sold within two years from the initial effective date. During that period, all material information must be added to the registration statement by means of post-effective amendments.

In the case of an "at the market" offering of equity securities eligible to use Form S-3, the registrant must employ an underwriter, and, where the offering is one of voting stock, the amount being registered may not exceed 10 percent of the aggregate market value of outstanding voting stock. Equity offerings other than "at the market" are not subject to these requirements, but the issuer must still be eligible to use Form S-3 in order to make the offering under Rule 415.

With the SEC's action making the shelf option a permanent part of the capital-raising mechanism, it is likely that it will continue to be used extensively. Certainly, as the data in Chapter 7 demonstrate, it has been heavily used thus far. Not only does it appear to result in significant cost savings, but it also gives the issuer enhanced flexibility to push an offering quickly through a temporary window of market opportunity.

Profile of Eligibility.   To obtain a profile of Form S-3 users, we drew up a list of qualifying firms and analyzed them, using the same set of corporate characteristics discussed in the previous section.[12] Approximately 1,400 companies filed

Form S-3 registration statements with the SEC in 1983. Not surprisingly, their industry classifications spanned the whole of the U.S. private sector. They are led by public utilities (8.8 percent of the group), machinery, except electrical (7.7 percent), banking (7.5 percent), electrical and electrical machinery (6.8 percent), chemicals and allied products (5 percent), and oil and gas companies (4.2 percent). Size distribution is broad.

Figure 8-23 shows that a quarter of the S-3 filers had sales of less than $260 million, and half had sales of less than $600 million (this is in sharp contrast to the typically larger sales profiles of the Rule 415 debt filers and even of the equity filers during the trial period). About a quarter of the universe had assets of less than $300 million, as compared with 3 percent among Rule 415 debt filers, and 21 percent among equity filers.

A large proportion of the S-3 filers did not have bond ratings by Standard & Poor's. In the lowest sales quartile 90 percent were unrated; 61 percent were unrated in the second lowest quartile, and even 20 percent were unrated in the largest quartile (see Figure 8-24). The nonrated portion of S-3 filers is thus even larger than that of the Rule 415 equity filers during the trial period. Of the handful (thirty-six) of lowest quartile firms with bonds that were rated by Standard & Poor's, more than half had a classification of single B or lower (Figure 8-25). Interestingly, while the proportion of such low bond ratings declined in the next two quartiles, the highest quartile of companies contained a significant proportion (105 companies, or 38 percent) in the B category or lower.

The lowest end of the size distribution was less levered financially than the highest end. Figure 8-26 shows that the ratios of debt to long-term capitalization were more modest, as were the ratios of total liabilities to total assets (Figure 8-27). Nevertheless, given the generally lower credit profiles revealed by the bond rating data, it is possible that the financial risk attached to many of these companies, particularly among the smaller firms, was significantly higher than average.

The Standard & Poor's equity ratings on their ownership

securities provides evidence of relatively higher business risk among some of these S-3 filing companies. Figure 8-28 shows that more than three-quarters of the companies in the lowest sales quartile had ratings of less than A −, compared with only one-third in the top quartile.

Institutional ownership also appears to vary with size. One-fifth of the lowest quartile of S-3 filing companies had less than 10 percent of their shares held by institutions (see Figure 8-29), as compared with only 5 percent in the top quartile. Moreover, 40 percent of the lowest quartile firms had less than 20 percent of their equity in institutional hands, versus 12 percent for the top size quartile.

As was true for the debt and equity filers during the trial period, the smaller companies qualified under the permanent rule appear to have grown faster. Figure 8-30 shows that in 44 percent of the lowest quartile, sales grew at more than 20 percent per year over the three-year period from 1980–82, whereas in only 11 percent of the top quartile did sales grow as fast. Figure 8-31 shows a similar trend with respect to the three-year growth rate in after-tax profits. The smallest quartile grew faster than any of the others.

In addition, Figure 8-32 shows that the smaller S-3 companies turned in a superior performance with respect to return on equity. Forty-two percent of the lowest quartile companies had a return on equity of more than 15 percent, whereas in the top quartile only 23 percent had a similar record. This higher growth rate is dramatically reflected in the price-to-earnings ratios accorded to the lowest quartile of S-3 filing firms. Figure 8-33 shows that more than half of the firms in that quartile had a P-E ratio in excess of twenty times current earnings, whereas in the highest quartile only 11 percent had a P-E ratio of more than twenty.[11] Despite these comparatively favorable results, the Standard & Poor's equity ratings of these smaller firms were substantially lower than those of the larger firms, reflecting the composite of risks attendant to those businesses (see Figure 8-28).

All of this suggests that the profiles of companies qualifying to use shelf registration under the permanent rule are substantially more diverse than those of firms which utilized

Figure 8-23 Reported Assets of 1366 Eligible Shelf Registrants
(by Volume of Sales)

Number of Companies

Total Assets

	Q1	Q2	Q3	Q4	
		18	46	146	Greater than $4 B
	14 16	20			$3 B to $4 B
	28	23	12		
	278	32	25		$2 B to $3 B
		51	69		
		88	92	46	$1 B to $2 B
				68	$600 M to $1 B
		109	81	60	$300 M to $600 M
			17	16	$0 M to $300 M

Q1 $0–$260 M
Q2 $260 M–$600 M
Q3 $600 M–$1700 M
Q4 Greater than $1700 M

B = Billion
M = Million

Note: Data points were available for 1361 companies.

Sales Volume Quartiles

Figure 8-24 Rated Debt of 1366 Eligible Shelf Registrants
(by Volume of Sales)

Number of Companies

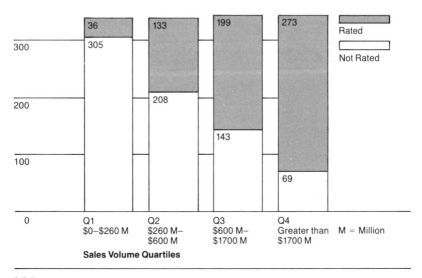

	Q1	Q2	Q3	Q4	
	36	133	199	273	Rated
	305	208	143	69	Not Rated

Q1 $0–$260 M
Q2 $260 M–$600 M
Q3 $600 M–$1700 M
Q4 Greater than $1700 M

M = Million

Sales Volume Quartiles

166

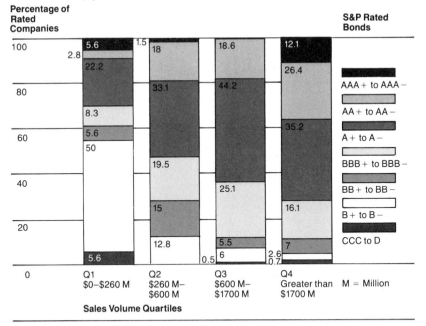

Figure 8-25 **Bond Ratings Among 1366 Eligible Shelf Registrants**
(by Volume of Sales)

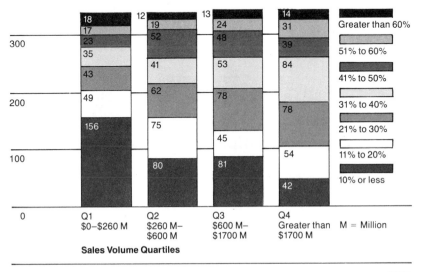

Figure 8-26 **Debt as Percent of Capitalization of 1366 Eligible Shelf Registrants**
(by Volume of Sales)

167

Figure 8-27 **Liabilities as Percent of Total Assets of 1366 Eligible Shelf Registrants**
(by Volume of Sales)

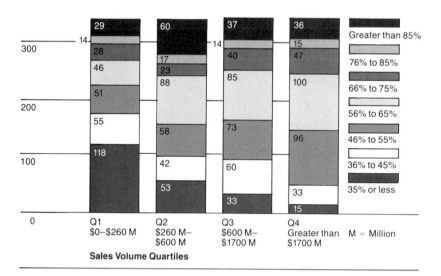

Figure 8-28 **S&P Equity Ratings of 1366 Eligible Shelf Registrants**
(by Volume of Sales)

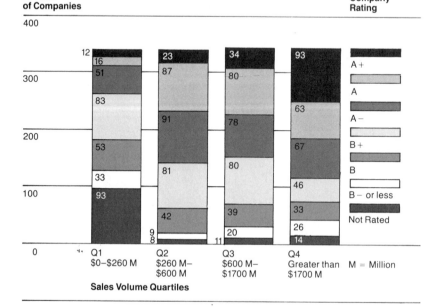

168

Figure 8-29 **Institutional Stock Ownership of 1366 Eligible Shelf Registrants**
(by Volume of Sales)

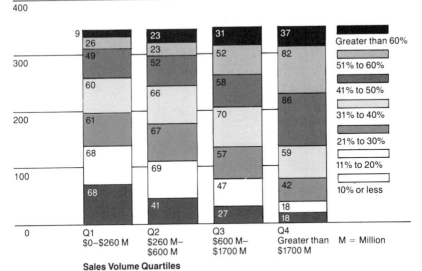

Number of Companies

Institutional Ownership

Greater than 60%
51% to 60%
41% to 50%
31% to 40%
21% to 30%
11% to 20%
10% or less

Q1 $0–$260 M
Q2 $260 M–$600 M
Q3 $600 M–$1700 M
Q4 Greater than $1700 M

M = Million

Sales Volume Quartiles

Figure 8-30 **Sales Growth of 1366 Eligible Shelf Registrants**
(by Volume of Sales)

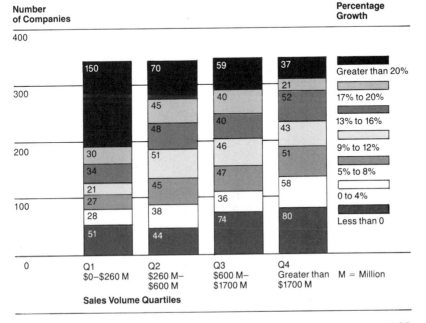

Number of Companies

Percentage Growth

Greater than 20%
17% to 20%
13% to 16%
9% to 12%
5% to 8%
0 to 4%
Less than 0

Q1 $0–$260 M
Q2 $260 M–$600 M
Q3 $600 M–$1700 M
Q4 Greater than $1700 M

M = Million

Sales Volume Quartiles

169

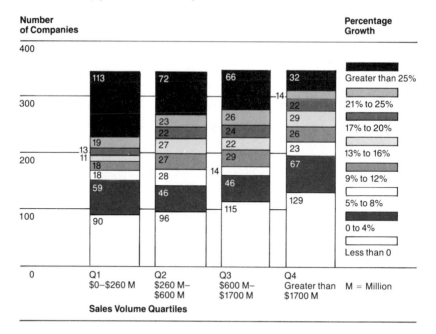

Figure 8-31 **Income Growth of 1366 Eligible Shelf Registrants**
(by Volume of Sales)

Number of Companies — Percentage Growth

Q1 $0–$260 M	Q2 $260 M–$600 M	Q3 $600 M–$1700 M	Q4 Greater than $1700 M	Percentage Growth
113	72	66	32	Greater than 25%
		14	22	21% to 25%
13	23	26	29	17% to 20%
11	22	24	26	13% to 16%
19	27	22	23	
18	27	29	67	9% to 12%
18	28	14		5% to 8%
59	46	46	129	0 to 4%
90	96	115		Less than 0

Sales Volume Quartiles   M = Million

Figure 8-32 **Return on Equity of 1366 Eligible Shelf Registrants**
(by Volume of Sales)

Number of Companies — Percentage Return

Q1 $0–$260 M	Q2 $260 M–$600 M	Q3 $600 M–$1700 M	Q4 Greater than $1700 M	Percentage Return
72	42	28	18	Greater than 20%
	64	67	62	16% to 20%
72		61	72	13% to 15%
	88			11% to 12%
72		54	42	
	59		68	7% to 10%
31		61		0 to 6%
33	48	45	46	
33				Less than 0
28	26	26	34	
	14			

Sales Volume Quartiles   M = Million

170

Figure 8-33 **Ratio of Market Price to Earnings of 1366 Eligible Shelf Registrants**
(by Volume of Sales)

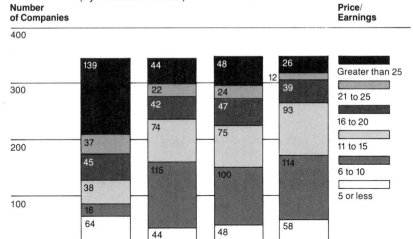

Number of Companies

Price/Earnings

Greater than 25	
21 to 25	
16 to 20	
11 to 15	
6 to 10	
5 or less	

Q1
$0–$260 M

Q2
$260 M–$600 M

Q3
$600 M–$1700 M

Q4
Greater than $1700 M

M = Million

Sales Volume Quartiles

171

Rule 415 under the temporary arrangement. That diversity extends from comparative recent operating performance to capital structure differences to size disparities to stock market evaluations. It is highly unlikely that market efficiency extends to the bulk of this group. And therefore it seems to us unlikely that the several procedures which the SEC has identified as substitutes for normal due diligence investigation in a shelf registration offering will suffice. In the next chapter we shall explore some implications of this conclusion.

NOTES

1. Sec. Act Rel. 6499 (November 17, 1983) [48 Fed. Reg. 52889 (1983)].
2. Ibid.
3. Figures obtained from Abrahamsen & Company, a leading private sector monitor of such filings, which is now a part of Securities Data Corporation in New York City.
4. The SEC's data report specifically identifying shelf filers for the period could not be obtained. The slightly shorter period which we are using and the fact that the larger SEC debt list included multiple filings by the same issuer may account in part for the differences in our debt issuer figures. In the case of the equity filings, the smaller number of SEC reported filers may be explained in part by the fact that, unlike our data, the commission's totals do not include preferred stock and convertible securities filings.
5. In a sample cross-check, we found only rare instances in which a company was rated by Moody's when it was not rated by Standard & Poor's.
6. Debt Rating Definitions, *Bond Guide*, Standard & Poor Corporation, (New York, September 1985), p. 10.
7. Sec. Act Rel. 6499 (November 11, 1983) [48 Fed. Reg. 227, 52889 (1983)], p. 8, states that equity shelf offerings were about 3 percent of the total equity registrations and 6 percent of the dollar volume from March 1982 through September 1983.
8. At the Fifteenth Annual Institute on Securities Regulation, sponsored by the Practicing Law Institute, it was reported that Thomas A. Saunders III of Morgan Stanley expressed the following views on November 10, 1983, the day before the permanent Rule 415 was adopted: (1) it was not supportable that the rule would lead to lower costs for the issuer, although the issuer's administrative costs would be reduced; (2) prospectus quality had substantially decreased; (3) bid shopping, "fire drills," and a mania for "bought deals" were examples of questionable business practices that were occurring; (4) the trend toward concentration of underwriters was accelerating; (5) issuer presentations discouraged underwriters' questions; and (6) interrogation of the biggest issuers was no longer happening, in part because of "competitive

pressure" among underwriters. Special Report, 15 *Securities Regulation and Law Report* (November 18, 1983), 2104.

9. While not accepting the problem of institutionalization of securities markets as a pertinent consideration in its adoption of Rule 415, the commission was clearly aware of its possible consequences to the individual investor. Speaking a year later with regard to the effect of the SEC's installation of EDGAR (see chap. 6), Commissioner Charles C. Cox noted that EDGAR might reverse the trend toward institutionalization. "By revolutionizing the method by which investment decisions are made and executed, EDGAR could bring individual investors back into the stock market," he is reported to have said. 16 *Securities Regulation and Law Report* (December 21, 1984), 1991.

10. Sec. Act Rel. 6499, p. 18.

11. The requirements of Form S-3 are codified at 17 C.F.R. §239.13 (1984).

12. The list was generated through the good offices of Goldman, Sachs & Company, New York.

9
Future Public Policy

While there has been a tendency to view the initiation of shelf registration as a watershed in capital market evolution and to refer to the "post-415 era," our appraisal suggests that Rule 415 is better viewed in the context of a series of developments involving corporate issuers, industry competitors, and changes in the world's capital markets.

In the private corporate sector, borrowers and capital raisers, as we have pointed out, have continued to rely importantly on external financings as the compounding of growth in their sales and asset bases has expanded their need for funds. From time to time, monetary inflation has exacerbated those needs. As the size and frequency of financings have grown, underwriting and selling compensation has tended to adjust to offset the increased size of the deals, particularly when the deals are placed institutionally. Thus, price concessions to institutional investors have been cutting into intermediary compensation at the same time that these intermediaries have shaved their pricing for issuers in order to keep their good will and business.

It is possible that an important impetus for the initiation of Rule 415 included the desire of the SEC to counteract capital issuers' and intermediaries' risks in the face of the increasingly volatile capital markets and relatively high real and/or nominal cost of capital. Clearly, however, the commission has also intimated that it hoped to encourage more de facto competition in bidding for these financings and thus broaden as well as deepen the competition among investment bankers.

The substantial actual volume, as well as the prospect of continued heavy use, of shelf registrations under the permanent rule raises the question as to the ability of issuers and their underwriters to meet the expectations of the 1933 Act for disseminating to potential investors all material information prior to these offerings.

As we have seen, the SEC has suggested that an increasingly efficient marketplace can compensate for any shortcomings in due diligence investigations that might arise because of the speed of the offering. Nevertheless, the commission does recognize that the underwriting intermediary remains responsible under the law for any failure to perform a sufficiently diligent investigation of the issuer. As the statistics in Chapter 8 suggest, the number of companies qualified to use shelf underwritings is large and diverse enough to raise serious questions about the reliance on market efficiency as a backup, let alone a substitute, for underwriter diligence in many cases.

In this chapter we shall explore some implications of the SEC's sources of comfort on the question of underwriter diligence. We shall also propose a modification of the permanent Rule 415 which, we believe, could preserve the benefits of the shelf registration concept while avoiding what we consider to be potential adverse consequences for the investor.

RELIANCE ON MARKET EFFICIENCY

In August 1984, eighteen years after his earlier examination of the concept of integrated disclosure, Milton Cohen took a new look at these issues. In remarks entitled "Truth in Secu-

rities Revisited—Again," he concluded that the SEC had accomplished a great deal in integrating disclosure under the
1933 and 1934 statutes. A question that concerned him, however, was whether "the quality of 1933 Act disclosures for a
public offering by a continuous registrant deteriorated under
the integrated system." If the results were, in fact, of lower
quality, Cohen attributed this to reduced due diligence, not
integrated disclosure. This is the same question that nagged
investment bankers and commentators during the gestation
of Rule 415, and many now would be in general agreement
with Cohen's conclusion. Others, however, might conclude
for the very reasons cited by Cohen for deterioration of due
diligence that integrated disclosure was also a factor in les-
sening reasonable investigation under the 1933 Act.[1]

Cohen stated the basis of his conclusion as follows:

> What makes due diligence very difficult, if not impossible,
> at the moment of offerings is mostly a combination of the ex-
> traneous circumstances that I mentioned at the outset: such as
> time pressures resulting from the volatility of interest rates
> and stock prices, weakening of ties between companies and
> underwriting firms, institutionalization and internationaliza-
> tion of securities markets, and greater reliance on house coun-
> sel. And, if those factors were not enough, what poses the due
> diligence dilemma in its severest form is something superim-
> posed on the integrated disclosure system rather than inher-
> ent in it, namely Rule 415, as made available for equity, as
> well as debt offerings, without a compulsory waiting period.[2]

In enacting Rule 415, the commission took the position that
the enhanced market efficiency presumed to be realized
under integrated disclosure would be an adequate practical
surrogate for disclosure required by the 1933 Act in the case
of "registrants that are widely followed in the marketplace."[3]
The reasonable investigation required by the act was assumed by the SEC to be superseded in a de facto manner by
integrated disclosure. Thus, the commission stated: "Forms
S-3 and F-3 recognize the applicability of the efficient market
theory to those companies which provide a steady stream of
high quality corporate information to the marketplace and
whose corporate information is broadly disseminated."[4]

It can be fairly argued, however, that reliance on this kind of information is not enough to fulfill the 1933 Act's intent unless there is also a specific process of reasonable investigation. The 1933 Act involves, if not requires,[5] the undertaking of that specific diligence function, and it establishes a disclosure requirement which is essentially the same as that provided under the 1934 Act. The issuer may subjectively conclude that it is *always* diligent in determining the content of its disclosure. But this lacks the verification of an outsider investigation of what may be seen as material for the prudent investor. Indeed, as Cohen commented in his 1984 remarks, "Disclosures for 1934 Act purposes still tend to be taken less seriously, and to be of lower quality, than those historically provided, and still aspired to, under the 1933 Act."[6]

Role of the Securities Analyst. In relying on the effective operation of an efficient market, the commission specifically referred in detail to the diligence concept embodied in the 1933 Act. It concluded, however, that reasonable investigation could effectively proceed through the private, unregulated function of the securities analyst rather than through the responsible securities underwriter: "Information about these companies is constantly digested and synthesized by financial analysts, who act as essential conduits in the continuous flow of information to investors, and is broadly disseminated on a timely basis by the financial press and other participants in the marketplace."[7] The commission further noted the "important role of research reports in the integrated disclosure system," and stated that it had proposed reducing "substantially" the previous existing restrictions on use of analysts' research reports by registrants using Form S-3.[8]

In relying on market efficiency to help validate the terms of Rule 415, the commission appears to have assumed that the combined activities of financial analysts, professional portfolio managers, and other market participants can serve as a sufficiently objective and reasonable surrogate for public investigation of a broad array of companies for the purposes of the 1933 Act. But there are many kinds of financial analysts performing a wide range of services. Some analysts or their employers give only the "buy, hold, or sell" variety of recommendations to their customer; others provide graded relative merit ratings for various securities; and still others purport to specialize in such special situations and speculative opportunities as hostile and arbitrage plays. Despite the obvious variety, the SEC's approach seems to assume a broad, unqualified, inherent integrity in the unregulated process of the analyst's "factual" analysis, unalloyed by the employer firm's commercial self-interests.

The BarChris Concept of Diligence. An important concern is whether the financial analyst who, in the SEC's view, plays a key role in the creation of the efficient market, meets the investigative requirement of *BarChris*, the leading judicial determination of the due diligence burden of the underwriter. In this decision, the court said with respect to an underwriter's investigation:

> In any event, it is clear that no effectual attempt at verification was made. The question is whether due diligence required that it be made. Stated another way, is it sufficient to ask questions, to obtain answers which, if true, would be thought satisfactory, and to let it go at that, without seeking to ascertain from the records whether the answers in fact are true and complete?. . .
>
> To effectuate the statute's purpose, the phrase, "reasonable investigation" must be construed to require more effort on the part of the underwriters than the mere accurate reporting in the prospectus of "data presented" to them by the company. It should make no difference that these data are elicited by questions addressed to the company officers by the underwriters, or that the underwriters at the time believe that the company's officers are truthful and reliable. . . . They may not rely solely on the company's officers or on the company's counsel. A prudent man in the management of his own property would not rely on them.[9]

It would seem that the investment banker who could not rely "solely on the company's officers or on the company's counsel" would in many instances be foolhardy to rely upon the disparate actions of one or more financial analysts to assure that all relevant information is in the public domain and that the market for the securities is, as a consequence, efficient.

FALLING BACK ON TRADITIONAL DILIGENCE

The SEC appears to be of two minds on this issue. In formulating its own integrated disclosure system under its rulemaking power, it has adopted a philosophy that holds that to the extent that "the market accordingly [referring to periodic reports] acts efficiently, and this information is adequately reflected in the price of a registrant's outstanding securities, there seems little need to reiterate this information in a prospectus in the context of a [new] distribution."[10] However, the commission also emphasizes that it does not treat the reasonable investigation provision of the 1933 Act as having been abrogated by Rule 415—nor, as we have noted, could it do so even if it had so wished, since it has no constitutional power to amend a law.

The commission thus has made it clear that hovering over Rule 415 is the law itself, which continues to hold underwriters liable for the results of reasonable investigation, regardless of the conclusion reached by the SEC about the degree of market efficiency surrounding the issuer's securities. The commission appears, accordingly, to be relying on both the underwriter's fear of litigation as well as the efficacy of forms of due diligence short of the traditional approach to ensure that the 1933 Act's "regulation-by-information" mandate is carried out where the forms of market efficiency prove inadequate.[11]

Given the competitive forces at work in the securities industry described in Chapter 5, however, it is not clear that the specter of litigation would be sufficient to influence underwriters' behavior decisively. In the event that an inadequate process of investigation were proved to have led to inadequate disclosure, thus precipitating suits by stockholders, what would be the reaction of the investment bankers involved? We surmise that they would probably attempt to settle out of court with the claimants rather than litigate for several reasons. First, the imprimatur of the securities firm's name (and its implied warranty for securities products sold) would be too valuable an asset to put at risk in a court action covered by the public press. In addition, they would probably have real doubts about the advisability and outcome of pursuing an expensive, drawn-out jury trial. Thus, both in terms of immediate economic gains and losses as well as maintaining public esteem, settlement out of court could well involve the lower costs.

Assume, for example, that Premier Investment Bank is the lead underwriter of a group of four bankers successfully competing to underwrite equally a $200 million long-term debt offering of the Octopus Manufacturing Company. Less than a year after the offering, adverse information comes into the public domain which diminishes Octopus's credit standing and prompts the market value of the bonds to decline from an initial offering price of $1,000 per bond to $700. Further assume that an investor then brings a class action suit against Octopus, its key officers and directors, as well as against Premier Bank and the investment banking underwriters participating in its syndicate, claiming that a reasonable investigation would have disclosed this adverse information at the time of the offering. The potential liability of the combined defendants would be $300 per bond, or a total of $60 million on the issue. Each of the bankers would be liable for the entire damage. If the aggrieved investors, convinced of their deep pockets, brought a class action solely against the bankers, it is likely they would share the maximum liability on a pro rata basis equal to their respective underwriting participation of $15 million.

Such an economic cost would probably not unduly distress Premier Bank, which in view of the size of the underwriting may be assumed to have had recent annual pretax earnings of many times such a liability, and capital amounting to hundreds of millions of dollars.[12] Thus, even in the unlikely event of the issuer's not remaining sufficiently solvent to share at least some of the liability and even if the suit were brought against Premier Bank alone, Premier could well afford to absorb at least one such setback in any given year.

Since investment bankers can be expected to settle their due diligence lawsuits in the most efficient manner, including pro rata sharing of liability, can we assume that when thus painfully chastised they would pull back from their aggressive stance of maximum participation in shelf registration? Would they refrain from bidding on underwritings that have received perfunctory, inadequate investigation, or would they at least withhold submitting offers until they were satisfied that all pertinent information about the issuer's circumstances had been disclosed? Given the competitive industry pressures described in earlier chapters, we must assume that in many instances they would not, even though the firm's reputation and public image could again be put at risk.

Issuers' Diligence Supports.   The SEC, however, is apparently convinced that sufficient new methods of accomplishing adequate investigation have been developed in recent years to reduce to tolerable levels the potential of investigatory injury flowing from the abbreviated time schedule of a typical Rule 415 offering. It stated that registrants—that is, the issuers of the securities—had described procedures for diligence investigation that had been and were being developed "to enable underwriters to adapt to the integrated disclosure system and the shelf registration environment." The SEC attributed to the registrants the information they cited concerning "use of continuous due diligence programs, which employ a number of procedures, including designated underwriters' counsel."[13]

The commission spoke of factual findings, but did not make findings as to the nature, degree, or adequacy of any of these new procedures purportedly facilitating Rule 415, except to note that moves by issuers to appoint counsel to act for the underwriters "is a particularly significant development." The commission considered this lone factual finding, if indeed it is such, to reflect "a sound practice because it. . . facilitates continuous due diligence by ensuring on-going access to the registrant on the underwriters' behalf."[14]

The SEC also favorably noted other substitute procedures, but without any specific administrative or quasijudicial findings as to frequency, effectiveness, or method. It remarked on registrants' claims that "drafting sessions" were being held in accordance with the 1934 Act, in which underwriters and their counsel could participate, and that due diligence sessions were being held following the release of periodic reports. An extraordinary "finding" of the SEC in this regard, and one that it seems to have regarded as significant —is the fact that "some registrants indicate that prospective underwriters and underwriters' counsel are able to schedule individual meetings with management at any time."[15]

In a speech to the securities industry shortly after Rule 415 was adopted in its permanent form, SEC Chairman John Shad neither agreed with nor equivocated on these matters. He stated that "the shelf due diligence approaches suggested by non-underwriters are of limited value." Criticizing a suggestion that collaborative drafting sessions be held between issuers, groups of underwriters, and their attorneys during the preparation of prospectuses, proxies, and other SEC filing documents, he said, "Such documents are difficult enough to draft with one underwriter participating, let alone half a dozen."[16]

Shad added that continued collaboration would entail more than drafting problems: "It would be very expensive for senior corporate and underwriting executives and their attorneys to spend hundreds of thousands of hours annually, attending such meetings on the speculative possibility that the companies concerned will decide to do public offerings, and that one of the underwriters attending such sessions will be the high bidder for the issue."[17]

The Lawyer as a Diligence Agency. The commission appropriately recognized that due diligence methods of investigation "may not be the same for all registrants."[18] But it failed to recognize that the appointment by the issuer of counsel to act for ultimate Rule 415 underwriters (which the SEC appears actually to have found to be a "sound" approach to diligence investigation), would be unlikely to be supported generally by sophisticated securities counsel as a satisfactory process for carrying out a reasonable investigation.

In 1969, David Henkel, a prominent member of the New York Bar, analyzed the investigative function of counsel in the light of the *BarChris* case. Many lawyers experienced in representing underwriters in public offerings of securities would agree with his analysis as being singularly apt now under Rule 415:

The client should be made well aware of the limited function by the nature of things counsel can play in the decisional process of materiality. . .and that the sole decision should not be left to counsel. In attempting to define what is material, the Commission and the courts have related it to what would affect an investment decision. This is the heart of investment banking. . . .

Utilization of counsel to investigate factual matters should be considered as just one of the underwriters' procedures, not the only one. The underwriters' personnel must also be used. Furthermore, there are other persons, such as engineers, appraisers and management consultants, whose professional training makes them better alternatives than counsel in investigating certain areas. . . .

There are some caveats I should point out. The tendency is for the lawyers to be assigned the role of residual investigator. As I have stated earlier, this should be avoided. There are many technical, financial and business areas where others are more competent to make the investigation. Counsel probably does not have sufficient time, manpower or familiarity with the business to perform this function properly. . . .

The procedures to be followed in updating to the effective date of the registration statement the earlier investigation made by counsel will vary from case to case, but they should include close liaison with company officials, counsel and accountants, bring down letters by accountants, reexamination of key files, certificates as to developments and the reading of current minutes of board and committee meetings.[19]

Whether or not the lawyer is otherwise competent to serve as an independent investigator under Rule 415, the court made clear in *BarChris* that counsel is not an "expert" as to matters of fact:

To say the entire registration statement is expertised because some lawyer prepared it would be an unreasonable construction of the statute. Neither the lawyer for the company nor the lawyer for the underwriters is an expert within the meaning of Section 11. . . .

Drexel is bound by their failure [of their attorneys]. It is not a matter of relying on counsel for legal advice. Here the attorneys were dealing with matters of fact. . . . It must bear the consequences of their failure to make an adequate examination.

The other underwriters, who did nothing and relied solely on Drexel and on the lawyers, are also bound by it.[20]

In its commentary on the initial experience with Rule 415, the SEC stated, as we have noted, that the trend toward appointing a single law firm to act as underwriters' counsel is "a sound practice because it provides for due diligence investigations to be performed continually throughout the effectiveness of the shelf registration statement."[21]

The commission's reliance on this technique as a sound practice is somewhat perplexing. As the SEC notes, the technique is borrowed from the procedures necessarily developed for public utility financing when the commission promulgated its Rule 50 some forty years ago, requiring sealed competitive bidding for securities being issued by public utility companies subject to the Public Utility Holding Company Act of 1935. Because of the compulsory bidding procedures, no proposed underwriting group could know whether it would have the deal until a few minutes before the issue would be taken to market. A reasonable investigation ("diligence" in the commission's discussion) could not be accomplished by the lead underwriter, because of the short time between the opening of the sealed bids and the commencement of the public offering by the successful bidder. Accordingly, in order to make its policy of compulsory competitive bidding work under the Holding Company Act, the SEC agreed to let the issuer select non-affiliated counsel both to participate with issuer's counsel in the preparation of the registration statement and offering documents (such as the frequently necessary mortgage indenture securing utility debt issues) and then to act as counsel for the successful underwriters after the bids were opened.

To apply this procedure to the equally short shelf registration process raises at least two questions of concern to underwriters. First, although the SEC has less than a quasijudicial function under the Securities Act of 1933, the Holding Company Act does require the commission to make certain specific, substantive regulatory findings. This comparative regulatory difference, which places a statutory burden on the SEC before the utility security can be sold, results in a form of approval by the commission of the security being offered under Rule 50. In effect, the commission itself is essentially doing the due diligence investigation in these offerings, whereas under the pure disclosure scheme of the Securities Act of 1933, the burden is on the underwriters. It is unlikely that an underwriter could successfully assert the fact of the commission's order having been issued under the Holding Company Act as a defense against a due diligence suit regarding a utility security, since Securities Act requirements are also fully applicable to securities issues under the Holding Company Act. However, the underwriters might plausibly claim to find at least a certain degree of comfort in the fact that the commission itself failed to spot the material falsity or omission before permitting the security to be sold.

Second, Rule 415 shelf registration has a life of two years. The underwriter must therefore be concerned not only about the performance of a reasonable investigation by issuer-selected counsel assumed to have the requisite competence, techniques, and experience for making a *factual* investigation in a matter in which (pursuant to *BarChris*) lawyers are not accepted by the courts as experts, but whether the lawyer-investigator will be available for two years and have kept the investigation thoroughly current over the period. In contrast to the possible lengthy postponement under Rule 415, Rule 50 transactions usually involve a relatively short time between preregistration drafting and actual public offering. Moreover, independent counsel selected by the issuers in Rule 50 bidding are publicly identified as having been continuously involved in the kind of business, public utility, involved in the proposed issue. This is particularly significant, as the work frequently involves expert review of detailed technical, as distinguished from factual, documentation. Thus, issues involving such matters as atomic energy problems, compliance of the terms of a proposed utility bond indenture with the requirements of the Trust Indenture Act, and disclosure of the legal remedies on debt default by public utility companies, would emerge as specialized legal questions.

Commenting on the hiring of attorneys to make due diligence investigations, SEC Chairman Shad noted that the "principal purpose [of due diligence reviews] is to protect investors," not to defend legal actions. He stressed that it is the underwriters' "capital and reputations that are at risk, if offerings are unsuccessful or perform poorly in the after-issue market," and added that "assessment of the underwriting and the after-issue market risks require market judgements and careful reviews by experienced underwriters. However, under accelerated offering schedules, the critical judgement has become the price at which there will be sufficient immediate institutional interest to absorb the issue."[22]

Regarding the validity of the analogy between Rule 415 diligence and the historical Rule 50 practice in competitive bidding on utility offerings, the chairman made the important distinction between the kinds of securities offerings being affected. He said: "Issuer hired attorneys are used in competitive utility offerings. However, utilities are the most predictable of corporate enterprises. They are not subject to the vagaries to which industrial and other issuers are subject. In addition, many publish their financing intentions a year in advance. The reasonable certainty that their financings will occur, permit and justify preparatory efforts by prospective bidders for such issues."[23]

Conflicts in Determining Materiality. The very nature of integrated disclosure information compounds the diligence problem. Reports filed by the registrant under the 1934 Act are not prepared in the investigatory context of a 1933 Act registration. There is no give and take in the 1934 Act reporting process between the issuer on the one hand determining what and how to report and a third party on the other hand, asking questions and testing the answers. In every 1934 Act report situation, there is reason to wonder whether an independent objective questioner as to what may be material might have elicited additional information. Furthermore, a registrant utilizing in its 1933 Act registration an incorporation by reference of its own 1934 Act report is unlikely to accept a diligence demand from independent counsel to modify the 1934 Act report to meet 1933 Act standards. Any such voluntary modification by the registrant would retrospectively raise questions in the marketplace concerning the adequacy of its original 1934 Act disclosure. Even lesser events than such modifications have in the past been regarded as an admission of fault and stimulated litigation.

One must question whether the savings in costs flowing from integrated disclosure (savings for issuers of the expense of duplicating information and for the government owing to reduced SEC workload) are sufficient to offset the potential costs to the public. We may take as given that independent security analysis is easier and less expensive to conduct under integrated disclosure than under the separate disclosures systems, but it does not necessarily follow that thus relying on the market's efficiency produces an adequate investigation. At most, the work of the analyst yields the expectation that the information released in publicly filed documents will be quickly incorporated into the market price of the relevant securities. While some analysts may aggressively seek out additional information, perhaps calling upon personal relationships with corporate officers, the latter must always be concerned with whether insider information is being improperly disclosed in such contacts. In a 1933 Act investigation, by contrast, seeking out this additional information is an absolute *requirement* and there is no such thing as "insider information" which is off limits to the investigating underwriter.

Rule 176 as a Safe Harbor.   As we have previously noted, the commission was aware of the problems posed for meeting the requirements of due diligence, whether the underwriter's investigatory obligation under section 11 was considered a mandatory requirement or merely a protective shield against investor redress. The SEC avoided the question in part by adopting Rule 176 as a statement of its views on what could be deemed compliance with the reasonable investigation provision of section 11.

As described by the commission, "Rule 176 sets forth a non-exclusive list of circumstances which the commission believes bear upon the reasonableness of the investigation and the determination of what constitutes reasonable grounds for belief under Section 11(b) of the Securities Act." The circumstances in the commission's judgment "which may be particularly relevant" to determining whether there has been due diligence by an underwriter of a Form S-3 issuance include the following:

> The type of issuer and security; the type of person on whom relied and office held, if an officer, and other relationship to the issuer if the person is a director or proposed director; the nature of reliance on persons through whose duties there should have been, as a matter of function and responsibility, knowledge of particular facts with respect to the issuer and the filing; the type of underwriting arrangement, the role of the underwriter and the availability of information with respect to the registrant; and whether, with respect to any incorporation by reference in the registration statement, the underwriter participated in the preparation or review of documents so incorporated.[24]

The significance of Rule 176 to the determination by a court as to whether an underwriter's investigation constituted due diligence has not yet been the subject of any litigation. The commission, of course, is not itself the finder of fact or law in a suit brought by a securities buyer under section 11. The federal court would hear that suit, and it would not be bound by the provisions of Rule 176 as to what the commission considers a reasonable investigation. The rule might realistically appeal to the court as a fair solution, treating the commission as a learned, impartial friend of the court. But even then, the rule which purports to be universal might not have any significant bearing on the particular investigation, notwithstanding the court's acceptance of its general applicability.

In applying Rule 176 to the conduct of an investment banker competing for the underwriting of an offering, the most significant problem for the banker's staff would be the time available for meeting the final two circumstances it cites. First, how is a determination to be made as to the "availability of information with respect to the registrant?" If information is readily available, is the underwriter entitled to any shield against liability? Where pertinent information is demonstrated to be extremely difficult to acquire, is an underwriter to be excused from liability under section 11?

In addition, the commission seems to assume that the underwriter will be familiar with the 1934 Act material incorporated by reference in the registration statement. More often than not, the underwriter will not have participated in filing that prior report, and will not have had direct knowledge of it at the time. Can the underwriter dare to accept this incorporated material as meeting the reasonable investigation requirements of the Securities Act? Suppose, for example, that the incorporated document is a report of an internal corporate investigation by a committee of nonmanagement directors triggered by a payment likely to be considered questionable under the Foreign Corrupt Practices Act. Or the summary of a disagreement between the commission's chief accountant and the registrant's independent auditors as to whether a particular accounting procedure constitutes generally accepted accounting practice. Or an engineering report on the causes of an accident in a foreign subsidiary of the registrant which produced a calamitous loss of life and property. The provisions of Rule 176 may protect an underwriter in these cases for SEC purposes, but they would not serve as an impenetrable shield against the arrows of litigation in a judicial proceeding.

POLICY PROPOSALS

In light of these observations, it may fairly be concluded that permanent Rule 415 in its present form does not adequately meet the requirements of the 1933 Act, and should be amended.[25] Any amendments should distinguish between easy situations, in which the existing flow of information is likely to ensure adequate investor protection (and thus the current rule is satisfactory), and hard situations, in which there is considerable doubt as to the process of ensuring adequate information.

Because the costs associated with undertaking due diligence investigations are not trivial, they ought to be minimized in the easy cases. The time period required for such an investigation should also be kept to a minimum so as not unnecessarily to miss a window for an advantageous public offering or to run into changes in the nature of the risk attached to the security itself. The shorter the period, the better an issuer and banker are able to determine and satisfy market preferences.

Conversely, in hard cases the security should not be offered to the public until the underwriter is completely satisfied with the disclosures made in the prospectus, no matter how long the investigation takes.

It would be tempting to employ the distinction between debt and equity financings as a basis for resolving the difference between "easy" and "hard" cases. It could be argued that a broader group of issuers should be permitted to utilize shelf registration of debt securities without a laborious due diligence process because such senior corporate obligations are protected by the law as a matter of creditor's rights and thus offer the investor less uncertainties than those inherent in an equity security issued by the same company. While we agree that one may assume there is less likelihood of serious injury to an investor in a "plain vanilla" senior debt obligation as compared to an equity security, we nonetheless conclude that a remedial modification in the current shelf registration rule should focus on distinctions among corporate *issuers* rather than among classes of securities being sold. In part, this is because risk distinctions between classes of securities—once relatively straightforward—are increasingly breaking down in the face of a proliferating array of hybrid instruments with subtle yet significant differences in their holders' claims on the issuing corporation.

Even more important, however, is the fact that the Securities Act of 1933 clearly directs its attention to the corporate *issuer*, not to a particular class of securities instruments being offered. The flotation of a new securities offer, as has been noted earlier, is the opportunity for the kind of exhaustive investigation of an *issuer's* affairs which, for the bulk of public financings, is not likely otherwise to be pursued adequately on a continuous basis.

Yet, even adopting distinctions based on issuers of securities rather than on types of securities offerings to identify groups of "easy" and "hard" cases does not describe all potential offerers. As we saw in Chapter 8, there is also a group of issuers qualified to use Form S-3 that stands somewhere in between these two poles. Moreover, since the market value of equity test is the fundamental qualification for Form S-3 eligibility, the future composition of this middle group may swell significantly in size (particularly in a speculative market) as the Dow Jones industrial average rises.

Categories of Issuers.   Thus it would appear that there are basically three broad categories of public issuers of corporate securities, rather than the two classes now either included in or excluded from Rule 415. These should be identified for purposes of current administrative interpretation of the public policy mandate of the Securities Act, and for establishing a revised policy for the future.

There is, first, a group of issuers who, by virtue of investment quality and availability of pertinent material information, warrant reliance wholly on a process of self-examination as a condition to effective registration under the 1933 Act. To the extent that there is a group of publicly owned companies for whom the markets are efficient in extracting relevant, material information and promptly incorporating that information into its securities prices, these "household name" companies would be the group. Even if the markets are less effective in this regard than adherents to the efficient market hypothesis maintain, one could still rationalize exemption for this group because they can be relied upon to exercise self-discipline effectively. Their presumed wide experience in due diligence requirements and the very substantial stake their managements would feel in upholding the issuer's image for integrity and forthcomingness is too valuable an asset to be squandered in one lapse into sloppiness or obfuscation in a public offering's factual documentation.

Thus, although these issuers should remain subject to section 11 of the 1933 Act, they alone would be liable for any failure to meet the disclosure standards. The act could be amended to permit the commission to exempt their underwriters from the reasonable investigation requirements of section 11(c). This amendment would merely authorize by law what is now in effect occurring under Rule 415 without any such legal sanction. In these cases, investment bankers would freely compete to underwrite and distribute new security offerings without any risk of liability for the content of the accompanying prospectus. Pricing of the offering by the underwriter would be purely a matter of applicable financial conditions, public taste, its own capital resources, and its distributing talents. Other bankers could join an underwriting group in such cases without any concern as to the investigative diligence of the lead underwriter. Prestige and public acceptance of the underwriter would still be important to the securities buyers, but the expenses of the offering would be minimized.

The rule defining eligibility for this privileged group of issuers would involve two distinct screens. The first screen would continue to be the registration requirement represented in Form S-3, which essentially involves an equity market valuation test (or qualification under other permitted uses). This screen is related to the quality of integrated disclosure and market efficiency. We consider, however, that if diligence is to be eliminated as a test for the "household names," a second screen is also required which establishes a hurdle which only the most credit-worthy issuers could leap, as determined from time to time by the SEC. The rule's eligibility requirement would need to recognize, moreover, that a history of having been credit-worthy does not ensure maintenance of that condition, notwithstanding that a large body of information might already exist in the public domain. The rule, accordingly, would be designed to assure investors that they have no need to fear exposure to other than the normal risks of the issuer's particular business. In short, the buyer need not beware.

The quality hurdle should take into account more than merely the issuer's equity market value, no matter how large. An earnings test based on previous fixed-charge coverage, return on equity, or return on sales would be relevant, as might various tests of the relationship of assets to liabilities. A combination formula embodying a number of investment quality earnings and assets indices could ensure that an issuer had not slipped below the minimum quality standards.[26]

For all cases other than those which we have characterized as "household names," the Securities Act would remain unmodified. The commission would, of course, have the right to change the composition of the Rule 415 universe, but that would not affect our proposed method of achieving diligence.

Authorization of Professional Diligence Agencies. The proposed treatment of the in-between group would, as in the easy cases, require amending the Securities Act. The objective would be to permit the commission to provide by rule that an underwriter may avoid liability under the 1933 Act when a reasonable investigation under section 11 had been conducted by a new class of experts meeting certain qualification tests. In effect, eligibility to join the Rule 415 universe could be met or possibly even enlarged by the commission. A process of assured diligent investigation might permit Form S-3 registration to be less stringent in terms of its equity market value test or its transaction limitations. The law could permit the investigation to be conducted by professional experts or agencies, other than underwriters, having specific expertise to perform diligence investigations under the 1933 Act. These experts would be financially responsible for the adequacy of the registration. The issuer in the in-between group would have discretion whether to employ such professionals. If the issuer chose not to, there would be an alternative incubation period before effectiveness of the registration during which the underwriter could complete a reasonable investigation. The period could be considerably shortened for this group under customary acceleration procedure, but this acceleration should be coupled with certain investor comfort requirements including, for example, a required diligence performance certificate from the underwriter and a restriction limiting the use of Rule 415 to situations where within a specified prior period, say within twelve months, a non-Rule 415 registration had become effective.

The definition of the acceptable professional investigator would establish standards both of expertise and financial responsibility. The rule's standard of financial ability could be expressed both directly, as in the case of establishing the size of the assets of an insurance company acting as an investigator, or indirectly, by establishing the terms of an irrevocable quality letter of credit where, for example, a law, accounting, or other qualifying firm would be serving as the investigator. Financial ability of the investigator would also be related to the size of the issue and the aggregate amount of all issuances financially backed by the investigator.

The underwriter would thus either have sufficient time to make a reasonable investigation or be removed from any responsibility for it. The buyer could continue to hold responsible both the issuer and either an underwriter or other responsible financial entity. Unlike the practice, suggested in Rule 415, of assigning an independent counsel to perform diligence, the professional investigator would not only employ counsel but would also bring to the task a broader array of talents (particularly financial analytic acumen) than are available from counsel. The professional investigator, unlike counsel under present law, would be personally liable for failure of due diligence, but counsel itself could elect to become a professional investigator under the terms of the applicable rule, by adding necessary personnel resources as well as assuring its financial responsibility.

Substituting a third party for the underwriter's reasonable investigation provision, while keeping the registration scheme of the Securities Act intact, would have the effect of removing the underwriter from the group of persons other than the issuer for whom the diligence provision is thought variously to be a requirement or a shield. The issuer itself is, of course, always responsible and never able to claim an investigative shield. Many persons other than the underwriter, however, are also responsible under section 11 for a reasonable investigation. Because of their relationship as either affiliates or employees of the issuer—by contrast with the underwriter's presumed arm's-length relationship with the issuer—their proper responsibility may be considered to be mandatory investigation, and not discretionary shielding of themselves or others from litigation. For these persons there would be no change from the present law.

Operation of the Proposals.   One significant consequence of distinguishing the underwriter from others who would remain subject to section 11 is that the ostensibly deep pockets of the investment banker who underwrote the sale of the issue would not be pickable for failure to investigate adequately whether the sales literature met the law's disclosure requirements. The fact that the issuer and a host of other individuals remain liable for damages would produce investor comfort to the extent of the financial strength of the issuer and the related responsible individuals. But, financial comfort may also be available other than from a balance sheet. The use of insurance or indemnification provisions based on letters of credit or similar reliance on third-party financial standing has become increasingly important in the sale of municipal obligations. Appropriate protection of this type promotes the issuer's credit standing to that of the third party and is designed to reduce financing costs.[27] Deep pocket sources of this nature—generally banks or insurance companies—would in many cases be superior in quality and quantity to those of the investment banker.

Effect of the Proposals. Eliminating the reasonable investigation provision from the act for an eligible class of quality issuers eliminates the nature of that investigation as a source of legal complaint. The plaintiff's case could still be maintained, however, against the issuer and other persons remaining subject to section 11, but would turn solely on the objective appraisal of adequacy of disclosure rather than of investigation. The question of adequate disclosure, of course, is always the principal issue under the Securities Act since it is at the heart of the act's regulatory scheme. The question of whether an investigation is mandatory or discretionary under the act would be mooted in such cases.

Clearly, we mean to suggest an end to the test of diligent investigation only in certain highly qualified cases. Indeed, our recommendations would, in effect, call for amplifying the investigatory process and making it more stringent in other cases. When an insurance carrier or other indemnifier becomes financially responsible for the investigation process, it will not have an underwriting fee, as such. Its reward for undertaking financial responsibilities will be wholly related to accomplishing an impeccable service function. Its insurance premium or standby credit fee will serve generally to increase its professional concern with the integrity of the registration and the investigation process. The commission's views, expressed in the adoption of Rule 415, as to the validity of the diligence process through the vehicle of independent counsel or securities analysts or through an integrated disclosure in which bankers would participate, would be realized more certainly in the emergence of full-time professional investigators. They could be employed on a permanent basis by frequent issuers in order to keep the issuer's affairs constantly under confidential review, much as independent accountants do in connection with preparing for annual audits. The professional investigators so retained would then be prepared, on short notice, to stand behind a proposed offering financially for the one-year period fixed in the statute.

This professional, financially responsible diligence review by a third party would essentially constitute a new function in the vetting of a proposed offering. It could engender a new service industry. Assuming they already had or acquired the necessary personnel resources, banks, insurance companies, investment bankers, public accountants, consulting organizations, lawyers, engineers, and securities analysts would be among those that might participate in this new industry, either solely or in groups, and either directly as investigators or indirectly as financial backers. They would act not as securities underwriters, but as professional securities investigators. Professional paid diligence would be substituted for the investigative function of the underwriter, which under Rule 415 may now actually be conducted by persons unrelated to the underwriter who, however, continues to have statutory and financial responsibility for the consequences of their investigation.

Exempted by law from liability under section 11 in the quality cases, the investment banker could price a security without regard to costs incurred either for factual investigation or through the burden of liability. The banker would have no responsibility to the public beyond carrying out the terms of the public offering in the registration statement, and none to the issuer beyond the terms of purchase and payment in the underwriting agreement.

The professional investigator could be paid a retainer by the frequent issuer or be compensated on an *ad hoc* basis. The issuer would continue to be liable for failure to comply with the Securities Act, and the professional investigator would be liable for failure to make a reasonable investigation.

From a cost standpoint, the professional investigation would mean an added expense to the offering only if it is assumed that the underwriter does not now include the cost of investigation in its pricing of an issue. If that is so, the adequacy of current investigations is open to even sharper questioning. However, even if this process is now a "free ride" for the issuer, it is not so for the issuer's outside directors, who must rely on management for the registration statement's accuracy, but are nevertheless required to sign the statement themselves. In such cases, the fee incurred by the issuer for a statutory investigation made on a professional basis and backed by financial responsibility should be reflected, as is the case in municipal debt issues, in enhanced quality and reduced transaction costs over the long term.

Many aspects of the securities markets have changed in the half-century since the original passage of the Securities Act. Organizational and marketing arrangements for issuing new securities have necessarily had to adapt to those changes. The shelf underwriting registration procedure is an effort in that direction which ought to be preserved in concept but not at the expense of an independent investigation on behalf of potential investors. At the time of the 1933 Act's passage, the investment banker was the only practical source of arm's-length investigation for the protection of investors. Fifty years later, the great depth and diversity of market participants in the United States argues not for abandoning that independent investigation but for modifying it to take into account both the impracticality of this role for underwriters in many shelf deals and the emergence of a number of experts capable of taking their place. The achievement of a meaningful due diligence investigation within a realistic time frame and with financial responsibility—a situation that existed during the first fifty years of the 1933 Act—should continue to be the objective for the future.

NOTES

1. Milton H. Cohen's remarks, which were addressed to the Committee on Federal Regulation of Securities of the Section of Corporation, Banking and Business Law of the American Bar Association, were subsequently published as "The Integrated Disclosure System— Unfinished Business," 40 *The Business Lawyer* 987 (1985).
2. Ibid., pp. 992–993.
3. Sec. Act Rel. 6499, p. 12.
4. Ibid.
5. Whether, as we have previously noted, the process is deemed mandatory or voluntary with the underwriter who is concerned only with building a defense against possible litigation, is a question that is not directly addressed in the legislative history of the 1933 Act.
6. Cohen, "The Integrated Disclosure System," p. 992.
7. Sec. Act Rel. 6499, p. 12.
8. Ibid., p. 12, note.
9. *Escott* v. *BarChris Const. Corp.*, 283 F.Supp. 643, 696–697 (S.D.N.Y., Mar. 29, 1968).
10. Sec. Act Rel. 6235 (September 2, 1980) [45 Fed. Reg. 63693 (1980)].
11. A prominent securities lawyer, William Williams, has been quoted as saying, concerning the adoption of Rule 415, that the position of underwriters has become "virtually untenable," and that SEC staff members were "deluding themselves a little bit as to what's going on in the real world." 16 *Securities Regulation and Law Report*, January 20, 1984, p. 122.
12. See various recent issues of *Wall Street Letter;* see also, *Institutional Investor*, June 1984.
13. Sec. Act Rel. 6499, p. 13.
14. Ibid., pp. 14, 15.
15. Ibid., p. 15.
16. Speech by John S. R. Shad, December 1, 1983, to the Securities Industry Association, entitled "Causes and Consequences," p. 6. See also his concurring opinion in the adoption of Rule 415, Sec. Act Rel. 6499.
17. Ibid.
18. Sec. Act Rel. 6499, p. 16.
19. David Henkel, "Liability of Counsel for Underwriter," 24 *The Business Lawyer* 641, 643, 652–653 (1969).
20. *Escott* v. *BarChris Const. Corp.*, 283 F.Supp. 643, 647 (S.D.N.Y., Mar. 29, 1968).
21. Sec. Act Rel. 6499, p. 15.
22. Shad, "Causes and Consequences," p. 6.
23. Ibid., p. 7.
24. Sec. Act Rel. 6499, p. 16.
25. In adopting Rule 415 in its permanent form, the commission adverted

to suggested modifications to the temporary rule which it had received from interested persons. These included: "(1) restricting eligibility for use of the Rule to (a) investment grade securities, (b) a combination of investment grade debt securities and limited types of equity securities or (c) registrants that are widely followed in the marketplace; (2) requiring advance notice to the marketplace of forthcoming offerings; and (3) imposing some form of 'cooling off period' between the announcement and sale of securities." The commission also noted that some commentators had suggested providing relief from liability under the 1933 Act for underwriters. Sec. Act Rel. 6499, p. 6.

26. By analogy to the *Fortune* "200" or "500," there might be a quality "500" exemption under the applicable easy case rule, representing part of the Rule 415 universe as it appears appropriate to the commission from time to time to do so.

27. The extension of this type of protection to securities other than tax-exempt debt in its various forms has already commenced. In 1985 Financial Security Assurance, Inc. was formed by Equitable Life Assurance, John Hancock Mutual Life, New England Mutual Life, Transamerica Corporation, Ford Motor Credit Company, and Westpac Banking Corporation with initial paid-in capital of $155 million, with thirty smaller companies also expected to invest, increasing capital to $235 million within six months. The corporation proposed to issue and reinsure financial guarantees on corporate debt obligations of various kinds. The obligations so insured by the corporation were expected to have a Standard & Poor's AAA rating, and the issuers to have a cost of about one-half of the interest savings which they would enjoy on their obligations by reason of having the insurance. The securities being insured would be required by the corporation to be of investment grade and to be collateralized by assets, receivables, or a bank letter of credit. *New York Times*, 31 July 1985, p. D17.

10
Summary and Overview

This book has traced some significant aspects of the public sale of new corporate securities in the United States for more than a half-century, beginning with the heady days of the 1920s. The underlying question that stimulated the book's exploration concerns the nature and thrust of American public policy in the marketing of new corporate securities, and thus the conditions by which such securities are permitted to be sold. This exploration led to a chronicling of the evolution in public capital raising procedures as they have adapted both to changes in the economic and business environment and to unfolding political exigencies in the United States.

The economic expansion in the aftermath of World War I spawned a free-wheeling securities market which brought with it excesses and fiduciary abuses during the 1920s. At that time there was no national expression of a public policy, but the states, with their blue sky laws, were attempting individually to meet the emerging demands from the public for protection. The aftermath of the experience of the 1920s and the commencement of harsh economic depression helped to elect a reform-minded Democratic administration and fostered the securities and banking legislative reforms of the mid-1930s. The thrust of this legislation was both to preserve the capitalist system, then in disarray, in the face of a new— and to most persons a frightening—economic and political alternative system which had only recently been established in Russia, and to create a series of protections for previously abused suppliers of capital to the system. Congress's notion of subjecting securities issuance to regulation by information on a national basis was essentially a renewed effort at industry self-regulation but with a fresh approach to public oversight via the creation of a new national regulatory body, the Securities and Exchange Commission. This solution also addressed the question of sanctions in a unique way. The regulatory agency would be provided with sheathed knives— only to be utilized if the participants should slip back into unacceptable habits.

That series of measures not only changed the rules by which capital was raised in the United States, but also fostered the growth of new information-generating and analytical industries which helped alter the competitive environment within which financial intermediaries competed for securities business.

The sparse record of prosecuted abuses suggests that the system devised for raising new capital has been largely effective in accomplishing its purpose. The legislative framers are now seen to have displayed uniquely good judgment in their decision to avoid assigning government regulators a role in assessing the quality of new securities products being offered for sale to the public. This new agency with its expert staff would intervene in these matters, which were so important to the efficient functioning of the economic system, only by exception—when they saw a gap in the public disclosure of full particulars surrounding a proposed offering.

We have dealt in this book with what we consider to have been particularly relevant changes in the financial markets in the fifty years since passage of the reform legislation. These markets have become significantly broader and deeper in the intervening years, and the growth of institutionalized capital pools has dramatically shifted both the holding of, and the trading in, financial assets from individual investors to professional investment managers.

An integral part of this shift has been the rise of a growing cadre of professional financial market participants and sources of new technology that have abetted the process of developing and transmitting information about publicly traded companies. The emergence of knowledgeable and sophisticated securities analysts, portfolio managers, and professional arbitrageurs, with analytic tools and communications links that were inconceivable in the 1930s, has greatly expanded the supply of information that works its way into the public domain.

Academic researchers have been much intrigued with the possible consequences of amplified and speedier information. Some have sought to prove that this much enhanced array of market participants and technological aids has produced free market prices for well-traded securities which now reliably reflect the true current circumstances and business prospects of the issuing companies. The empirical findings as to the *degree* of this enriched market efficiency, however, still seem equivocal to us, and there is thus far no wide agreement among scholars and practitioners in the field of security analysis as to the efficacy of the market's information-incorporating mechanism. The search for technical patterns, the application of market-action theories ranging from reliance on the indications from sunspots to the signals to be derived from variations identified in the Dow theory, and the digging for the special situation go on and on. We conclude, along with many others, that the presumption of market efficiency has a significant bearing on market-making in a large number of securities but in the bulk of cases cannot be relied upon as a substitute for the rigorous due diligence investigation which underlies the intent, if not the text, of the Securities Act of 1933.

To paraphrase loosely what has been attributed to Lincoln

in discussing forfeiture of public confidence, we believe that efficient markets may reflect all material securities information some of the time, and even some of the material information all of the time, but they never reflect all of the material information all of the time.

Even if statistical results were to indicate that the economic cost of the failure to provide adequate material information was less than the cost of the remedies that might be imposed on issuers and their financial intermediaries to prevent abuses or failures, we would be reluctant to see the adoption of a laissez-faire regulatory posture as to the continued need for due diligence. It seems clear to us that the reform legislation of the 1930s was not directed primarily toward economic optimization on a broad basis, but rather toward buttressing the public's confidence in the integrity of the free market system on a more narrow basis.

Thus, unless one embraces fully the position of the strong form proponents of the efficient market hypothesis, who believe that the market provides a nearly infallible proxy for all manner of due diligence, one is left with the conviction that managements and other insiders are likely to know more about an issuing company's affairs than outsiders, who must necessarily include not only unsophisticated individual investors but also professional observers. The speed of analysis and the soundness of judgment applied to information must lag and be influenced by its untested sponsorship.

There is the further notion that framers of the securities legislation sought to provide both an occasion (a new offering) and a vehicle (the registration statement) by which new or updated independently tested information could be introduced occasionally into the public domain. In that sense, the due diligence exercise takes on an importance that goes beyond the provision of more immediate protection for potential buyers of newly offered securities.

One does not have to embrace blindly the recent push for deregulation in a number of U.S. industry sectors to acknowledge the common sense inherent in continually modifying the rules governing various aspects of commerce—including securities sales. After all, changes are constantly occurring in economic and market conditions. It was in response to just such changes that the commission introduced the shelf registration option. Our reservations are not with the considerations that led to its introduction but with the filter subsequently used to identify the qualified users. We recognize that there is a subset of the Form S-3 universe of companies that is more likely than others to fit the mold of the efficient market that the commission has put forward. For those issuers deemed to be household names, due diligence as an obligation should be expressly eliminated rather than honored in the breach. For another group of issuers we have advanced the idea of professional third-party due diligence, provided by vendors that would be financially responsible for their conclusions. Finally, for the remaining issuers we believe it is important that the securities intermediary itself undertake careful investigation of the issuing company's affairs prior to a securities offering; these issuers should be foreclosed from using the shelf procedure altogether.

It is important that the proven benefit and comfort of due diligence not be sacrificed in the quest for the fruits of deregulation. In our view public policy has, over a period of a half-century of operation, significantly altered the definition of what is required by the concept of regulation by information, and how it is to be provided. But we have no doubt that the validity of and mandate for the concept continues, and should continue, to exist under the Securities Act of 1933.

Nor do we have any doubt that the effective realization of the objectives of the concept depends on diligent, independent investigation tailored to specific circumstances.

APPENDIX I

1,000,000 Shares*
YOUNGCORP
Common Stock

AGREEMENT AMONG UNDERWRITERS

_____ , 19__

---

* Plus an option to purchase from Youngcorp up to 100,000 additional shares to cover over-allotments.

1,000,000 Shares*
YOUNGCORP
Common Stock

AGREEMENT AMONG UNDERWRITERS

———————————— , 19——

Universal Investment Banker, Incorporated,

As Representative of the Several Underwriters

New York, New York

Gentlemen:

We wish to confirm as follows the agreement among you, the undersigned and the other underwriters named in Schedule I to the form of Underwriting Agreement attached hereto as Exhibit A (herein called the "Underwriting Agreement") as it is to be executed (all such parties being herein called the "Underwriters") with respect to the purchase by the Underwriters from Youngcorp, a Delaware corporation (herein called the "Company") and the selling stockholders named in the Underwriting Agreement (the "Selling Stockholders") and the sale by the Company and the Selling Stockholders to the several Underwriters, of the respective numbers of shares of Common Stock of the Company (such shares of Common Stock to be purchased by the Underwriters being herein called the "Underwritten Stock") set forth opposite the name of each of the Underwriters in said Schedule I. The Underwriting Agreement also provides for the granting by the Company to the Underwriters of an option, on the terms and conditions set forth therein, to purchase up to the number of additional shares of Common Stock set forth therein from the Company (said additional shares being herein called the "Option Stock" and with the Underwritten Stock herein collectively called the "Stock"). We also understand that changes may be made in those who are to be Underwriters and in the respective numbers of shares of Stock which they agree to purchase, but that the number of shares of Stock to be purchased by us, as set forth in

———————————

* Plus an option to purchase from the Company up to 100,000 additional shares to cover over-allotments.

Schedule I, will not be changed without our consent except as provided herein and in the Underwriting Agreement.

1. *Authority of the Representative.* We authorize you as our Representative and on our behalf (a) to complete, execute and deliver the Underwriting Agreement in substantially the form attached hereto, with such variations, if any, as in your judgment are appropriate and are not material, provided that the number of shares of stock set forth opposite our name in Schedule I thereto shall not be increased without our consent, (b) to take such action as in your discretion may be necessary or advisable to carry out the Underwriting Agreement, this Agreement and the transactions for the accounts of the several Underwriters contemplated thereby and hereby and (c) to waive performance or satisfaction by the Company of the obligations and conditions included in the Underwriting Agreement if, in your judgment, such waiver will not have a material adverse effect upon the interests of the Underwriters; provided that the time in which the registration statement on Form S-1 filed with the Securities and Exchange Commission (the "Commission") in respect of the Stock (herein called the "Registration Statement") is required to become effective pursuant to the Underwriting Agreement shall not be extended more than 48 hours without the approval of a majority in interest (based upon the number of shares of Stock allocated) of the Underwriters (including yourselves). We also authorize you to determine all matters relating to the public advertisement of the Stock.

2. *Public Offering and Sale of the Stock.* A public offering of the Stock is to be made, as herein provided, as soon after the Registration Statement relating thereto becomes effective as in your judgment is advisable. The Stock shall initially be offered to the public at the public offering price set forth on the cover page of the prospectus relating to the Registration Statement (herein called the "Prospectus"). You will advise us by telegraph or telephone when the Stock shall be released for offering. We authorize you, as Representative of the Underwriters, after the initial public offering of Stock hereunder has commenced, to vary the public offering price, in your sole discretion, by reason of changes in general market conditions or otherwise. The public offering price at any time in effect is herein called the "Offering Price."

We authorize you to reserve for offering and sale, and on our behalf to sell, to institutions or other retail purchasers (such sales being herein called "Retail Sales") and to dealers selected by you (such dealers being herein called "Selected Dealers"), among whom you may include any of the Underwriters, all or any part of the Stock as you may determine. Such sales, if any, shall be made (i) in the case of Retail Sales, at the Offering Price and (ii) in the case of sales to Selected Dealers, at the Offering Price less such concessions as you may from time to time determine.

Any Retail Sales of the Stock made for our account shall be as nearly as practicable in the ratio that our underwriting obligations bear to the underwriting obligations of all the Underwriters, except that if our proportion of the shares of the Stock sold in Retail Sales, when added to the shares of the Stock theretofore sold by you for our account (in sales to Selected Dealers or otherwise) plus the shares of the Stock theretofore sold by us for our own account and the shares of the Stock then retained for direct sale by us, would exceed the number of shares of the Stock which we shall then be obligated to purchase or shall then have purchased, you may, in your discretion, allocate all or any part of such excess shares to the other Underwriters in computing the proportion of Retail Sales made for the accounts of the several Underwriters. Any Stock reserved for sale to selected Dealers for our account need not be in the ratio that our underwriting obligations bear to the underwriting obligations of all the Underwriters, but sales of the Stock to Selected Dealers shall be as nearly as practicable in the ratio that Stock reserved for our account for offering to Selected Dealers bears to the aggregate of all the Stock of all the Underwriters so reserved.

You agree to notify us promptly as to the number of shares, if any, of the Stock which we may retain for direct sale. Prior to the termination of this Agreement, you may reserve for offering and sale as hereinabove provided any of the Stock remaining unsold theretofore retained by us and we may, with your consent, retain any of the Stock remaining unsold theretofore reserved by you. Upon the termination of this Agreement you shall, or prior thereto at your discretion you may, deliver to us any of the Stock purchased by us and then reserved for sale in Retail Sales or to Selected Dealers but not so sold, except that if the aggregate of all reserved but unsold and undelivered Stock is less than the number of shares which constitutes the Option Stock, you are authorized to sell such Stock for the accounts of the several Underwriters at such price or prices as you may determine.

We authorize you to determine the form and manner of any communications or agreements with Selected Dealers. In the event that there shall be any such agreements with Selected Dealers, you are authorized to act as manager thereunder and we agree in such event, to be governed by the terms and conditions of such agreements. The form of Selected Dealer Agreement attached hereto as Exhibit B is satisfactory to us. In the event there shall not be any agreements with Selected Dealers, we agree to be governed by the terms and conditions of Exhibit B.

Underwriters and Selected Dealers may reallow a concession, initially not in excess of the amount per share set forth in the Prospectus, to other dealers, who are (a) members of the National Association of Securities Dealers, Inc. ("NASD") and who agree in writing to comply with Section 24 of the Rules of Fair Practice of the NASD or (b) foreign dealers who are not eligible for such membership but who agree to comply with the Interpretation with Respect to Free-Riding and Withholding of the NASD in making sales to purchasers outside the United States and who agree in writing to comply with Sections 8, 24 and 36 of the Rules of Fair Practice of the NASD and with Section 25 of such Rules as that Section applies to non-member brokers or dealers in a foreign country.

After advice from you that the Stock is released for sale to the public, we will offer to the public in conformity with the terms of offering set forth in the Prospectus such of our shares of Stock as you advise us are not reserved. We authorize you after the Stock is released for sale to the public, in your discretion, to change the Offering Price of the Stock and the concessions at any time or from time to time.

3. *Repurchase in the Open Market* . Any shares of the Stock sold by us (otherwise than through you), which, prior to the termination of this Agreement or such earlier date as you may determine, shall be contracted for or purchased in the open market by you on behalf of any Underwriter or Underwriters, shall be repurchased by us on demand at a price equal to the cost of such purchase plus commissions and taxes on redelivery. In lieu of delivery of such shares to us, you may (i) sell such shares in any manner for our account and charge us with the amount of any loss or expense or credit us with the amount of any profit, less any expense, resulting from such sale or (ii) charge our account with an amount not in excess of the concession to Selected Dealers for such shares.

4. *Delivery and Payment for the Stock.* We agree to deliver to you before 10:00 A.M., New York time, on the Closing Date referred to in the Underwriting Agreement, at your office,   Street, New York, New York, or at such other place as you shall designate, a certified or official bank check in New York Clearing House funds payable to the order of Universal Investment Banker, Incorporated for the full purchase price of the Stock which we have agreed to purchase from the Company and the Selling Stockholders. Upon delivery to you for our account of the Stock, you will deliver your checks to the Company and the Selling Stockholders for our account. You are authorized to accept delivery of the Stock from the Company, to give a receipt therefor and to make deliveries thereof, for our account of such shares, if any, as shall be reserved for sale in Retail Sales or to Selected Dealers, as aforesaid. You may in your discretion cause some or all of our reserved Stock to be delivered to you registered in your name or in such other name as you shall designate, but such registration shall be for administrative convenience only and shall not affect our title to such reserved Stock or the severalty of the obligations of the Underwriters to the Company and the Selling Stockholders. If we are a member of Shareholder Trust Company, you may at your discretion deliver our participation through its facilities. You agree to cause to be delivered to us at said office promptly, as aforesaid, any Stock reserved for us which has not been sold for our account or reserved for sale.

Upon receipt by you of payment for the Stock sold by or through you for our account, you will remit to us as promptly as practicable an amount equal to the purchase price paid by us to the Company for such Stock and credit or debit our account on your books with the difference between the selling price, less any concessions as aforesaid, and such purchase price.

As compensation for your services in connection with the purchase of the Stock and the managing of the offering thereof, we agree to pay you, and you may charge our account on your books with, an amount not in excess of $ per share for each share of the Stock which we agree to purchase pursuant to Section 3 of Exhibit A and, if the notice referred to in the first paragraph of Section 3 of Exhibit A shall be given, a like amount for each share of the Option Stock which we shall be obligated to purchase.

5. *Authority to Borrow.* In connection with the transactions contemplated in the Underwriting Agreement or this Agreement, we authorize you, in your discretion, to advance your own funds for our account, charging current interest rates, to arrange loans for our account, and in connection therewith to execute and deliver any notes or other instruments and hold or pledge as security all or any of our Stock or any other securities purchased for our account hereunder. Any lender may rely upon your instructions in all matters relating to any such loan.

Any of our Stock and any other securities purchased for our account hereunder held by you may from time to time be delivered to us for carrying purposes, and if so delivered will be redelivered to you upon demand.

6. *Allocation of Expense and Liability.* We authorize you to charge our account with and we agree to pay (a) any transfer taxes on sales of Stock made by you for our account and (b) our proportionate share (based upon our underwriting obligation) of all expenses incurred by you in connection with the purchase, carrying and distribution of the Stock or other shares of Common Stock and all other expenses arising under the terms of the Underwriting Agreement or this Agreement and in connection with the purchase, carrying, sale and distribution of the Stock. Your determination of such expenses and your allocation thereof shall be final and conclusive. Funds for our account at any time in your hands as our Representative may be held in your general funds without accountability for interest.

As soon as practicable after termination of the provisions referred to in Section 11 of this Agreement, the accounts hereunder shall be settled, but you may reserve from distribution such amount as you deem necessary to cover possible additional expenses. You may at any time make partial distribution of credit balances or call for payment of debit balances. Any of our funds in your hands may be held with your general funds without accountability for interest. Notwithstanding any settlement, we will pay (a) our proportionate share (based upon our underwriting obligation as related to the aggregate underwriting obligations of all nondefaulting Underwriters) of all expenses and liabilities which may be incurred by or for the accounts of the Underwriters, including any liability based on the claim that the Underwriters constitute a partnership, association, unincorporated business or other separate entity, and of any expenses incurred by you or any other Underwriter with your approval in contesting any such claim or liability and (b) any transfer taxes paid after such settlement on account of any sale or transfer for our account. In the event of the default of any Underwriter in carrying out its obligations hereunder, the expenses chargeable to such Underwriter pursuant to this Agreement and not paid by it, as well as any additional losses or expenses arising from such default, may be proportionately charged by you against the other Underwriters not so defaulting, based upon their respective underwriting obligations as related to the aggregate underwriting obligations of all nondefaulting Underwriters, without, however, relieving such defaulting Underwriter from its liability therefor.

We and you will each indemnify and hold harmless each Underwriter and each person, if any, who controls any Underwriter within the meaning of Section 15 of the Securities Act of 1933, as amended ("1933 Act"), to the extent and upon the terms upon which each Underwriter agrees to indemnify the Company and certain other persons in the Underwriter Agreement.

In the event that at any time any claim or claims shall be asserted against you, as Representative of the Underwriters or otherwise, or against any other Underwriter (in which case such Underwriter will promptly give you notice) involving the Underwriters generally, relating to any Preliminary Prospectus, the Prospectus, the Registration Statement, the public offering of the Stock, or any transaction contemplated by this Agreement, we authorize you to make such investigation, to retain such counsel and to take such other action as you shall deem necessary or desirable under the circumstances, including settlement of any such claim or claims. We agree to pay to you, on request, our proportionate share (based upon our underwriting obligation) of all expenses incurred by you (including, but not limited to, the disbursements and fees of counsel retained by you) in investigating and defending against such claim or claims. Each Underwriter (including you) agrees to pay its proportionate share (based upon its underwriting obligation) of the aggregate liability incurred by all Underwriters in respect of such claim or claims (after deducting from the amount of such liability the amount of any contribution or indemnification obtained pursuant to the Underwriting Agreement or otherwise from persons other than Underwriters), whether such liability shall be the result of a judgment against any Underwriter or Underwriters or as a result of any such settlement. In the event that one or more Underwriters default in the payment of any amount required to be paid by this paragraph, each nondefaulting Underwriter agrees to pay, on request, its proportionate share (based upon its underwriting obligation and without regard to the underwriting obligations of such defaulting Underwriter or Underwriters) of such amount. Each person, if any, who controls an Underwriter within the meaning of Section 15 of the 1933 Act shall have the same rights under this paragraph as such Underwriter.

In case any Stock reserved for sale in Retail Sales or to Selected Dealers shall not be purchased and paid for in due course as contemplated hereby, we agree (i) to accept delivery when tendered by you of any Stock so reserved for our account and not so purchased and paid for and (ii) in case we shall have received payment from you in respect of any such Stock, to reimburse you on demand for the full amount which you shall have paid us in respect of such Stock.

7. *Trading and Stabilization.* We authorize you, in your discretion, (i) until termination of this Agreement, to make purchases and sales of the Common Stock, in the open market or otherwise, on a when issued basis or otherwise, for long or short account, and on such terms and at such prices, all as you in your discretion may deem desirable, (ii) in arranging for sales of the Stock to Selected Dealers, to over-allot and (iii) either before or after the termination of this Agreement, to cover any short position incurred pursuant to this Section 7; subject, however, to the applicable rules and regulations of the Commission under the Securities Exchange Act of 1934, as amended ("1934 Act"). It is understood that such purchases and sales and over-allotments shall be made for our account as nearly as practicable in proportion to our underwriting commitment; provided that our net position in the case of short account, computed on the assumption that all the Option Stock is acquired from such purchases and sales and over-allotments shall not at any time exceed, either for long or short account under the foregoing provisions of this Section, 10% of the number of shares of the Underwritten Stock, which we agree to purchase from the Company pursuant to Section 3 of the Underwriting Agreement. Notwithstanding the foregoing limitation, we agree to assume our proportionate share (based upon our underwriting obligation) of the liability of any Underwriter in default with respect to its obligations under this Section 7; provided that such assumption shall not relieve such defaulting Underwriter from its obligations hereunder. We agree, either before or after the termination of this Agreement, to pay you as our Representative, on demand, the cost of any such shares of Common Stock so purchased for our account and to deliver to you as our Representative, on demand, any shares of Common Stock sold or over-allotted for our account pursuant to the authority conferred by this Section 7.

On demand, we will take up and pay for at cost any Stock so purchased and deliver any of said Stock so sold or over-allotted for our account, and if any other Underwriter shall fail to comply with such a demand, we will assume our proportionate share of such obligations, based upon our underwriting obligation as related to the aggregate underwriting obligations of all nondefaulting Underwriters, without, however, relieving such defaulting Underwriter from its liability therefor. The existence of this provision is no assurance that the price of the Stock will be stabilized or that stabilizing, if commenced, may not be discontinued at any time. If you engage in any stabilizing transactions as Representative of the Underwriters, you shall notify us of the fact and shall, as such Representative, make the requisite reports of such transactions as required by Rule 17a-2 of the Commission under the 1934 Act. We authorize you on our behalf to file any reports required to be filed with the Commission in connection with any transactions made by you for our account pursuant to this Section, and we agree to furnish you with any information needed for such reports. We understand that, in the event that you effect stabilization pursuant to this Section, you will notify us promptly of the date and time when the first stabilizing purchase is effected and the date and time when stabilizing is terminated. If stabilizing is effected we will provide you, for filing with the Commission, a signed original copy of a "not as manager" report on Form X-17a-1 not later than five business days following the day on which stabilizing is terminated. We authorize you to submit our name to the Commission if we fail timely to submit such reports to you. Each Underwriter represents that in connection with the offering of the Stock it has complied, and agrees that it will comply, with the provisions of Rule 10b-6 under the 1934 Act, as interpreted by the Commission with regard to trading in the Common Stock, any security of the same class and series as the Common Stock and any right to purchase the Common Stock or any such security.

We agree to advise you from time to time, upon request, prior to the termination of this Agreement, of the amount of the Stock purchased by us under the Underwriting Agreement not reserved and remaining unsold at the time of such request and, if in your opinion of any such Stock shall be needed to make deliveries of the Stock sold or over-allotted for the account of one or more of the several Underwriters, we will forthwith upon your request grant to you, for the account or accounts of such Underwriter or Underwriters, the right, exercisable promptly after receipt of notice from us that such right has been granted, to purchase, at such price as you shall determine, but not less than the net price to Selected Dealers nor more than the Offering Price, such number of shares of the Stock owned by us as shall have been specified in your request.

8. *Open Market Transactions.* We agree that, except with your consent and except as herein provided, we will not, prior to the termination of this Agreement, directly or indirectly, bid for, purchase for any account in which we have a beneficial interest or attempt to induce any person to purchase or sell, in the open market or otherwise, either before or after issuance of the Stock and either for long or short account, any Common Stock or any right to purchase Common Stock. Nothing contained in this Section 8 shall prohibit us from acting as broker or agent in the execution of unsolicited orders of customers for the purchase or sale of any securities of the Company.

9. *Reports and Blue Sky Matters.* Prior to the public offering by the Underwriters, you will inform us as to the jurisdictions under the respective securities or blue sky laws of which it is believed that the Stock has been qualified or is exempt for sale, but you do not assume any responsibility or obligation as to the accuracy of such information or as to the right of any Underwriter or dealer to sell the Stock in any jurisdiction. In addition to the reports described in Section 7 hereof, we authorize you to file with the Commission and any other governmental agency any reports required in connection with any transaction effected by you for our account pursuant to this Agreement, and we will furnish any information needed for such reports.

10. *Effect of Cancellation or Termination of Underwriting Agreement.*

If the Underwriting Agreement shall be cancelled or terminated in accordance with the terms thereof, our obligations hereunder shall nevertheless continue with respect to payment by us of our proportionate share of all expenses and liabilities.

11. *Termination of Agreement.* Unless earlier terminated by you, this Agreement shall terminate 30 full business days after the date hereof, but may be extended by you for an additional period or periods not exceeding 30 full business days in the aggregate. No such termination shall affect our obligations under Sections 3, 4, 6 and 10 hereof.

12. *General Position of the Representative.* In taking action under this Agreement, you shall act only as agent of the several Underwriters. Your authority as Representative of the several Underwriters shall include the taking of such action as you may deem advisable in respect of all matters pertaining to any and all offers and sales of the Stock, including the right to make any modifications which you consider necessary or desirable in the arrangements with Selected Dealers or others. You shall not be under any liability for or in respect of the value of the Stock, the validity or the form thereof or the Registration Statement, any preliminary prospectus, the Prospectus, the Underwriting Agreement or other instrument executed by the Company or by others, the delivery of the Stock, the performance by the Company or by others of any agreement on its or their part, or the exercise or failure to exercise the option granted pursuant to Section 3 of the Underwriting Agreement, you shall not, as such Representative or otherwise, be liable under any of the provisions hereof or for any matters connected herewith, except for want of good faith, and except for any liability arising under the third and fourth paragraphs of Section 6 hereof or the 1933 Act; and any obligation that you have expressly assumed as such Representative herein shall not be implied by this Agreement. In representing the Underwriters hereunder, you shall act as the Representative of each of them respectively. Nothing herein shall constitute the several Underwriters a partnership, association, unincorporated business or other separate entity, and the rights and liabilities of the Underwriters are several and not joint. Except as otherwise provided in Section 7 hereof and Section 3 of the Underwriting Agreement, nothing herein contained shall render any Underwriter liable for the commitments of any other Underwriter. If for Federal income tax purposes the Underwriters should be deemed to constitute a partnership, then each Underwriter elects to be excluded from the application of Subchapter K, Chapter 1, Subtitle A, of the Internal Revenue Code of 1954, as amended. Each Underwriter authorizes you, in your discretion, on behalf of such Underwriter, to execute such evidence of such election as may be required by the Internal Revenue Code.

If we fail (whether or not such failure shall constitute a default hereunder) to deliver to you, or you fail to receive, our check for the Stock which we have agreed to purchase, at the time and in the manner provided in Section 4 hereof, you, in your individual capacity and not as Representative of the Underwriters, are authorized (but shall not be obligated) to make payment to the Company for such Stock for our account, but any such payment by you shall not relieve us of any of our obligations under the Underwriting Agreement or under this Agreement, and we agree to repay to you on demand the amount so advanced for our account.

13. *Acknowledgment of Registration Statement.* We hereby confirm that we have examined the Registration Statement (including all amendments thereto) relating to the Stock as heretofore filed with the Commission, that we are familiar with the final form of the Prospectus proposed to be filed, that we are willing to accept the responsibilities of an Underwriter thereunder, and that we are willing to proceed as therein contemplated. We further confirm that the statements made under the heading "Underwriting" in such proposed final form of the Prospectus, insofar as they relate to us, are correct, and we authorize you so to represent and warrant to the Company on our behalf. We understand that the aforementioned documents are subject to further change and that we will be supplied with copies of any amendment or amendments to the Registration Statement and of any amended or supplemented Prospectus promptly, if and when received by you, but the making of such changes, amendments or supplements shall not release us or affect our obligations hereunder or under the Underwriting Agreement.

14. *Reimbursement of the Representative.* We understand that you will receive from the Company $ as a non-accountable reimbursement of your expenses (in addition to the expenses referred to in Section 6 hereof), in connection with the transactions contemplated by the Underwriting Agreement, which amount you will retain.

15. *Contribution.* We will pay, upon your request, as contribution, our proportionate share (based upon our underwriting obligation as related to the aggregate underwriting obligation of all Underwriters) of any losses, claims, damages or liabilities, joint or several, paid or incurred by any Underwriter to any person other than an Underwriter (including amounts paid by any Underwriter as contributor pursuant to the Underwriting Agreement or otherwise), arising out of or based upon an untrue statement or alleged untrue statement of a material fact contained in the Registration Statement, the Prospectus, any amendment or supplement thereto or any related preliminary prospectus or any other selling or advertising material approved by you for use by the Underwriters in connection with the sale of the Stock, or the omission or alleged omission to state therein a material fact required to be stated therein or necessary to make the statements therein not misleading; and will pay such proportionate share of any legal or other expenses reasonably incurred by you or with your consent in connection with investigating or defending against any such loss, claim, damage or liability, or any action in respect thereof. In determining the amount of our obligation under this paragraph, appropriate adjustment may be made by you to reflect any amounts received by any one or more Underwriters in respect of such claim from the Company pursuant to the Underwriting Agreement or otherwise. There shall be credited against any

amount paid or payable by us pursuant to this Section any loss, damage, liability or expense which is incurred by us as a result of any such claim asserted against us, and if such loss, claim, damage, liability or expense is incurred by us subsequent to any payment by us pursuant to this Section, appropriate provision shall be made to effect such credit, by refund or otherwise. If any such claim is asserted, you may take such action in connection therewith as you deem necessary or desirable, including retention of counsel for the Underwriters, and in your discretion separate counsel for any particular Underwriter or group of Underwriters, and the fees and disbursements of any counsel so retained by you, including fees and disbursements for a successful defense, shall be included in the amount payable pursuant to this Section. You may, in your discretion, consent to being named as the representative of a defendant class of Underwriters. Any Underwriter may elect to retain at its own expense its own counsel. You may settle or consent to the settlement of any such claim on advice of counsel retained by you. Whenever you receive notice of the assertion of any claim to which the provisions of this Section would be applicable, you will give prompt notice thereof to each Underwriter. Whenever we receive notice of the assertion of any such claim, we will give prompt notice thereof to you. You will also furnish each Underwriter with periodic reports, at such times as you deem appropriate, as to the status of any such claim and the action taken by you in connection therewith. If any other Underwriter defaults in its obligation to make any payments under this Section, we shall be obligated to pay our proportionate share of all defaulted payments, based upon our underwriting obligation as related to the aggregate underwriting obligations of all nondefaulting Underwriters. Nothing herein shall relieve a defaulting Underwriter from liability for its default. In determining amounts payable pursuant to this Section, any loss, claim, damage, liability or expense paid or incurred, and any amount received, by any person controlling any Underwriter within the meaning of Section 15 of the 1933 Act which has been paid or incurred or received by reason of such control relationship shall be deemed to have been paid or incurred or received by such Underwriter. No person guilty of fraudulent misrepresentation (within the meaning of Section 11(f) of the 1933 Act) shall be entitled to contribution from any person who was not guilty of such fraudulent misrepresentation.

16. *NASD Matters.* We understand that on behalf of the several Underwriters you will file with the NASD such documents and information, if any, which are available or have been furnished to you for filing pursuant to the applicable rules, statements and interpretations of the NASD. You represent that you are members in good standing of the NASD and we (a) represent that we are a member in good standing of the NASD or (b) represent that we are a foreign dealer not eligible for such membership and agree (i) that, in making sales of Stock outside the United States, we will comply with the requirements of the NASD's Interpretation with Respect to Free-Riding and Withholding and (ii) that we will not offer or sell any

Stock in the United States except through you. In connection with our sales of Stock, we agree to comply with Section 24 of the Rules of Fair Practice of the NASD or, if we are a foreign dealer and not a member of the NASD, we agree to comply as though we were a member, with Sections 8, 24 and 36 of such Rules and with Section 25 of such Rules as that Section applies to a non-member broker or dealer in a foreign country.

17. *Financial Responsibility Requirements.* We represent and warrant that our commitment to purchase the Stock we are obligated to purchase hereunder and under the Underwriting Agreement will not result in a violation by us of the financial responsibility requirements of Rule 15c-1 under the 1934 Act.

18. *Miscellaneous.* Any notice hereunder from you to us or from us to you shall be deemed to have been duly given if sent by mail or by telegram to us at our address as set forth in Schedule I to the Underwriting Agreement or to you at the address first above written.

19. *Applicable Law.* This Agreement shall be governed by, and be construed in accordance with, the laws of

This instrument may be signed by the Underwriters in various counterparts which together shall constitute one and the same agreement among all the Underwriters and shall become effective at such time as all the Underwriters shall have signed such counterparts and you shall have confirmed all such counterparts.

By. . . . .

Attorney-in-fact for the Several Underwriters

Confirmed as of the date first above written.

Universal Investment Bankers, Incorporated, As Representative

By. . . . .

Authorized Signature

EXHIBIT A
TO
APPENDIX I

1,000,000 Shares*
YOUNGCORP
Common Stock

—————————— , 19—

Universal Investment Banker, Incorporated,
  As Representative of the Several Underwriters

  New York, New York

Gentlemen:

Youngcorp, a Delaware corporation (the "Company") and the stockholders of the Company listed in Schedule II hereto (the "Selling Stockholders") each address you as the representative (the "Representative") of each of the persons listed in Schedule I hereto (the "Underwriters," which term shall also include any underwriter purchasing Stock, hereinafter defined, pursuant to Section 3 hereof). The Company and the Selling Stockholders confirm their agreements with the several Underwriters as follows:

1. *Description of Securities.* The Company proposes to issue and sell to the several Underwriters 850,000 shares of its authorized but unissued common stock and the Selling Stockholders propose to sell to the several Underwriters 150,000 shares of the Company's outstanding Common Stock (the Company's issued and unissued common stock being herein called the "Common Stock," and said 1,000,000 shares of Common Stock, proposed to be sold by the Company and the Selling Stockholders being herein called the "Underwritten Stock"). The respective amount of Underwritten Stock to be sold by the Selling Stockholders is set forth opposite their names in

—————————————————

* Plus an option to purchase from the Company up to 100,000 additional shares to cover over-allotments, if any.

218

Schedule II hereto. The Common Stock is more fully described in the Registration Statement and the Prospectus hereinafter mentioned. The Company proposes to grant to the Underwriters of the Underwritten Stock an option to purchase up to 100,000 additional shares of Common Stock (the "Option Stock"). The Underwritten Stock and the Option Stock are collectively referred to herein as the "Stock."

2. *Representations and Warranties of the Company and the Selling Stockholders.* Each of the Company and the Selling Stockholders represents and warrants to, and agrees with, each Underwriter that:

(a) A Registration statement on Form S-1 (File No.   ) with respect to the Stock, including a preliminary form of prospectus, has been prepared by the Company in conformity with the requirements of the Securities Act of 1933, as amended (the "1933 Act"), and the rules and regulations of the Securities and Exchange Commission (the "Commission") thereunder and has been filed with the Commission; one or more amendments to such registration statement have been so prepared and have been, or will be, so filed, including an amendment containing a final form of prospectus. Copies of such registration statement and amendments, each related preliminary prospectus (the "Preliminary Prospectus") and the final form of prospectus have been delivered to you. Such registration statement (including all documents, exhibits and financial statements included therein) as amended at the time it becomes effective is herein referred to as the "Registration Statement." In the event of any amendment to the Registration Statement after the effective date and prior to the Closing Date, hereinafter defined, the term Registration Statement shall also mean such Registration Statement (from and after the effectiveness of such amendment) as so amended. The term "Prospectus" as used herein shall mean the prospectus relating to the Stock as included in such Registration Statement at the time it becomes effective (unless the form of prospectus first filed pursuant to Rule 424(b) under the 1933 Act shall differ therefrom, in which event it shall mean such form of prospectus as so filed). Reference herein to any Preliminary Prospectus or to any Prospectus or to any amendment or supplement to the Prospectus includes all documents and information incorporated by reference therein.

(b) No order preventing or suspending the use of any Preliminary Prospectus has been issued by the Commission and each Preliminary Prospectus, at the time of filing thereof, did not contain an untrue statement of a material fact or omit to state a material fact required to be stated therein or necessary to make the statements therein, in the light of the circumstances under which they were made, not misleading; except that the foregoing shall not apply to statements in or omission from any Preliminary Prospectus in reliance upon, and in conformity with, written information furnished to the Company by you, or by any Underwriter through you, specifically for the use in the preparation thereof.

(c) When the Registration Statement becomes effective, upon the filing of any supplement to the Prospectus and at the Closing Date (hereinafter defined), (i) the Registration Statement and Prospectus will conform in all material respects to the requirements of the 1933 Act and the rules and regulations of the Commission thereunder and (ii) no such document will contain an untrue statement of a material fact or omit to state a material fact required to be stated therein or necessary to make the statements therein, in the light of the circumstances under which they were made, not misleading; except that the foregoing shall not apply to statements in or omissions from any such document in reliance upon, and in conformity with, written information furnished to the Company by you, or by any Underwriter through you, specifically for use in the preparation thereof.

(d) The consolidated financial statements of the Company and its subsidiaries set forth in the Registration Statement and the Prospectus present fairly the position of the Company and such subsidiaries as at the dates indicated and the results of their operations and the changes in their financial position for each of the years and for the periods therein specified in conformity with generally accepted accounting principles consistently applied throughout the periods involved. As used herein, "subsidiary" means any corporation or other entity of which the Company owns or holds with power to vote, at any applicable time, directly or indirectly, outstanding securities or other interests which entitle it to elect or otherwise designate more than 50% of the members of the board of directors of such corporation or entity or persons having powers similar to those of directors in respect of such corporation or entity.

(e) Each of the Company and its subsidiaries has been duly incorporated and is an existing corporation in good standing under the laws of its jurisdiction of incorporation, has full power and authority (corporate and other) and franchises to conduct its business and to own or lease its properties as described in the Registration Statement and the Prospectus and is duly qualified, licensed and registered to do business and is in good standing in each jurisdiction in which it owns or leases real property or in which the conduct of its business requires such qualification, licensing or registration, except where the failure to be so qualified, licensed or registered, considering all such cases in the aggregate, does not involve a material risk to the business, properties, financial condition or results of operations of the Company and its subsidiaries taken as a whole; and all of the outstanding shares of capital stock of each subsidiary have been duly authorized and validly issued, are fully paid and non-assessable and, except as otherwise stated in the Registration Statement, are owned beneficially and of record by the Company subject to no security interest, mortgage, pledge, lien, equity, other encumbrance or adverse claim.

(f) The outstanding shares of Common Stock of the Company and the Stock have been duly authorized and are, or when issued as contemplated hereby will be, validly issued, fully paid and non-assessable and conform, or when so issued will conform, to the description thereof in the Registration Statement and no pre-emptive rights of stockholders exist with respect to the Stock or the issue and sale thereof. Except as disclosed in the Registration Statement, the Company has not granted any options, warrants or other rights to purchase shares of its Common Stock, and has not granted to any person any right to require or participate in the registration of Common Stock of the Company under the 1933 Act ("Registration Right"). No person holds any Registration Right with respect to the registration to be effected by the Registration Statement, which right has not been effectively waived by the holder hereof as of the date hereof. No further approval or authority of the stockholders or the Board of Directors of the Company will be required for issuance and sale of the shares of the Stock to be sold by the Company as contemplated hereby.

(g) Except as contemplated in the Prospectus, subsequent to the respective dates as of which information is given in the Registration Statement and the Prospectus, (1) neither the Company nor any subsidiaries have incurred any liabilities or obligations, direct or contingent, or entered into any transactions, not in the ordinary course of business, that are material to the Company and such subsidiaries, taken as a whole; (2) there has not been any material change, on a consolidated basis, in the capital stock, short-term debt (other than in the ordinary course of business) or long-term debt of the Company and its subsidiaries, or any material adverse change, or any development involving a prospective material adverse change, in the condition (financial or other), business, prospects, net worth or results of operations of the Company and subsidiaries taken as a whole; (3) no loss or damage which is material to the Company's business or assets (whether or not insured) to the property of the Company or any subsidiary has been sustained; and (4) no material legal or governmental proceeding, domestic or foreign, adversely affecting the Company or any subsidiary or the transactions contemplated by this Agreement has been or will have been instituted or, to the best knowledge of the Company, threatened.

(h) Except as set forth in the Prospectus, there is not pending or, to the best knowledge of the Company, threatened, any action, suit or proceeding to which the Company or any subsidiary is a party, before or by any court or governmental agency or body, which might result in any material adverse change in the condition (financial or other), business, prospects, net worth or results of operations of the Company and subsidiaries taken as a whole, or might materially and adversely affect the properties or assets thereof.

(i) There is no contract or document of the Company or any of its subsidiaries that is required to be filed as an exhibit to the Registration Statement by the 1933 Act or by the rules and regulations of the Commission thereunder that has not been so filed.

(j) The execution, delivery and performance of this Agreement and the consummation of the transactions herein contemplated will not result in a breach or violation of any of the terms and provisions of, or constitute a default under, any statute, any agreement or instrument to which the Company or any of its subsidiaries is a party or by which any of them are bound or to which any of the property of the Company or its subsidiaries is subject, the charter or by-laws of the Company or any subsidiary, or any order, rule or regulation of any court or governmental agency or body having jurisdiction over the Company or any such subsidiary or any of their properties; the Company has (other than with respect to the qualification of the Stock for offer and sale under the applicable securities or blue sky laws) obtained every consent, approval, authorization or order of, and has made every filing with, any court or governmental agency or body which is required for the consummation of the transactions contemplated by this Agreement in connection with the issuance or sale of the Stock by the Company; and the Company has full power and authority to authorize, issue and sell the Stock as contemplated by this Agreement.

(k) The Company and each subsidiary has good and marketable title, except as otherwise indicated in the Registration Statement and Prospectus, to all of its assets and properties described therein as being owned by it, free and clear of all liens, encumbrances and defects except such encumbrances and defects as do not, in the aggregate, materially affect or interfere with the use made and proposed to be made by the Company or any subsidiary, described in the Registration Statement and Prospectus, of such property; and neither the Company nor any subsidiary has any material leased properties except as disclosed in the Registration Statement and Prospectus.

(l) Neither the Company nor any Selling Stockholder knows of any outstanding claims for services in the nature of a finder's fee, brokerage fee or otherwise with respect to the offering of Stock contemplated hereby for which either the Company or any Selling Stockholder may be responsible other than as disclosed in the Registration Statement and Prospectus.

(m) The Company and its subsidiaries have filed all federal, state, local and foreign income tax returns relating to any material liability which are required to be filed and have paid all taxes indicated by said returns to be due and all assessments received by them or any of them to the extent that such taxes have become due.

(n) The Stock to be sold hereunder by each Selling Stockholder has been validly authorized and issued and is fully paid and nonassessable.

(o) Each Selling Stockholder has, and at the Closing Date (as such date is hereinafter defined) will have, good and valid title to the Stock to be sold by such Selling Stockholder, free of any liens, encumbrances, equities, pledges and claims, and full right, power and authority to effect the sale and delivery of such Stock; and upon the delivery of and payment for such Stock pursuant to this Agreement, good and valid title thereto, free of any liens, encumbrances, equities, pledges and claims, will be transferred to the several Underwriters.

(p) Each Selling Stockholder has duly executed and delivered, in the forms heretofore furnished to you, a custody agreement, as described in Section 4 hereof (the "Custody Agreement") and a Power of Attorney appointing   or any of them, attorneys-in-fact (the "Attorneys"), with authority to execute and deliver this Agreement and to act thereunder on behalf of such Selling Stockholder; all authorizations and consents necessary for the execution and delivery of this Agreement on behalf of such Selling Stockholder and for the sale and delivery of the Stock to be sold by such Selling Stockholder hereunder have been given; and such Selling Stockholder has full right, power and authority to execute the Power of Attorney and to execute and perform the Custody Agreement and this Agreement.

(q) No Selling Stockholder has taken nor will take, directly or indirectly, any action designed to, or which has constituted, or which might reasonably be expected to cause or result in stabilization or manipulation of the price of the Common Stock of the Company.

(r) No offering, sale or other disposition of any Common Stock of the Company will be made for a period of 90 days after the effective date of the Registration Statement, directly or indirectly, by any Selling Stockholder otherwise than hereunder or with the prior written consent of the Representative.

3. *Purchase of the Stock by the Underwriters.* On the basis of the representations, warranties and agreements herein contained, but subject to the terms and conditions herein set forth, the Company agrees to issue and sell to each Underwriter, and the Selling Stockholders agree, severally and not jointly, to sell to each Underwriter, and each Underwriter agrees, severally and not jointly, to purchase pro-rata from the Company and the Selling Stockholders respectively, the number of shares of the Underwritten Stock which bears the same proportion to the total number of shares of the Underwritten Stock to be issued and sold by the Company or to be sold by the Selling Stockholders, as the case may be, as the number of shares of the Underwritten Stock set forth opposite the name of such Underwriter in Schedule I hereto bears to the total number of shares of the Underwritten Stock, to be purchased by all of the Underwriters under this Agreement, at a purchase price of $ per share. The Company grants an option (the "Option") to the several Underwriters to purchase, severally and not jointly, up to 100,000 shares in the aggregate of Option Stock at the same price per share as the Underwriters shall pay for the Underwritten Stock. Said Option may be exercised only to cover over-allotments in the sale of the Underwritten Stock by the Underwriters. Said Option may be exercised twice in whole or in part at any time (but if exercised more than once, one such exercise notice shall provide that the First Option Closing Date as defined below shall be on the Closing Date, as defined in section 4 hereof) within 30 days after the effective date of the Registration Statement by written or telegraphic notice by the Representative to the Company setting forth the aggregate number of shares of the Option Stock as to which the several Underwriters are exercising the Option and the date (not earlier than the Closing Date) and hour and place at which such certificates are to be delivered (such date and hour therefor being called the "First Option Closing Date" and if there is to be a second delivery of Option Stock, being herein called the "Section Option Closing Date"). The Sec-

ond Option Closing Date, together with the place of delivery of Option Stock there to be made, shall be determined by the Representative, but the Second Option Closing Date shall not be earlier than three or later than eight full business days after delivery to the Company of such written or telegraphic notice. Delivery of certificates for the shares of the Option Stock, and payment therefor, shall be made as provided in this Section 3. The number of shares of the Option Stock to be purchased by each Underwriter on either of the First Option Closing Date or the Second Option Closing Date, as the case may be, shall be the same percentage of the total number of shares of Option Stock to be purchased by the several Underwriters on either of the First Option Closing Date or the Second Option Closing Date, as the case may be, as the percentage of the Underwritten Stock being purchased by such Underwriter, as adjusted by the Representative in such manner as it deems advisable to avoid fractional shares.

If for any reason one or more of the Underwriters shall fail or refuse (otherwise than for a reason sufficient to justify the termination of this Agreement under the provisions of Sections 6 and 9 hereof) to purchase and pay for the number of shares of the Stock agreed to be purchased by such Underwriter, the Company shall immediately give notice thereof to the Representative, and the non-defaulting Underwriters shall have the right within 24 hours after the receipt by the Representative of such notice, to purchase, or procure one or more other Underwriters to purchase, in such proportions as may be agreed upon between the Representative and such purchasing Underwriter or Underwriters and upon the terms herein set forth, the shares of the Stock which such defaulting Underwriter or Underwriters had agreed to purchase. If the non-defaulting Underwriters fail so to make such arrangements with respect to all such shares, the number of shares which each non-defaulting Underwriter is otherwise obligated to purchase under this Agreement shall be automatically increased pro rata to absorb the remaining shares which the defaulting Underwriter or Underwriters had agreed to purchase; provided, however, that the non-defaulting Underwriters shall not be obligated to purchase the shares which the defaulting Underwriter or Underwriters had agreed to purchase if the aggregate number of such shares exceeds 10% of the total number of shares which all Underwriters had agreed to purchase hereunder. If the total number of Shares which the defaulting Underwriter or Underwriters had agreed to purchase shall not be purchased in accordance with the two preceding sentences, the Company shall have the right, within the 24 hours next succeeding the 24-hour period above referred to, to make arrangements with other underwriters or purchasers satisfactory to the Representative for the purchase of such shares on the terms set forth herein. In any such case, either the Representative or the Company shall have the right to postpone the Closing Date determined as provided in Section 4 hereof for not more than seven business days after the date originally fixed as the Closing Date pursuant to said Section 4 in order that any necessary changes in the Registration Statement, the Prospectus or any other documents or arrangements may be made. If neither the non-defaulting Underwriters nor the Company shall make arrangements within the 24-hour periods stated above for the purchase of all the shares which the defaulting Underwriter or Underwriters had agreed to purchase hereunder, this Agreement shall be terminated without further act or deed and without any liability on the part of the Company or the Selling Stockholders, except as provided in Section 5(i) and Section 7, to any non-defaulting Underwriter and without any liability on the part of any non-defaulting Underwriter to the Company or the Selling Stockholders. Nothing in this paragraph, and no action taken hereunder, shall relieve any defaulting Underwriter from liability in respect of any default of such Underwriter under this Agreement.

The obligation of each Underwriter to the Company and the Selling Stockholders shall be to purchase pro rata from the Company and the Selling Stockholders, respectively, that number of shares of the Underwritten Stock which bears the same proportion to the total number of shares of the Underwritten Stock to be sold by the Company and the Selling Stockholders pursuant to this Agreement as the number of shares of the Underwritten Stock set forth opposite the name of such Underwriter in Schedule I hereto bears to the total number of shares of the Underwritten Stock to be purchased by all Underwriters under this Agreement. In making this Agreement, each Underwriter is contracting severally, and not jointly, and except as provided in this Section 3, the agreement of each Underwriter is to purchase only the respective number of shares of Underwritten Stock specified in Schedule I.

The terms of the initial public offering by the Underwriters of the Stock to be purchased by them shall be set forth in the Prospectus. The Underwriters may from time to time change the public offering price and increase or decrease the concessions, discounts and reallowances to dealers as they may determine.

4. *Delivery of and Payment for the Stock.* Certificates in negotiable form for all the shares of Stock to be sold hereunder by the Selling Stockholders have been placed in custody for delivery under this Agreement with   , as custodian (the "Custodian") pursuant to a Custody Agreement executed by each Selling Stockholder. Each of the Selling Stockholders specifically agrees that the Stock represented by the certificates held in custody for the Selling Stockholders under the Custody Agreement is subject to the interests of the Underwriters hereunder, that the arrangements made by the Selling Stockholders hereunder shall not be terminable by any act or deed of the Selling Stockholders (or by any other person, firm or corporation including the Company, the Custodian or the Underwriters) or by operation of law (including the death or incapacity of an individual Selling Stockholder) or by the occurrence of any other event or events. If any such event should occur prior to the delivery to the Underwriters of any of the Stock hereunder, certificates for such Stock shall be deliverable by the Custodian in accordance with the terms and conditions

of this Agreement as if such event had not occurred. The Custodian is authorized to receive and acknowledge receipt of the proceeds of sale of the Stock held by it against delivery of such Stock. Delivery of certificates for the shares of the Stock, and payment therefor, shall be made at the offices of Universal Investment Banker, Incorporated, at 10:00 A.M. New York time, on the fifth full business day after the day on which the Registration Statement shall become effective, or at such time on such other day as shall be agreed upon in writing by the Company and the Representative. The date and hour of such delivery and payment (which may be postponed as provided in Section 3 hereof) are herein called the "Closing Date." Payment for the Stock shall be made by the several Underwriters, or for their respective accounts, by one or more certified or official bank check or checks in New York Clearing House funds, to the Company or the Selling Stockholders, as the case may be, or their respective orders. Such payment shall be made upon delivery of certificates for the Stock to the Representative for the respective accounts of the several Underwriters against receipt therefor signed by the Representative. The certificates for the Stock to be delivered upon break-up of the certificates delivered at the closing shall be registered in such name or names and shall be in such denominations as the Representative, at least three business days before the Closing Date in the case of Underwritten Stock, may request, and will be made available to the Underwriters for inspection, checking and packaging at the offices of Transfer Agent Bank, New York, New York, not less than one full business day prior to the Closing Date.

It is understood that Universal Investment Banker, Incorporated, in its individual capacity and not as the Representative, may (but shall not be obligated to) make payment to the Company and the Selling Stockholders for Stock to be purchased by any Underwriter whose check shall not have been received by the Representative on the Closing Date for the account of such Underwriter. Any such payment by the Representative shall not relieve such Underwriter from any of its obligations hereunder.

5. *Covenants.* The Company and, as provided below, each of the Selling Stockholders covenants and agrees, with each Underwriter that:

(a) The Company will use its best efforts to cause the Registration Statement and any subsequent amendments thereto to become effective as promptly as possible; it will notify you promptly (and confirm such notice in writing) of the time when the Registration Statement or any subsequent amendment to the Registration Statement has become effective or any supplement to the Prospectus has been filed and of any request by the Commission for any amendment or supplement to the Prospectus has been filed and of any request by the Commission for any amendment or supplement to the Registration Statement or Prospectus or for additional information; it will, at the Company's sole expense, prepare and file with the Commission, promptly upon your reasonable request, any amendments or supplements to the Registration Statement or Prospectus that in your opinion may be necessary or advisable in connection with the distribution of the Stock by the Underwriters in order to assure that the Registration Statement or Prospectus does not contain an untrue statement of a material fact or omit to state a material fact required to be stated therein or necessary to make the Statements therein, in the light of the circumstances under which they were made, not misleading; and it will file no amendment or supplement to the Registration Statement or Prospectus to which you shall reasonably object by notice to the Company after having been furnished a copy thereof a reasonable time prior to any such proposed filing.

(b) The Company will advise you, promptly after it shall receive notice or obtain knowledge thereof, of the issuance by the Commission of any stop order suspending the effectiveness of the Registration Statement, or the suspension of the qualification of the Stock for offering or sale in any jurisdiction, or of the initiation or threatening of any proceeding for any such purpose; and it will promptly use its best efforts to prevent the issuance of any stop order or to obtain its earliest possible withdrawal if such stop order should be issued.

(c) A reasonable time prior to the filing thereof with the Commission, the Company will submit to the Representative, for its information, a copy of any post-effective amendment to the Registration Statement, any supplement to the Prospectus or any amended prospectus proposed to be filed and will not file any such amendment, supplement or amended prospectus to which you shall object in writing.

(d) If at any time when a Prospectus relating to the Stock is required to be delivered under the 1933 Act, the Securities Exchange Act of 1934 (the "1934 Act") or the rules and regulations under either, any event relating to or affecting the Company, or of which the Company shall be advised in writing by the Representative, shall occur as a result of which it is necessary, in the opinion of counsel for the Company or of counsel for the Underwriters, to supplement or amend the Prospectus in order to make the Prospectus not misleading in the light of the circumstances existing at the time it is delivered to a purchaser of the Stock, the Company will forthwith prepare and file with the Commission a supplement to the Prospectus or an amended prospectus so that the Prospectus as so supplemented or amended will not contain any untrue statement of a material fact or omit to state any material fact necessary in order to make the statements therein, in the light of the circumstances existing at the time such Prospectus is delivered to such purchaser, not misleading. If after the initial public offering of the Stock by the Underwriters, when a Prospectus relating to the Stock is required to be delivered under the 1933 Act or 1934 Act, the Underwriters shall propose to vary the terms of offering thereof by reason of changes in general market conditions or otherwise, the Representative will advise the Company in writing of the proposed variation, and, if in the opinion of counsel for the Company or of counsel for the Underwriters such proposed variation requires that the Prospectus be supplemented or amended, the Company will forthwith prepare and file with the Commission a supplement to the Prospectus or an amended prospectus setting forth such variation. The Company authorizes the Underwriters and all dealers to whom any of the Stock may be sold by the several Underwriters to use the Prospectus, as from time to time amended or supplemented, in connection with the sale of the Stock in accordance with the applicable provisions of the 1933 Act and applicable rules and regulations thereunder.

(e) The Company and each of the Selling Stockholders will cooperate, when and as requested by the Representative, in the qualification of the Stock for offer and sale under the securities of blue sky laws of such jurisdictions as the Representative may designate and, during the same period after the Registration Statement becomes effective when a Prospectus relating to the Stock is required to be delivered, in keeping such qualifications in good standing under said securities or blue sky laws; provided, however, that the Company shall not be obligated to file any general consent to service of process or to qualify as a foreign corporation in any jurisdiction in which it is not so qualified, except as to matters and transactions relating to the offer and sale of the Stock.

(f) During a period of five years commencing with the date hereof, the Company will furnish to the Representative and to each Underwriter who may so request in writing, copies of all periodic and special reports furnished to stockholders of the Company and of all information, documents and reports filed with the Commission (including the Report on Form SR required by Rule 463 of the Commission under the 1933 Act).

(g) The Company will furnish to the Underwriters copies of the Registration Statement (three of which will be signed and will include all exhibits), each Preliminary Prospectus, the Prospectus and all amendments and supplements to such documents (together with, in each case, all exhibits thereto unless previously furnished to the Representative), in each case as soon as available. The Company will also (i) deliver to the Representative, for distribution to the Underwriters, a sufficient number of additional conformed copies of each of the foregoing (but without exhibits) so that one copy of each may be distributed to each Underwriter; (ii) as promptly as possible and in no event later than 24 hours after the Registration Statement shall become effective, deliver to the Representative and send to the several Underwriters, at such office or offices as the Representative may designate, copies of the Prospectus; and (iii) thereafter from time to time, likewise send to the Representative as many copies of any supplement to the Prospectus and of any amended prospectus, filed by the Company with the Commission, as the Representative may reasonably request for the purposes contemplated by the 1933 Act.

(h) The Company will make generally available to its security holders as soon as practicable, but in any event not later than the fifteenth full calendar month following the effective date of the Registration Statement, and will deliver to the Representative, an earnings statement (which need not be audited) covering a 12-month period beginning after the effective date of the Registration Statement that shall satisfy the provisions of Section 11(a) of the 1933 Act.

(i) Whether or not the transactions contemplated hereunder are consummated or this Agreement is prevented from becoming effective under the provisions of Section 3 hereof or is terminated, the Company and the Selling Stockholders, will pay all expenses incident to the performance of its obligations hereunder (including, without limitation, all expenses necessary to effect the matters described in Section 5(a) and 5(e), including fees and disbursements of Company's counsel, filing and qualification fees and expenses for such matters, expenses of the transfer agent and registrar, if any, and costs of certificates evidencing the Stock), will pay the expenses of printing all documents relating to the offering (including the cost of printing this Underwriting Agreement and other underwriting agreements and related documents), and will reimburse the Underwriters for any expenses (including fees and disbursements of counsel) incurred by them in connection with the matters referred to in Section 5(e) hereof and the preparation of memoranda relating thereto and for any filing fee of the National Association of Securities Dealers, Inc. relating to the Stock. The Company and the Selling Stockholders also agree to reimburse the Representative the sum of $ for non-accountable expenses incurred by the Representative, and not charged in whole or in part to the other Underwriters, in connection with the offering contemplated by this Agreement. If the sale of the Stock provided for herein is not consummated by reason of action by the Company pursuant to Section 9(a) hereof which prevents this Agreement from becoming effective, or by reason of any failure, refusal or inability on the part of the Company or the Selling Stockholders to perform any agreement on their respective parts to be performed, or because any other condition of the Underwriters' obligations hereunder required to be fulfilled by the Company or the Selling Stockholders is not fulfilled, the Company and the Selling Stockholders will reimburse the several Underwriters for all accountable out-of-pocket disbursements (including fees and disbursements of counsel) incurred by the Underwriters in connection with their investigation, preparing to market and marketing the Stock or in contemplation of performing their obligations hereunder, provided that the aggregate amount of such reimbursements shall not exceed $. The Company and the Selling Stockholders shall not in any event be liable to any of the Underwriters for loss of anticipated profits from the transactions covered by this Agreement.

(j) The Company agrees, and will use its best efforts to cause its principal stockholders (meaning those persons or entities having beneficial ownership of 5% or more of the outstanding Common Stock of the Company) to agree, that neither the Company nor any of such principal stockholders will in the public market issue or sell, offer or contract to sell, or grant any option for the purchase of any Common Stock within 90 days after the commencement of the public offering of the stock by the Underwriters without the prior written consent of the Representative of the Underwriters.

(k) The Company will apply the net proceeds from the sale of the Stock to be sold by it hereunder for the purposes set forth in the Prospectus.

6. *Conditions of Underwriters' Obligations.* The obligations of the several Underwriters to purchase and pay for the Stock, as provided herein, shall be subject to the accuracy, as of the date hereof and the Closing Date (as if made on and as of the Closing Date), of the representations and warranties of the Company and Selling Stockholders herein, to the performance by the Company and the Selling Stockholders of their respective obligations hereunder and to the following additional conditions:

(a) The Registration Statement shall have become effective not later than 12:00 A.M., New York time on the day following the date of this Agreement, or such later date as shall be consented to in writing by you; and no stop order or other order suspending the effectiveness of the Registration Statement shall have been issued and no proceeding for that purpose shall have been instituted or, to the knowledge of the Company, any of the Selling Stockholders or any Underwriter, threatened by the Commission, and any request of the Commission for additional information (to be included in the Registration Statement or the Prospectus or otherwise) shall have been complied with to the satisfaction of the Representative.

(b) No Underwriter shall have advised the Company that the Registration Statement or Prospectus, or any amendment or supplement thereto, contains an untrue statement of fact which in the opinion of the Representative is material or omits to state a fact which in the opinion of the Representative is material and is required to be stated therein or is necessary to make the statements therein not misleading.

(c) Subsequent to the respective dates as of which information is given in the Registration Statement and the Prospectus, there shall not have been any change, on a consolidated basis, in the capital stock, short-term debt (other than in the ordinary course of business) or long-term debt of the Company and its subsidiaries, except as contemplated in the Prospectus, or any adverse change, or any event or development involving a potential adverse change, in the condition (financial or other), business, prospects, net worth or results of operations of the Company and its subsidiaries or any change in the rating assigned to any securities of the Company, which, in the judgment of the Representative, would make it impractical or inadvisable to offer or deliver the Stock on the terms and in the manner contemplated in the Prospectus.

(d) The Representative shall have received the opinion of Messrs. , counsel for the Company and the Selling Stockholders, dated the Closing Date, to the effect that as of the Closing Date:

(i) The Company and each of its subsidiaries has been duly incorporated and is an existing corporation in good standing under the laws of its jurisdiction of incorporation, has full power and authority (corporate and other) and franchises to conduct its business and to own or lease its properties as described in the Registration Statement and the Prospectus and, to the best knowledge of such counsel, is duly qualified, licensed and registered to do business in each jurisdiction in which it owns or leases real property or in which the conduct of its business requires such qualification, licensing or registration, except where the failure to be so qualified, licensed and registered, considering all such cases in the aggregate, does not involve a material risk to the business, properties, financial condition or results of operations of the Company and its subsidiaries taken as a whole;

(ii) The authorized, issued and outstanding capital stock of the Company consists, to the best knowledge of such counsel after making due inquiry with respect thereto, of 2,500,000 shares of Common Stock. Upon the issuance of the Underwritten Stock there will be outstanding 3,350,000 shares, plus, upon the issuance thereof, the number of shares of Option Stock, if any, that shall have been exercised to be issued; all necessary corporate proceedings have been taken validly to authorize such authorized capital stock and all of the outstanding shares of Common Stock (including the Underwritten Stock and shares of Option Stock issued, if any) have been duly and validly issued and are fully paid and non-assessable and conform to the description thereof in the Prospectus; the stockholders of the Company have no pre-emptive rights with respect to the Stock; and the forms of certificates used to evidence the Stock are in due and proper form; all of the issued and outstanding shares of capital stock of each subsidiary have been duly authorized and validly issued, are fully paid and non-assessable and, to the best knowledge of such counsel after making due inquiry with respect thereto, are owned by the Company free and clear of all mortgages, pledges, liens, encumbrances, claims and equities whatsoever; to the best knowledge of such counsel after making due inquiry with respect thereto, the shares of Stock being sold by each Selling Stockholder pursuant hereto are held of record by such Selling Stockholder, and no person holds any Registration Right with respect to the registration to be effected by the Registration Statement, which right has not been effectively waived;

(iii) The Registration Statement is in effect under the 1933 Act and, to the best knowledge of such counsel, no stop or other order suspending the effectiveness of the Registration Statement or suspending or preventing the use of the Prospectus has been issued or is in effect, and no proceeding for that purpose has been instituted, or to the best knowledge of such counsel, threatened under the 1933 Act;

(iv) The Registration Statement and the Prospectus, and any amendment or supplement thereto, comply as to form in all material respects with the requirements of the 1933 Act and the rules and regulations of the Commission thereunder; such counsel has no reason to believe that either the Registration Statement or the Prospectus or any amendment or supplement thereto contained or contains as of their respective dates an untrue statement of a material fact or omitted or omits to state a material fact required to be stated therein or necessary to make the statements therein not misleading, it being understood that such counsel will express no opinion as to the financial statements or other financial data included in any of the documents mentioned in this clause (iv);

(v) The descriptions in the Registration Statement and Prospectus of statutes and regulations, and, to the best knowledge of such counsel, legal and governmental proceedings, contracts and other documents are accurate and fairly present the information required to be shown; and to the best of their knowledge and belief there are no statutes, regulations or legal or governmental proceedings required to be described in the Prospectus that are not described as required;

(vi) This Agreement has been duly authorized, executed and delivered by the Company and constitutes the valid and binding agreement of the Company in accordance with its terms, except as to rights of indemnity (and reimbursements as part of such indemnity) which may be limited under federal securities laws; the issuance and sale of the Stock by the Company, the execution, delivery and performance of this Agreement and the consummation of the transaction herein contemplated do not and will not result in a breach or violation of any of the terms and provisions of, or constitute a default under, any statute, any agreement or instrument known to such counsel to which the Company or any subsidiary is a party or by which it is bound or to which any of the property of the Company or any subsidiary is subject, the Company's or any subsidiary's charter or by-laws, or any order, rule or regulation, or injunction or decree known to such counsel of any court or governmental agency or body having jurisdiction over the Company or any subsidiary or any of its or any subsidiary's properties; and no consent, approval, authorization or order of, or filing with, any court or governmental instrumentality is required for the consummation of the transactions contemplated by this Agreement in connection with the issuance or sale of the Stock by the Company, except such as have been obtained or made under the 1933 Act and such as may be required under state securities laws in connection with the purchase and distribution of the Stock by the Underwriters as to which such counsel need express no opinion;

(vii) To the best of their knowledge and information, there are no material contracts, indentures, mortgages, loan agreements, leases or other documents of a character required to be described or referred to in or filed as exhibits to the Registration Statement other than those described or referred to therein or filed as exhibits thereto, and the existing such contracts so described or referred to or those filed are valid in accordance with their terms, and the description thereof or reference thereto is correct and complete, and no default exists in the due performance or observance of any material obligation, agreement, covenant or condition contained in any thereof so described, referred to or filed;

(viii) No approval, consent, order, authorization, designation, declaration or filing by or with any regulatory, administrative or other governmental body is necessary in connection with the execution and delivery of this Agreement or the Custody Agreement by the Selling Stockholders and the consummation by the Selling Stockholders of the transactions herein and therein contemplated (other than as required by state securities or blue sky laws as to which such counsel need express no opinion) except such as have been obtained or made under the 1933 Act, specifying the same;

(ix) To the best knowledge of such counsel after making due inquiry with respect thereto, the execution and delivery of this Agreement and the Custody Agreement and the consummation of the transactions herein and therein contemplated do not and will not conflict with or result in a breach or violation of any of the terms, provisions or conditions of any agreement or instrument to which any Selling Stockholder is a party or by which any Selling Stockholder may be bound;

(x) Each of this Agreement and the Custody Agreement has been duly executed and delivered by the Selling Stockholders and constitutes their respective valid and binding agreements;

(xi) To the best knowledge of such counsel after making due inquiry with respect thereto, good and marketable title to the Stock being sold by the Selling Stockholders, certificates for which have been delivered to the Representative against payment therefor pursuant to this Agreement, has been conveyed to the several Underwriters. Such counsel may assume for this purpose as to any Underwriter that such Underwriter has no knowledge of any adverse claim; and

(xii) Each of the Custody Agreement and the Power of Attorney executed and delivered by each Selling Stockholder is a valid instrument which is legally sufficient for the purposes intended thereby.

In rendering such opinions such counsel may rely as to matters of fact on certificates of officers of the Company and public officials.

(e) You, as Representative, shall have received from Messrs. , counsel for the several Underwriters, such opinions, dated the Closing Date, with respect to the validity of the Stock, the Registration Statement, the Prospectus and other related matters as you reasonably may request, and such counsel shall have received such papers and information, in form and substance satisfactory to them, as they shall have requested to enable them to pass upon such matters.

(f) You shall have received from a letter dated the date the Registration Statement becomes effective and stating:

(i) that they are independent public accountants within the meaning of the 1933 Act and the applicable published rules and regulations thereunder and the response to the Item of the Registration Statement relating to interests of named experts and counsel is correct insofar as it relates to them;

(ii) that, in the opinion of such accountants, the consolidated financial statements and schedules to which their opinions and consents included in the Registration Statement and the Prospectus refer comply as to form in all material respects with the applicable accounting requirements of the 1933 Act and the published rules and regulations thereunder with respect to registration statements on Form S-1;

(iii) that on the basis of a reading of the unaudited consolidated financial information in the financial statements following their opinion in the Prospectus and included under the captions "Selected Consolidated Financial Information" and "Selected Consolidated Financial Data" in the Prospectus and of inquiries of officers of the Company responsible for financial and accounting matters and a reading of the minutes of the Board of Directors of the Company, nothing came to their attention which caused them to believe that (A) such unaudited consolidated financial information does not agree with the Company's unaudited consolidated financial information for the _____ months' period ended _____, and _____; and (B) such unaudited consolidated financial information is not fairly presented in conformity with that of the consolidated financial statements to which their opinions included in the Registration Statement and the Prospectus refer.

(iv) that on the basis of a reading of the latest available unaudited consolidated financial statements of the Company, of inquiries of officers of the Company responsible for financial and accounting matters and a reading of the minutes of the Board of Directors of the Company, nothing came to their attention which caused them to believe that, except for decreases (increases) which the Prospectus discloses have occurred or may occur, (A) at a date not more than five business days prior to the date of such letter, there was any change in the capital stock of the Company or any decrease in stockholders' equity as compared with the amounts shown in the _____, balance sheet included in the Registration Statement or (B) for the period from _____, to such date not more than five business days prior to the date of such letter, there were any decreases (increases) in the total or per share amounts of consolidated net income (loss) as compared to the corresponding amounts thereof for the corresponding period in the preceding year; and

(v) that as a result of carrying out specified procedures, all of which have been agreed to by the Representative, performed for the purpose of comparing additional financial information included in the Registration Statement and Prospectus, other than the audited and unaudited consolidated financial information referred to above (which additional financial information is limited to financial information derived from accounting records which are subject to the Company's system of internal accounting controls) with indicated amounts in the financial statements or accounting records of the Company, and excluding any questions of legal interpretation, nothing came to their attention which caused them to believe that such additional financial information does not substantially conform to such indicated amounts.

(g) You shall have received a letter from _____, dated the

Closing Date, confirming the information set forth in the letter referred to in paragraph (f) and stating that nothing has come to their attention during the period from the date referred to in that letter to a date not more than five days prior to the Closing Date which would require any change in such letter if it were to be dated the Closing Date.

(h) On the Closing Date you shall have received from the Company a certificate, signed by the Chairman of the Board and Chief Executive Officer and by its principal financial or accounting officer, and by the Directors of the Company who are Selling Stockholders as such, dated the Closing Date, stating that the respective signers of said certificate have carefully examined the Registration Statement and the Prospectus and that:

(i) as of the effective date of the Registration Statement, the statements made in the Registration Statement and the Prospectus were true and correct and neither the Registration Statement nor the Prospectus contained any untrue statement of a material fact or omitted to state any material fact required to be stated therein or necessary to make the statements therein not misleading;

(ii) since the effective date of the Registration Statement, no event has occurred which should have been set forth in a supplement or amendment to the Registration Statement or the Prospectus which has not been set forth in such a supplement or amendment;

(iii) since the respective dates of which information is given in the Registration Statement and the Prospectus, there has not been any change in the capital stock or consolidated long-term debt of the Company and its subsidiaries or any material adverse change in the business prospects, properties, management, financial condition or results of operations of the Company and its subsidiaries, whether or not arising from transactions in the ordinary course of business, and, since such dates, except in the ordinary course of business, neither the Company nor any of its subsidiaries has entered into any material transaction not referred to in the Prospectus;

(iv) neither the Company nor any of its subsidiaries has any material contingent obligation which is not disclosed in the Prospectus;

(v) there is not any pending or, to their knowledge, threatened, legal proceedings to which the Company or any of its subsidiaries is a party or of which the property of the Company or any of its subsidiaries is the subject which either is material or which is a governmental action relating to health, safety or environmental matters and which is not disclosed in the Prospectus;

(vi) there are not any franchises, contracts, leases or other documents which are required to be described in the Prospectus or filed as exhibits to the Registration Statement which have not been described and filed as required;

(vii) the representations and warranties of the Company herein are true and correct at and as of, and as though made on, the Closing Date and the Company has complied with all agreements and satisfied all conditions on its part to be performed or satisfied at or prior to the Closing Date; and

(i) On the Closing Date you shall have received from each Selling Stockholder a certificate signed by him representing and warranting that (1) the representations and warranties of such Selling Stockholder herein are true and correct at and as of, and as though made on, the Closing Date, and such Selling Stockholder has complied with all agreements and satisfied all conditions on his part to be performed or satisfied at or prior to the Closing Date and (2) the shares of Stock being sold by him pursuant hereto have been duly authorized and validly issued, are fully paid and non-assessable and are owned by him free and clear of all mortgages, pledges, liens, encumbrances, claims and equities whatsoever.

7. *Indemnification and Contribution.*

(a) The Company and the Selling Stockholders, jointly and severally, will indemnify and hold harmless each Underwriter against and from all losses, costs, claims, damages and liabilities, joint or several, to which such Underwriter may become subject, under the 1933 Act or otherwise insofar as such losses, costs, claims, damages or liabilities (or actions in respect thereof) arise out of or are based upon an untrue statement or alleged untrue statement of a material fact contained in the Registration Statement or Preliminary Prospectus, the Prospectus or any amendment or supplement thereto, or arise out of or are based upon the omission or alleged omission to state in any thereof a material fact required to be stated therein or necessary to make the statement therein not misleading, and will reimburse each Underwriter for all legal and other expenses reasonably incurred by it in connection with investigating or defending against such loss, cost, claim, damage, liability or action; provided, however, that neither the Company nor any of the Selling Stockholders shall be liable in any such case to the extent that any such loss, cost, claim, damage or liability arises out of or is based upon an untrue statement or alleged untrue statement or omission or alleged omission made in or omitted from the Registration Statement, any Preliminary Prospectus, the Prospectus, or any such amendment or supplement, in reliance upon and in conformity with written information furnished to the Company by the Representative, or by any Underwriter through the Representative, specifically for use in the preparation thereof. Notwithstanding the foregoing, the obligations of the Selling Stockholders who are not directors of the Company to indemnify the Underwriters will be limited to the amount of the proceeds which such Selling Stockholders receive on the sale of their Common Stock. In addition, the Company agrees to purchase an insurance policy in favor of the Underwriters, in the face amount of at least $, on behalf of the Company and all of the Selling Stockholders (whether or not directors of the Company). The proceeds of such policy shall be available to reimburse the Underwriters for any expenses or losses to which the Underwriters may become subject under this Section 7.

(b) Each Underwriter will indemnify and hold harmless the Company and each Selling Stockholder against and from all losses, costs, claims, damages and liabilities to which the Company or such Selling Stockholders may become subject, under the 1933 Act or otherwise, insofar as such losses, costs, claims, damages or liabilities (or actions in respect thereof) arise out of or are based upon an untrue statement or alleged untrue statement of a material fact contained in the Registration Statement, any Preliminary Prospectus, the Prospectus or any amendment or supplement thereto, or arise out of or are based upon the omission or alleged omission to state in any thereof a material fact required to be stated therein or necessary to make the statements therein not misleading, in each case to the extent, but only to the extent, that such untrue statement or alleged untrue statement or such omission or alleged omission was made in or omitted from the Registration Statement, any Preliminary Prospectus, the Prospectus, or any such amendment or supplement, in reliance upon and in conformity with written information furnished to the Company and the Selling Stockholders by the Representative, or by such Underwriter through the Representative, specifically for use in the preparation thereof, and will reimburse the Company and such Selling Stockholder for all legal and other expenses reasonably incurred by the Company or such Selling Stockholders in connection with investigating or defending against any such loss, cost, damage, liability or action.

(c) Reasonably promptly after receipt by an indemnified party under subsection (a) or (b) above of notice of the commencement of any action, such indemnified party shall, if a claim in respect thereof is to be made against the indemnifying party under such subsection, notify the indemnifying party in writing of the commencement thereof; but the omission so to notify the indemnifying party shall not relieve such indemnitor from any liability that such indemnitor may have to any indemnified party otherwise than under such subsection. In case any such action shall be brought against any indemnified party, it shall notify the indemnifying party of the commencement thereof, and the indemnifying party shall be entitled to participate in, and, to the extent that it shall wish, jointly with any other indemnifying party, to assume the defense thereof, with counsel satisfactory to such indemnified party (who shall not, except with the consent of the indemnified party, be counsel to the indemnifying party), and after notice from the indemnifying party to such indemnified party of its election so to assume the defense thereof, the indemnifying party shall not be liable to such indemnified party under such subsection for any legal or other expense subsequently incurred by such indemnified party in connection with the defense thereof other than reasonable costs of investigation.

(d) If the indemnification provided for in this Section 7 is unavailable or insufficient to hold harmless an indemnified party under subsection (a) or (b) above, then each indemnifying party shall contribute to the amount paid or payable by such indemnified party as a result of the losses, costs, claims, damages or liabilities referred to in subsection (a) or (b) above, (i) in such proportion as is appropriate to reflect the relative benefits received by the Company and the Selling Stockholders on the one hand and the Underwriters on the other from the offering of the Stock or (ii) if the allocation provided by clause (i) above is not permitted by applicable law, in such proportion as is appropriate to reflect not only the relative benefits referred to in clause (i) above but also the relative fault of the Company, the Selling Stockholders and the Underwriters in connection with the statements or omissions that resulted in such losses, costs, claims, damages or liabilities, as well as any other relevant equitable considerations. The relative benefits received by the Company and the Selling Stockholders on the one hand and the Underwriters on the other shall be deemed to be in the same proportion as the total net proceeds from the offering (before deducting expenses) received by the Company and the Selling Stockholders bear to the total underwriting discounts and commissions received by the Underwriters, in each case as set forth in the table on the cover page of the Prospectus. The relative fault shall be determined by reference to, among other things, whether the untrue or alleged untrue statement of a material fact or the omission or alleged omission to state a material fact relates to information supplied by the Company and the Selling Stockholders or the Underwriters and the parties' relative intent, knowledge, access to information and opportunity to correct or prevent such untrue statement or omission. The Company and the Selling Stockholders and the Underwriters agree that it would not be just and equitable if contributions pursuant to this subsection (d) were to be determined by pro rata allocation (even if the Underwriters were treated as one entity for such purposes) or by any other method of allocation which does not take account of the equitable considerations referred to in the first sentence of this subsection (d). The amount paid by an indemnified party as a result of the losses, costs, claims, damages or liabilities referred to in the first sentence of this subsection (d) shall be deemed to include any legal or other expenses reasonably incurred by such indemnified party in connection with investigating or defending against any action or claim which is the subject of this subsection (d). Notwithstanding the provisions of this subsection (d), no Underwriter shall be required by this subsection (d) to contribute any amount in excess of the amount by which the total price at which the Stock underwritten by it and distributed to the public was offered to the public exceeds the amount of any damages that such Underwriter has otherwise been required to pay by reason of such untrue or alleged untrue statement or omission or alleged omission. No person guilty of fraudulent misrepresentation (within the meaning of Section 11(f) of the 1933 Act) shall be entitled to contribution from any person who was not guilty of such fraudulent misrepresentation. The Underwriters' obligations in this subsection (d) to contribute are several in proportion to their respective underwriting obligations and not joint.

(e) The obligations of the Company and each Selling Stockholder under this Section 7 shall be in addition to any liability which the

Company and each Selling Stockholder may otherwise have and shall extend, upon the same terms and conditions, to each person, if any, who controls any Underwriter within the meaning of the 1933 Act; and the obligations of the Underwriters under this Section 7 shall be in addition to any liability that the respective Underwriters may otherwise have and shall extend, upon the same terms and conditions, to each director of the Company, to each officer of the Company who has signed the Registration Statement and to each person, if any, who controls the Company within the meaning of the 1933 Act.

8. *Representations and Agreements to Survive Delivery.* All representations, warranties and agreements of the Company and the Selling Stockholders herein or in certificates delivered pursuant hereto, and the agreements of the several Underwriters contained in Section 7 hereof, shall remain operative and in full force and effect regardless of any investigation made by or on behalf of any Underwriter or any controlling person, or any Selling Stockholder or the Company or any of its officers, directors or any controlling person, and shall survive delivery of the Stock to the Underwriters hereunder.

9. *Effective Date of this Agreement and Termination.*

(a) This Agreement shall become effective at 10 A.M., New York time, on the first full business day following the effective date of the Registration Statement, or at such earlier time after the effective date of the Registration Statement as the Representative in its discretion shall first release the Stock for sale to the public. For purposes of this Section, the Stock shall be deemed to have been released for sale to the public upon release by the Representative of the publication of a newspaper advertisement relating thereto or of telexes releasing the Stock for sale to the public, whichever shall first occur. By giving notice as hereinafter specified before the time this Agreement becomes effective, the Representative of the several Underwriters, or the Company may prevent this Agreement from becoming effective without liability of any party to any other party, except that the provisions of Section 5(i) and Section 7 hereof shall at all times be effective.

(b) The Representative of the several Underwriters, shall have the right to terminate this Agreement by giving notice as hereinafter specified at any time at or prior to the Closing Date if (i) the Company shall have failed, refused or been unable, at or prior to the Closing Date, to perform any agreement on its part to be performed hereunder, (ii) any other condition of the Underwriters' obligations hereunder is not fulfilled, (iii) trading on the New York Stock Exchange or the American Stock Exchange shall have been wholly suspended, (iv) minimum or maximum prices for trading shall have been fixed, or maximum ranges for prices for securities shall have been required, on the New York Stock Exchange or the American Stock Exchange, by such Exchange or by order of the Commission or any other governmental authority having jurisdiction, (v) a banking moratorium shall have been declared by federal or New York authorities, or (vi) an outbreak of major hostilities in which the United States is involved, a declaration of war by Congress, any other substantial national or international calamity or any other event or occurrence of a similar character shall have happened since the execution of this Agreement that, in the judgment of the Representative, makes it impracticable or inadvisable to proceed with the completion of the sale of and payment for the Stock. Any such determination shall be without liability of any party to any other party except that the provisions of Section 5(i) and Section 7 hereof shall at all times be effective.

(c) If the Representative elects to prevent this Agreement from becoming effective or to terminate this Agreement as provided in this Section, the Company shall be notified promptly by the Representative by telephone or telegram, confirmed by letter. If the Company elects to prevent this Agreement from becoming effective, the Representative shall be notified promptly by the Company by telephone or telegram, confirmed by letter.

10. *Notices.* All notices or communications hereunder, except as herein otherwise specifically provided, shall be in writing and if sent to the Representative shall be mailed, delivered or telegraphed and confirmed to the Representative,   Street, New York, New York, Attention: President, or if sent to the Company or Selling Stockholders, shall be mailed, delivered or telegraphed and confirmed to the Company,   Street,   , Attention: President. Notice to any Underwriter pursuant to Section 7(c) shall be mailed, delivered or telegraphed and confirmed to such Underwriter's address as it appears in such Underwriter's questionnaire or other notice furnished to the Company in writing for the purpose of communications hereunder. Any party to this Agreement may change such address for notices by sending to the parties to this Agreement written notice (in the manner provided herein) of a new address for such purpose.

11. *Parties.* This Agreement shall inure to the benefit of and be binding upon the parties hereto and their respective successors and the controlling persons, officers and directors referred to in Section 7, and no other person will have any right or obligation hereunder.

In all dealings with the Company and the Selling Stockholders under this Agreement, you shall act on behalf of each of the several Underwriters, and any action under this Agreement taken by you will be binding upon all the Underwriters.

12. *Applicable Law.* This Agreement shall be governed by, and construed in accordance with, the laws of

If the foregoing correctly sets forth the understanding between the Company, the Selling Stockholders, and the several Underwriters, please so indicate in the space provided below for that purpose, whereupon this letter shall constitute a binding agreement among the Company, the Selling Stockholders, and the several Underwriters.

Very truly yours,

Youngcorp

By............................

Selling Stockholders Listed on Schedule II hereto

By............................

Attorney-in-fact

Accepted at

    as of the date first above written,

    on behalf of ourselves and as Representative

    of the other Underwriters named in Schedule I hereto.

    Universal Investment Banker, Incorporated

By............................

President

SCHEDULE I

Underwriter	Number of Shares of Common Stock to be Purchased
Universal Investment Banker, Incorporated.........	
Total..	1,000,000

SCHEDULE II

Names of Selling Stockholders	Number of Shares
....	30,000
....	30,000
....	30,000
....	30,000
....	30,000
Total..	150,000

EXHIBIT B
TO
APPENDIX I

1,000,000 Shares*

YOUNGCORP

Common Stock

——————————— , 19 ——

Gentlemen:

1. We and the other Underwriters named in the Prospectus of even date herewith, acting through us as Representative, have severally agreed to purchase, subject to the terms and conditions set forth in the Underwriting Agreement referred to in the Prospectus, an aggregate of 1,000,000 shares of Common Stock of Youngcorp, a Delaware corporation (the "Company"), from the Company and certain Selling Stockholders, plus up to an additional 100,000 shares from the Company to cover over-allotments (such 1,000,000 shares and any such additional 100,000 shares being herein called the "Stock"). The Stock and the terms upon which it is to be offered for sale by the several Underwriters are more particularly described in the Prospectus.

2. The Stock is to be offered to the public by the several Underwriters at a public offering price of $ per share (herein called the "Offering Price") and in accordance with the terms of offering set forth in the Prospectus.

3. Some of or all the several Underwriters are severally offering, subject to the terms and conditions hereof, a portion of the Stock for sale to certain dealers which are members of the National Association of Securities Deal-

---

* Plus an option to purchase from Youngcorp up to 100,000 additional shares to cover over-allotments.

ers, Inc. (the "NASD") and to foreign dealers or institutions not eligible for membership in the NASD which agree not to resell the Stock (i) to purchasers in, or to persons who are nationals of, the United States of America or (ii) when there is a public demand for the Stock, to persons specified as those to whom members of the NASD participating in a distribution may not sell (such dealers and institutions agreeing to purchase the Stock hereunder being hereinafter referred to as "Selected Dealers") at the Offering Price less a selling concession of $ per share, payable as hereinafter provided, out of which concession an amount not exceeding $ per share may be reallowed by Selected Dealers to members of the NASD or to foreign dealers or institutions ineligible for membership therein which agree as aforesaid. Some or all of the Underwriters may be included among the Selected Dealers.

4. On behalf of the Underwriters we shall act as Representative under this Agreement and shall have full authority to take such action as we may deem advisable in respect of all matters pertaining to the public offering of the Stock.

5. If you desire to purchase any of the Stock, your application should reach us promptly by telephone or telegraph at the office of Universal Investment Banker, Incorporated, and we will use our best efforts to fill the same. We reserve the right to reject all subscriptions in whole or in part, to make allotments and to close the subscription books at any time without notice. The number of shares of Stock allotted to you will be confirmed, subject to the terms and conditions of this Agreement.

6. The privilege of purchasing the Stock is extended to you only on behalf of the Underwriters, if any, as may lawfully sell the Stock to dealers in your state.

7. Any of the Stock purchased by you under the terms of this Agreement may be immediately reoffered to the public in accordance with the terms of offering thereof set forth herein and in the Prospectus, subject to the securities or blue sky laws of the various states. Neither you nor any other person is or has been authorized to give any information or to make any representations in connection with the sale of the Stock other than as contained in the Prospectus.

8. This Agreement will terminate when we shall have determined that the public offering of the Stock has been completed and upon telegraphic notice to you of such termination, but if not previously terminated, this Agreement will terminate at the close of business on the   full business day after the date hereof; provided, however, that we shall have the right to extend this Agreement for an additional period or periods not exceeding   full business days in the aggregate upon telegraphic notice to you. Promptly after the termination of this Agreement there shall become payable to you the selling concessions on all shares of Stock which you shall have purchased hereunder and which shall not have been purchased or contracted for including those issued upon transfer by us, in the open market or otherwise (except pursuant to Section 10 hereof),

during the term of this Agreement for the account of one or more of the several Underwriters.

9. For the purpose of stabilizing the market in the Stock, we have been authorized to make purchases and sales thereof, in the open market or otherwise, and, in arranging for sale of the Stock to over-allot.

10. You agree to advise us from time to time upon request, prior to the termination of this Agreement, of the number of shares of Stock purchased by you hereunder and remaining unsold at the time of such request, and, if in our opinion any such Stock shall be needed to make delivery of the Stock sold or over-allotted for the account of one or more of the Underwriters, you will, forthwith upon our request, grant to us for the account or accounts of such Underwriter or Underwriters the right, exercisable promptly after receipt of notice from you that such right has been granted, to purchase, at the Offering Price less the selling concession or such part thereof as we shall determine, such number of shares of Stock owned by you as shall have been specified in our request.

11. On becoming a Selected Dealer, and in offering and selling the Stock, you agree to comply with all applicable requirements of the Securities Act of 1933, as amended (the "1933 Act"), and the Securities Exchange Act of 1934, as amended, and all the rules and regulations under each including, without limitation, the requirements of the 1933 Act Release No. 4968, and to complete distribution of preliminary prospectuses as required therein.

12. Upon application, you will be informed as to the jurisdictions in which we have been advised that the Stock has been qualified for sale under the respective securities or blue sky laws of such jurisdictions, but neither we nor any of the Underwriters assume any obligation or responsibility as to the right of any Selected Dealer to sell the Stock in any jurisdiction or as to any sale therein.

13. Additional copies of the Prospectus will be supplied to you in reasonable quantities upon request.

14. It is expected that public advertisement of the Stock will be made on the first day after the effective date of the Registration Statement. Twenty-four hours after such advertisement shall have appeared but not before, you will be free to advertise at your own expense, over your own name, subject to any restrictions of local laws, but your advertisement must conform in all respects to the requirements of the 1933 Act, and neither we nor the Underwriters shall be under any obligation or liability in respect of your advertisement.

15. No Selected Dealer is authorized to act as our agent or as agent for the Underwriters, or otherwise to act in our behalf or on behalf of the Underwriters, in offering or selling the Stock to the public or otherwise.

16. We and the several Underwriters shall not be under any liability for or in respect of the value, validity or form of the certificates of Stock, or delivery thereof, or the performance by anyone of any agreement on his part, or the qualification of the Stock for sale under the laws of any jurisdic-

tion, or for or in respect of any matter connected with this Agreement, except for lack of good faith and for obligations expressly assumed by us or by the Underwriters in this Agreement. The foregoing provisions shall not be deemed a waiver of any liability imposed under the 1933 Act.

17. Payment for the shares of Stock sold to you hereunder is to be made at the Offering Price, on or about   ,   , or such later date as we may advise, by certified or official bank check payable to the order of Universal Investment Banker, Incorporated in New York Clearing House funds at such place as we shall specify on one day's notice to you against delivery of the Stock.

18. We agree that delivery of any Stock purchased by us may be made through the facilities of Shareholder Trust Company if we are a member thereof, unless we are otherwise notified by you in your discretion. If we are not a member of Shareholder Trust Company, such delivery shall be made through a correspondent who is such a member, if we shall have furnished instructions to you (in connection with the purchase of the Stock) naming such correspondent, unless we are otherwise notified by you in your discretion.

19. Notice to us should be addressed to Universal Investment Banker, Incorporated,   ,   , Attention: Syndicate Department. Notices to you shall be deemed to have been duly given if telegraphed or mailed to you at the address to which this letter is addressed.

20. If you desire to purchase any of the Stock, please confirm your application by signing and returning to us your confirmation on the duplicate copy of this letter enclosed herewith even though you have previously advised us thereof by telephone, teletype or telegraph.

21. This Agreement shall be governed by, and construed in accordance with, the laws of   .

Universal Investment Banker, Incorporated,

   As Representative

By............................

   (Authorized Officer)

Universal Investment Banker, Incorporated

New York, New York

Gentlemen:

   We hereby agree to purchase   shares of the Common Stock of Youngcorp, a Delaware corporation, in accordance with all terms and conditions stated in the foregoing letter. We hereby acknowledge receipt of the Prospectus referred to in the first paragraph thereof relating to such Common Stock. We further state that in purchasing such Common Stock we have relied upon said Prospectus and upon no other statement whatsoever, written or oral. We hereby confirm that (i) we are a member of the National Association of Securities Dealers, Inc. or (ii) we are a foreign dealer or institution ineligible for membership in said Association, and we hereby agree not to resell such Common Stock (x) to purchasers in, or to persons who are nationals of, the United States of America or (y) when there is a public demand for such Common Stock, to persons specified as those to whom members of said Association participating in a distribution may not sell.

....

(Name of corporation or firm)

By............................

(Authorized Representative)

Dated: , 19

APPENDIX II

3,900,000 Shares

The Travelers Corporation

COMMON CAPITAL STOCK

($1.25 par value)

The Common Capital Stock, par value $1.25 per share (the "Common Stock"), of The Travelers Corporation (the "Company") is traded on the New York and Pacific Stock Exchanges under the symbol "TIC" and on The London Stock Exchange. On August 30, 1985, the last reported sale price of the Common Stock on the New York Stock Exchange was $41⅝ per share.

THESE SECURITIES HAVE NOT BEEN APPROVED OR DISAPPROVED BY THE SECURITIES AND EXCHANGE COMMISSION NOR HAS THE COMMISSION PASSED UPON THE ACCURACY OR ADEQUACY OF THIS PROSPECTUS. ANY REPRESENTATION TO THE CONTRARY IS A CRIMINAL OFFENSE.

PRICE $41⅜ A SHARE

	Price to Public	Underwriting Discount and Commission (1)	Proceeds to Company (2)
Per Share	*$41.375*	*$0.82*	*$40.555*
Total	*$161,362,500*	*$3,198,000*	*$158,164,500*

---

(1) The Company has agreed to indemnify Morgan Stanley & Co. Incorporated against certain liabilities, including liabilities under the Securities Act of 1933. See "Underwriting".

(2) Before deducting expenses payable by the Company estimated at $140,000.

The shares of Common Stock are offered, subject to prior sale, when, as and if accepted by Morgan Stanley & Co. Incorporated, and subject to approval of certain legal matters by Davis Polk & Wardwell, counsel for Morgan Stanley & Co. Incorporated. It is expected that delivery of the certificates for the shares will be made on or about September 10, 1985, at the office of Morgan Stanley & Co. Incorporated, 55 Water Street, New York, New York, against payment therefor in New York Clearing House funds.

MORGAN STANLEY & CO.
Incorporated

September 3, 1985

No person is authorized in connection with the offering made hereby to give any information or to make any representation not contained or incorporated by reference in this Prospectus, and any information or representation not contained or incorporated by reference herein must not be relied upon as having been authorized by the Company or Morgan Stanley & Co. Incorporated. This Prospectus is not an offer to sell, or a solicitation of an offer to buy, by any person in any jurisdiction in which it is unlawful for such person to make such an offer or solicitation.

AVAILABLE INFORMATION

The Company is subject to the informational requirements of the Securities Exchange Act of 1934 (the "Exchange Act") and in accordance therewith files reports and other information with the Securities and Exchange Commission (the "Commission"). Reports, proxy statements and other information concerning the Company may be inspected and copied at the public reference facilities maintained by the Commission at 450 Fifth Street, N.W., Washington, D.C. 20549, and at the Commission's Regional Offices at Jacob K. Javits Building, 26 Federal Plaza, New York, New York 10278; Room 1204, Everett McKinley Dirksen Building, 219 South Dearborn Street, Chicago, Illinois 60604; and at Room 500 East, 5757 Wilshire Boulevard, Los Angeles, California 90036. Copies of such material may be obtained by mail from the Public Reference Section of the Commission at 450 Fifth Street, N.W., Washington, D.C. 20549, at prescribed rates. In addition, reports, proxy statements and other information concerning the Company may be inspected at the offices of the New York Stock Exchange, 20 Broad Street, New York, New York 10005 and the Pacific Stock Exchange, 115 Sansom Street, San Francisco, California 94104.

The Company has filed with the Commission a registration statement on Form S-3 (herein, together with all amendments and exhibits thereto, referred to as the "Registration Statement") under the Securities Act of 1933. This Prospectus does not contain all of the information set forth in the Registration Statement, certain parts of which are omitted in accordance with the rules and regulations of the Commission. For further information, reference is hereby made to the Registration Statement.

INCORPORATION OF CERTAIN DOCUMENTS BY REFERENCE

The following Company documents filed with the Commission (File No. 1-5799) are incorporated herein by reference:

1. Annual Report on Form 10-K for the year ended December 31, 1984.

2. Quarterly Reports on Form 10-Q for the quarters ended March 31, 1985 and June 30, 1985.

3. All other documents filed by the Company pursuant to Section 13(a), 13(c), 14 or 15(d) of the Exchange Act subsequent to the date of this Prospectus and prior to the termination of the offering of the Common Stock.

Any statement incorporated by reference herein shall be deemed to be modified or superseded for purposes of this Prospectus to the extent that a statement contained herein or in any other subsequently filed document which also is or is deemed to be incorporated by reference herein modifies or supersedes such statement. Any statement so modified or superseded shall not be deemed, except as so modified or superseded, to constitute a part of this Prospectus.

The Company will provide without charge to each person to whom a copy of this Prospectus is delivered, upon the request of such person, a copy of any or all of the documents which are incorporated by reference herein, other than exhibits to such documents (unless such exhibits are specifically incorporated by reference into such documents). Written or telephone requests should be directed to John R. Kenney, Associate General Counsel and Corporate Secretary, The Travelers Corporation at One Tower Square, Hartford, Connecticut 06183-1050, telephone: (203) 277-3752.

IN CONNECTION WITH THIS OFFERING, MORGAN STANLEY & CO. INCORPORATED MAY OVER-ALLOT OR EFFECT TRANSACTIONS WHICH STABILIZE OR MAINTAIN THE MARKET PRICE OF THE OUTSTANDING COMMON STOCK AT A LEVEL ABOVE THAT WHICH MIGHT OTHERWISE PREVAIL IN THE OPEN MARKET. SUCH TRANSACTIONS MAY BE EFFECTED ON THE NEW YORK STOCK EXCHANGE AND THE PACIFIC STOCK EXCHANGE. SUCH STABILIZING, IF COMMENCED, MAY BE DISCONTINUED AT ANY TIME.

THE COMPANY

The Company and its subsidiaries constitute one of the largest multi-line insurance businesses in the United States. The Travelers Insurance Company and its subsidiaries ("Travelers Insurance") write individual and group life insurance, annuities, accident and health insurance, and workers' compensation insurance. With $143 billion of life insurance in force at December 31, 1984, Travelers Insurance is one of the largest stock life insurance groups in the United States. The Company's casualty and property business is carried on principally by The Travelers Indemnity Company ("Travelers Indemnity") and its subsidiaries. With 1984 revenues of $4.2 billion, Travelers Indemnity and its subsidiaries are one of the largest stock casualty and property insurance groups in the United States. They write most types of casualty and property insurance, including accident and health insurance. The insurance and related investment operations of the Company account for substantially all of its consolidated assets and net income. The principal market is the United States, where over 96% of premiums are written and investment income is earned. The Company's subsidiaries also offer pension and other investment management services.

The Company's principal executive offices are located at One Tower Square, Hartford, Connecticut 06183, telephone: (203) 277-0111.

USE OF PROCEEDS

The Company will add the net proceeds from the sale of the Common Stock to its general funds to be used for general corporate purposes.

DIVIDENDS AND PRICE OF COMMON STOCK

The following table sets forth the high and low sale prices, as reported on the consolidated transaction reporting system of the New York Stock Exchange, and the dividends for the Company's Common Stock for each quarter since January 1, 1983.

	High	Low	Dividends
1983			
First Quarter	$32	$22⅜	$0.45
Second Quarter	34¼	28¾	0.45
Third Quarter	32¾	24¼	0.45
Fourth Quarter	34	30¼	0.45
1984			
First Quarter	$36⅝	$28¼	$0.48
Second Quarter	35¼	27½	0.48
Third Quarter	36	25½	0.48
Fourth Quarter	38¼	32⅜	0.48
1985			
First Quarter	$45⅜	$36⅞	$0.51
Second Quarter	48⅜	40	0.51
Third Quarter (through August 30, 1985)	49¼	41½	*

* The Company has declared a dividend of $0.51 per share payable on September 10, 1985 to holders of Common Stock of record on July 31, 1985. Purchasers of Common Stock offered hereby will not be entitled to payment of this dividend.

See "Description of Common Stock" for information relating to dividend rights and dividend restrictions.

CAPITALIZATION

The capitalization of the Company at June 30, 1985 and as adjusted to reflect the sale by the Company of the shares of Common Stock offered hereby (after giving effect to the underwriting discount and commission and other expenses) is set forth below:

	At June 30, 1985	
	Outstanding	As Adjusted
	(Dollars in millions)	
Short-Term Debt	$ 352.8	$ 352.8
Long-Term Debt	64.0	64.0
Total indebtedness	$ 416.8	$ 416.8
Shareholders' Equity:		
Series A Convertible Exchangeable Preferred Stock	$ 200.0	$ 200.0
Common Stock	114.5	114.5
Additional paid-in capital	53.4	136.0
Unrealized investment gains (losses)	(32.7)	(32.7)
Retained earnings	3,413.1	3,413.1
Treasury stock, at cost	(106.9)	(31.5)
Total shareholders' equity	$3,641.4	$3,799.4
Total capitalization	$4,058.2	$4,216.2

SELECTED FINANCIAL INFORMATION

The amounts in the following table for the years 1980-1984 are derived from the consolidated financial statements included in the Company's 1984 Annual Report to Shareholders, which financial statements are incorporated herein by reference. Such amounts should be evaluated in light of the additional information set forth in those financial statements and notes thereto and in the related management's discussion and analysis, which also are incorporated herein by reference.

Amounts at June 30, 1985 and 1984 and for the six months then ended are derived from the consolidated financial statements included in the Company's Quarterly Report on Form 10-Q filed with the Securities and Exchange Commission for the quarter ended June 30, 1985. Such financial statements, notes thereto, and related management's discussion and analysis are also incorporated herein by reference.

	Six months ended June 30		Year ended December 31				
	1985	1984	1984	1983	1982	1981	1980
	(Dollars in millions except per share amounts)						
Premiums	$ 5,579.1	$ 5,050.2	$ 10,330.7	$ 9,252.4	$ 9,071.8	$ 7,897.1	$ 7,242.3
Investment income	1,743.4	1,530.6	3,146.0	2,749.7	2,308.9	1,903.7	1,547.7
Federal income taxes	14.4	11.1	(91.6)	71.9	20.8	39.5	92.5
Operating income	151.6	145.0	346.1	342.6	309.9	359.4	365.6
Realized investment gains (losses), net of taxes	16.3	26.4	27.0	(30.2)	(14.1)	.7	—
Net income	167.9	171.4	373.1	312.4	295.8	360.1	365.6
Cash provided by operations	1,732.9	1,451.0	3,560.8	3,514.9	3,059.3	1,817.3	1,845.4
Assets	39,049.3	34,090.9	36,434.7	32,875.8	27,988.7	23,982.3	21,637.9
Shareholders' equity	3,641.6	3,137.5	3,293.7	3,058.0	2,970.7	2,812.8	2,635.8
Per share of Common Stock:							
Operating income	$1.74	$1.73	$4.11	$4.08	$3.67	$4.23	$4.32
Net income	1.93	2.04	4.43	3.72	3.51	4.24	4.32
Dividends	1.02	.96	1.92	1.80	1.64	1.44	1.24

BUSINESS

General

The Company's business may be generally categorized as follows: (i) life business, (ii) casualty-property business, and (iii) other business, which is not material in any reported period. The following table shows the contributions to revenues and insurance operating income before Federal income taxes of the life business and casualty-property business during the past five years and the six months ended June 30, 1985 and 1984.

	Revenues*				Insurance operating income before Federal income taxes**			
	Life Business		Casualty-Property Business		Life Business		Casualty-Property Business	
	(Dollars in millions)				(Dollars in millions)			
Six months ended June 30								
1985	$4,899.5	67%	$2,432.9	33%	$211.3	132%	$(50.9)	(32)%
1984	4,445.1	67	2,145.8	33	197.1	128	(43.0)	(28)
Year ended December 31								
1984	9,324.4	69	4,171.0	31	474.2	190	(224.5)	(90)
1983	8,319.0	69	3,701.2	31	323.5	80	80.6	20
1982	7,641.4	67	3,761.3	33	326.8	103	(9.2)	(3)
1981	6,307.2	64	3,514.3	36	305.4	78	83.8	22
1980	5,518.3	63	3,286.8	37	295.9	65	156.4	35

* Revenues consist of written premiums and investment income.

** Excluding investment gains and losses.

The casualty-property business generally has been more volatile than the life business. This volatility has resulted principally from changing market conditions which affect policy pricing and is also influenced by the unpredictable nature of claims arising from catastrophies. In addition, claims under some casualty-property coverages emerge over a long period of time. During this period there may be significant unforeseen developments which can affect claims experience.

Life Business

The Company's life business may be separated into two subcategories. The first, Individual Life, Health and Financial Services, includes products and services sold to individuals and small businesses for protection from financial loss due to death, illness, disability or retirement, and for the accumulation, preservation and management of financial assets. Individual life insurance products include virtually all forms of non-participating life insurance, both permanent and term. Accident and health insurance products include hospital, medical, disability income and accidental death coverages. The Company offers fixed income annuities which are used for retirement funding purposes and structured claim settlements and also variable annuity products under which premiums are directed to separate accounts with investment in common stocks, money market obligations, debt obligations or a portfolio with a combination of such investments or into a variable interest rate deposit fund in the general account.

The products of the second subcategory, Group Insurance, which include life insurance, accident and health insurance and pensions, are sold through group contracts to employers, employer associations and trusts, and other organizations ranging in size from small local employers to very large multi-national corporations. Group life insurance is primarily renewable term life insurance. Group accident and health insurance includes coverage for reimbursement of hospital, medical, and dental expenses, as well as indemnity payments for both short and long-term disability. Group pension products include single premium annuity contracts, guaranteed fixed income contracts, separate accounts and managed account contracts issued in connection with tax-qualified pension and profit-sharing plans.

Casualty—Property Business

The casualty-property business may also be separated into two subcategories. The first, Personal Insurance, includes primarily automobile and homeowners insurance. Automobile policies provide coverage for liability to others both for bodily injury and for property damage, for physical damage to the insured's own vehicle from collision and various other perils. In addition, many states require policies to provide first-party personal injury, or no-fault, protection. Homeowners policies are available for owner-occupied dwellings, condominiums, mobile homes and tenants, providing against losses to dwellings and contents from a wide variety of perils, as well as coverage for liability arising from ownership or occupancy.

The products of the second subcategory, Commercial Insurance, provide protection to businesses and other institutions for the risks of property loss such as fire and windstorm and financial loss such as business interruption, liability claims and compensation benefits. Such coverages include fire and allied lines, commercial multiple peril, inland and ocean marine, workers' compensation, automobile liability and physical damage, liability other than automobile, and fidelity and surety bonds.

Other Business

The Company is engaged in providing investment services and certain related activities for mutual funds, institutional accounts, trusts, pension and profit-sharing plans, managed separate accounts of the Company and broker-dealers. These services are provided primarily through five subsidiaries: The Massachusetts Company, Inc., MassCo Investment Management Corp., Keystone Custodian Funds, Inc., The Travelers Investment Management Company and Securities Settlement Corporation. The Company also engages in real estate development and mortgage banking activities primarily through two other subsidiaries: The Prospect Company and Brokers Mortgage Service, Inc., respectively.

Recent Developments

On May 29, 1985, President Reagan submitted to the Congress proposals for tax reform. It is not possible to predict whether and in what form these proposals might be adopted. However, if enacted in their current form, they could have a significant adverse impact on the Company's operations, including the Company's Federal income taxes and the sale of its products.

Among other claims received and to be received in the ordinary course of its business, the Company is receiving claims in connection with the damage caused by the recent Hurricane Elena. Based on preliminary estimates of damage, the Company does not expect the claims related to Hurricane Elena to have a material effect on the Company's consolidated operating income for 1985.

DESCRIPTION OF COMMON STOCK

The following statements constitute a brief outline of information relating to the Common Stock. Such statements are subject to, and qualified in their entirety by reference to, all the provisions of the Charter and the By-Laws of the Company, both of which documents have been filed as exhibits to the Registration Statement.

The Charter authorizes the issuance of 200,000,000 shares of Common Stock, of which 86,539,178 shares were outstanding on July 31, 1985, and 10,000,000 shares of Preferred Stock, of which 4,000,000 shares are outstanding. The currently issued shares of Common Stock, including the shares offered hereby, are fully paid and nonassessable. Shares of Common Stock do not have any conversion rights and are not subject to any sinking fund or other redemption provisions.

Subject to the senior rights of the Preferred Stock, holders of the Common Stock are entitled to receive such dividends as the Board of Directors may lawfully declare. Under the Connecticut Insurance Holding

Company Act, the amount of dividends and other distributions which may be paid to shareholders without approval by the Connecticut Insurance Commissioner is subject to various restrictions based on the Company's surplus with respect to policyholders and its net investment income. Dividend payments to the Company from its insurance subsidiaries are subject to similar restrictions. Upon dissolution and liquidation, holders of the Common Stock are entitled to a ratable share of the net assets of the Company remaining after payment to the holders of the Preferred Stock of the full preferential amounts to which they are entitled.

The holders of Common Stock are entitled to one vote per share for the election of directors and on all other matters submitted to a vote of shareholders. The holders of any series of Preferred Stock may be granted the right to vote together with the holders of Common Stock on any such matters and shall have class or series voting rights (including rights to elect additional directors) under certain specified circumstances.

The Charter provides that shares of Common Stock shall have the pre-emptive rights provided by the Connecticut Stock Corporation Act (the "Act"). Accordingly, upon an offering or sale by the Company for cash of authorized but unissued shares of Common Stock, other than pursuant to employee rights or options approved by shareholders or upon release of the shares from pre-emptive rights by requisite shareholder action, the holders of Common Stock would have pre-emptive rights to purchase such shares in proportion to their holdings, within the time and on the terms fixed by the Board of Directors. The shares of Common Stock offered hereby are treasury shares, which the Act provides are not subject to pre-emptive rights.

UNDERWRITING

Under the terms of and subject to the conditions contained in an Underwriting Agreement dated the date hereof, Morgan Stanley & Co. Incorporated has agreed to purchase, and the Company has agreed to sell, the shares of Common Stock.

The Underwriting Agreement provides that the obligation of Morgan Stanley & Co. Incorporated to pay for and accept delivery of the shares of Common Stock is subject to the approval of certain legal matters by counsel and to certain other conditions. The nature of the obligation of Morgan Stanley & Co. Incorporated is such that it is committed to take and pay for all of the shares of Common Stock offered hereby if any are taken.

Morgan Stanley & Co. Incorporated proposes to offer part of the shares of Common Stock directly to the public at the public offering price set forth on the cover page hereof and part to dealers at a price which represents a concession not in excess of $0.35 per share under the public offering price. Morgan Stanley & Co. Incorporated may allow and such dealers may reallow a concession, not in excess of $0.15 per share, to certain other dealers.

The Company has agreed to indemnify Morgan Stanley & Co. Incorporated against certain liabilities, including liabilities under the Securities Act of 1933, as amended, or to contribute with respect to payments which Morgan Stanley & Co. Incorporated may be required to make in respect thereof.

LEGAL OPINIONS

The validity of the Common Stock will be passed upon for the Company by Ropes & Gray and for Morgan Stanley & Co. Incorporated by Davis Polk & Wardwell. Both of such firms will rely on the opinion of the General Counsel of the Company as to matters of Connecticut law. Partners and associates of Ropes & Gray have a beneficial interest in an aggregate of 1,200 shares of the Company's Common Stock and are trustees or other fiduciaries with respect to 106,860 additional shares. John R. Kenney, Associate General Counsel of the Company, owns 207 shares of the Company's Common Stock and holds options to purchase 2,654 shares.

EXPERTS

The consolidated financial statements and schedules included or incorporated by reference in the Annual Report on Form 10-K of the Company incorporated by reference in this Prospectus have been examined by Coopers & Lybrand, independent certified public accountants, whose report thereon is incorporated herein by reference. These financial statements and schedules are incorporated herein by reference in reliance on the report of Coopers & Lybrand, given on their authority as experts in accounting and auditing.

Glossary

acceleration In a public offering of securities, the action by which the SEC permits the registration statement to become effective and the offering to commence prior to the otherwise applicable waiting period provided by the 1933 Act in the circumstances.

Advisory Committee Report A report in 1977 of a committee appointed by the SEC, entitled Report of the Advisory Committee on Corporate Disclosure to the Securities and Exchange Commission, 95th Cong., 1st. sess. 451 (Comm. Print 1977), recommending integration of 1933 Act and 1934 Act reports.

agreement among underwriters A contract among investment bankers regarding the intended public offering of a security, fixing the terms and authority of an underwriter as a representative to enter into an agreement with the issuer of the security and to manage the offering on behalf of all the underwriters.

apex group A small group of approximately six to ten U.S. investment banking firms whose leadership in underwriting and trading securities and in counseling capital issuers gives them a particularly strong competitive position in the securities industry.

BarChris The decision of the federal district court in the Southern District of New York in *Escott v. BarChris Const. Corp.* 283 F. Supp. 643 (March 29, 1968) dealing with the nature of diligent investigations of issuers by underwriters.

bears, bear raid A colloquial term referring to investors or securities speculators with a pessimistic outlook on either particular securities or the stock market in general. A group of speculators could, in the days before government securities regulation, exert downward pressure on a stock price by concerted and coordinated selling efforts, thus precipitating a "bear raid" on a stock. (see **pools.**)

best efforts An arrangement between a securities issuer and an investment banking intermediary in which the intermediary uses its "best efforts" to sell all of the offered securities, but does not provide the standard guarantee of sale which is normally at the center of an "underwriting" agreement and referred to as a "firm commitment."

blue sky laws The laws of the several states generally regulating the public issuance and sale of securities within the state, and the transactions and activities of persons engaging in the securities business within state boundaries.

boiler room A colloquial term relating to a dealer in the sale of securities through "high pressure" sales tactics, generally by telephone, directed to unsophisticated persons.

bond A written obligation of a corporation or municipality, either secured or unsecured, usually having a maturity of more than one year from its date of issuance, and promising to pay specific sums of principal and interest to the holder or bearer.

bond rating A relative credit quality assessment assigned to a company or municipality having outstanding or prospective bonds in the public market. Moody's and Standard & Poor's ratings are the two most frequently cited. Duff & Phelps and Fitch also have well-established analysts' rating groups.

bought deal A reference to a securities issuance in which a single securities dealer acquires an entire block of offered securities for its own inventory and subsequent resale.

churn Refers to a practice alleged of certain securities brokers who use their influence or discretionary decision making with certain customers' accounts to cause frequent purchases and sales of securities for the purpose of generating large brokerage commissions.

Clayton Act An antitrust law enacted in 1914 prohibiting (a) mergers which substantially lessen competition or tend to create a monopoly, (b) certain anticompetitive interlocking directorates, and (c) discriminatory or anticompetitive marketing practices.

closing In the purchase and sale of a security, the act of delivering money or other consideration as well as pertinent documentation between the issuer and the representative of the underwriters in accordance with the terms of the underwriting agreement.

cold comfort, comfort At a closing, the letter addressed to the representative of the underwriters by an issuer's independent public accountants, currently updating financial statements or opinions previously reviewed or rendered by the accountants.

commission The colloquial shortened identifying term used herein for the Securities and Exchange Commission.

corporate check The process, generally carried out by attorneys for the underwriters, reviewing an issuer's articles of incorporation, by-laws, minutes of board, board committee, and shareholders meetings, contracts and other pertinent documentation sufficient to permit a legal opinion that: the issuer is in good standing under the laws of its state of domicile and elsewhere; that all necessary authorizations for the proposed issuance are in effect; that upon issuance the security will be fully paid and entitled to specified rights and privileges; and that there has been compliance with laws applicable to the transaction.

cumulative voting A procedure for crediting votes in an election of corporate directors by written ballot which permits minority interests to aggregate their votes solely for one or more candidates rather than for an entire slate, and thus avoid being outvoted mathematically. For this purpose each shareholder has total votes equal to the number of his/her shares times the number of directors being elected.

deficiency letter A letter from a staff officer of the SEC to the registrant of a proposed security offering prior to effectiveness of a registration statement, citing perceived failures of compliance with the requirements of the 1933 Act, requesting additional information, suggesting changes in form and style of the prospectus, or raising questions of adequacy of content.

distribution A term used to refer to the selling channels through which investment securities are placed with investors.

dog and pony show A somewhat pejorative expression to describe a smoothly prepared oral presentation by an issuer to professionals, including bankers and analysts, prior to a proposed public offering.

due diligence The "reasonable investigation" referred to in section 11(b)(3) of the 1933 Act which permits a person (other than an issuer) to avoid liability for material misstatements or omissions contained in a registration statement when it becomes effective. Under section 11(b)(3), the defendant must prove that he made a reasonable investigation of, and had reasonable grounds to believe in, the accuracy of the non-expertised portions of the registration statement or, with respect to any part presented upon the authority of an expert other than the defendant, that he had no reasonable ground to believe and did not believe there was a material omission or misstatement.

Dutch Auction A form of competitive bidding in which all bonds are awarded at a uniform price at the highest yield accepted once the full amount is spoken for.

effective, effectiveness The compliance of a registration statement with the filing and incubation requirements of the 1933 Act, so that a public offering of the subject securities may begin.

efficient market A term identifying a theory that public markets for certain stocks are sufficiently liquid and the flow of information about the issuer is so quickly and efficiently incorporated into the price of the securities that the value of those securities in the market at any point in time may be presumed to be fair.

equity In the United States, it refers to the securities (generally common stock) representing ownership of a business, as distinct from the company's outstanding debt securities which represent a creditor claim. In Europe, the term is used to refer to any capital supplier's interest in a business firm, and thus, in addition to references to "shareholder equity," there are also references to such terms as "loan equity."

equity financing The use in the United States of equity securities to raise new capital funds or effect an acquisition.

equity rating A quality and earnings prospect designation given to a number of publicly traded common stocks by rating agencies such as Moody's and Standard & Poor's. (see **bond rating**.)

Euromarket Refers to the supranational, unregulated market for corporate and government securities which has been physically centered in London with activities which may be worldwide except for the United States. U.S. dollars are the most important currency in this market, but Japanese yen, Swiss francs, and German marks are frequently the medium.

Foreign Corrupt Practices Act The 1977 federal statute establishing (a) standards of accounting controls, administered by the SEC, and (b) making it unlawful to make corrupt payments to foreign governmental officers or politicians to secure or retain business, administered by the Department of Justice.

Form 10K A reporting form required to be filed annually by registrants of securities under the 1934 Act.

Form 10Q A reporting form required to be filed quarterly by registrants of securities under the 1934 Act.

Forms S-1, S-2, S-3 Forms prescribed by the SEC under the 1933 Act for the registration by issuers of securities generally involved in underwritten public offerings. Form S-1 is to be used by all registrants (except foreign governments or their political subdivisions) when no other form is authorized or prescribed.

Form S-2 may be used by any registrant (for issuances other than an offer of exchange for securities of another person) which is incorporated in and has its principal business operations in the United States and meets specified prior reporting and financial requirements; it may also be used by a foreign issuer meeting the reporting requirements.

Form S-3 may be used by a registrant otherwise eligible to use Form S-2 where it has outstanding at least $150 million in market value of voting stock held by nonaffiliates, or at least $100 million in market value of voting stock and trading volume in such stock of 3 million or more shares annually and: the securities being registered are offered for cash; or the registrant is offering certain "investment grade" securities; or the registrant is offering certain securities in connection with a call or redemption of warrants or convertible securities; or the registrant is offering securities on the exercise of pro rata rights, or in a dividend or reinvestment plan, or on conversion of convertible securities or on exercise of warrants.

Glass-Steagall Act The Banking Act of June 16, 1933 which was designed to separate the functions of commercial banking and investment banking, with the intent of prohibiting a banking entity from both taking public deposits and making loans on the one hand and underwriting issuances of securities (primarily corporate) to the public on the other.

going public The process of issuing securities to public investors for the first time. Also referred to as an "initial public offering."

insider trading Trades in a company's securities by persons deemed to be affiliated with that company, either because of a formal relationship or because of possession of as-yet-undisclosed ("insider") information.

institutional investor A professional manager with a pool of investment funds lodged in a financial institution such as an investment company, insurance company, trust company, or pension fund which is managed and supervised on behalf of savers, investors, or pensioners.

integrated disclosure The system by which the SEC unified its separate disclosure rules under the 1933 Act and the 1934 Act with the aim of current information pertinent under both statutes being continuously published so as to be applicable not only in the ongoing trading markets of the issuer's securities, but also by reference (rather than repetition) at the time of a public offering.

Interstate Commerce Act Enacted in 1887, and dealing only with railroads, it was the first federal law embodying such antitrust concepts as preventing discrimination, predatory business practices, and undue concentration of economic power.

Interstate Commerce Commission Created by the Interstate Commerce Act to administer that act, it became the first federal administrative agency to be granted powers to regulate, to act like a court in making quasi-judicial decisions, and to impose sanctions for violations of the act or its rules.

investment banker In the United States, a term used to refer to a financial intermediary who deals in securities and other financing and related counseling activities on behalf of corporate and municipal issuers and, to a lesser extent, individuals.

Investment Banker Association, IBA A securities dealers trade association formed before World War I which after merging with another such group formed the current, all-encompassing Securities Industry Association.

investment company or trust An aggregation of capital or portfolio of securities, in a corporate form (having publicly held shares), or a trust form (having publicly held transferable trustees certificates), and generally utilizing professional management.

issuer The person, corporation, company or trust against whose assets or cash flow an outstanding investment security has a creditor claim or represents an ownership interest.

leverage In the United States, the financial supplementing of shareholder-supplied (equity) capital with creditor-supplied (debt) capital bearing essentially fixed returns, thus enlarging the capital pool in order to permit equity capital to enjoy the benefits of successful operating results exceeding the fixed returns on the debt capital being employed. In Great Britain, this is known as "gearing."

listing agreement The written undertaking by an issuer of securities to observe the conditions, and thus utilize the benefits, of a securities exchange as a precondition to having the issuer's securities traded by members of the exchange under its rules.

materiality, material information The characterization of information required to be disclosed under the 1933 Act, the 1934 Act, and the SEC's rules thereunder; it has been broadly defined variously as those matters as to which an average prudent investor ought reasonably to be informed, or as to which a reasonable person would attach importance in determining a choice of action in a proposed securities transaction.

May Day The colloquial reference to May 1, 1975, the date designated by the SEC when commission rates on investment security purchases and sales fixed by exchanges were eliminated, and such fees became completely subject to negotiation.

merchant banker Historically, the term refers to the private banks in Europe that engaged in a variety of securities-related as well as deposit- and loan-related financial activities. In contemporary United States usage, it generally refers to a cluster of corporate finance-related activities interpreted to be permissible under the Glass-Steagall Act for non-commercial banks.

NASD The National Association of Securities Dealers. A trade association encompassing almost all of the securities firms which deal in the trading markets for corporate securities, self-regulating but subject to SEC jurisdiction and review.

over-trading In an underwriting distribution, the practice of the issuer acquiring portfolio securities from an investment banker or investor at above-market prices in exchange for the substantially concurrent sale of new securities to that investment banker or investor for resale at a price constituting a de facto discount from the published offering price of the new securities.

pools A device historically employed by investment bankers and other professional traders, intended to control the market, often times manipulating a security's market price. (see **Rule 10b-5**).

pre-emptive rights A legally sanctioned right (granted either by corporate charter or state law) giving incumbent equity shareholders a right prior to any proposed public offering by an issuer to acquire the additionally offered equity securities in proportion to the shareholder's current holdings.

preferred lists In an earlier day, an investment banker's customers whose relationships with the banker warranted favoring them with advance or inside trading information affecting a security before it was made available to the general public.

price amendment The amendment to a registration statement under the 1933 Act filed by an issuer immediately prior to the commencement of a public offering, stating the price at which the security is being offered and the terms of the underwriting.

private bank Usually refers to a closely held banking house not normally doing business with the general public. In the United States before the 1930s and in Europe, it would often be another term for a merchant bank (see above).

prospectus The sales piece or brochure or other means of communication under the 1933 Act by which the public offering of a security may be made by the issuer and the underwriters; it also refers to that part of a registration statement under the 1933 Act setting forth the portions of the registration statement so intended to be utilized.

regional broker A U.S. securities firm, usually doing a substantial amount of commission business with individual investors, having its principal office outside of New York City.

registrant The party filing a registration statement under the 1933 Act as an issuer for the offering of a security for sale to the public; it also refers to the party registering a security under the 1934 Act for public trading.

registration   The act of compliance by an issuer with the requirements of the 1933 Act and pertinent rules of the SEC as a precondition to the public offering of a security; it also refers to similar compliance by an issuer with the requirements of the 1934 Act prerequisite to the public trading of a security.

registration statement   The documentation, including exhibits, contained in a registration under the 1933 Act.

Regulation S-K   The SEC regulation applicable to the content of non financial data being filed under the 1933 Act, the 1934 Act and the SEC's general rules and regulations pertinent to each of the acts.

Regulation S-X   The SEC regulation setting forth the form and content of, and requirements for, financial statements required to be filed under the 1933 Act, the 1934 Act, the Public Utility Holding Company Act of 1935, the Investment Company Act of 1940, and certain accounts under the Energy Policy and Conservation Act of 1975, and Energy Supply and Environmental Coordination Act of 1974.

Rule 50   An SEC rule under the Public Utility Holding Company Act of 1935 generally requiring persons subject to the act to submit for sealed competitive bids securities being offered publicly.

Rule 415, Temporary Rule 415   Rule 415 is an SEC rule adopted November 17, 1983, effective as of December 31, 1983, under the 1933 Act relating to the registration of securities to be offered or sold publicly on a delayed or continuous basis, referred to colloquially as "shelf registration;" Temporary Rule 415 was a version adopted on a trial basis on March 3, 1982, and significantly changed in its final form.

Rule 176   An SEC rule under the 1933 Act setting forth the circumstances deemed relevant by the SEC for determining what constitutes a "reasonable investigation" or a "reasonable ground for belief." (see **due diligence.**)

Rule 10b-5   The SEC rule adopted under section 10(b) of the 1934 Act prohibiting anyone, in connection with the purchase or sale of a security, from employing a device or engaging in an act or practice which operates or would operate as a fraud, or from making an untrue statement of a material fact, or omitting a material fact necessary to make pertinent statements not misleading.

SEC The Securities and Exchange Commission, the regulatory body established by the Securities Exchange Act of 1934 to carry out the mandate of the Securities Act of 1933 and other contemporary and subsequent reform legislation affecting securities or corporations.

secondary distribution An organized sale through a brokerage intermediary of securities previously issued and currently outstanding.

Securities Act of 1933, 1933 Securities Act, 1933 Act, Securities Act A law administered by the SEC, 17 CFR Part 230, and set forth in 15 U.S.C. 77a *et seq.*, generally dealing with the public offering and sale of securities.

Securities Exchange Act of 1934, 1934 Act A law administered by the SEC, 17 CFR Part 230, and set forth in 15 U.S.C. 78a *et seq.*, generally regarding the trading of publicly outstanding securities.

securities industry Refers collectively to the brokerage and investment banking firms who deal in various types of outstanding securities (subject to occasional specialization) issued by either public or private issuers, and both as principals and agents.

selected dealer agreement In the marketing and distribution of a publicly offered security, the form of contract entered into by the representative of the underwriters with brokers and dealers in securities who are not in the group underwriting the offering, which fixes the terms of the dealer participation in the offering and their allowances.

selling groups Groups of securities firms enlisted by an underwriter to participate in the sale of underwritten securities to investors. They are not usually members of the underwriting syndicate and receive only a specified portion of the underwriter's selling commission as compensation for their efforts.

shelf registration An SEC filing by an issuer of securities to the public invoking, where eligible, the authorization to hold "on the shelf" over a maximum two-year period all or part of the securities proposed to be offered for possible future sale at times deemed opportune by the issuer. (see **Rule 415**).

Sherman Act Enacted in 1890, it was the first federal law specifically designed on the concept that the public interest demanded competition; it prohibited agreements or acts in restraint of trade or commerce, and monopolies generally.

soft dollars The dollar value of securities transaction commissions incurred by an investor which is permitted by the broker to be directed to the same or another securities firm as compensation for other financially related services rendered. Because the agreed commission cost is presumed to be incurred in any case, the dollar value of the directed benefits is, in effect, a discount which the service vendor will credit as payment for specific benefits which are otherwise charged in cash.

Standard & Poor One of the leading U.S. securities research and evaluation organizations, known particularly for its independent quality ratings of publicly outstanding debt and equity issues.

stop order The sanction under the 1933 Act authorizing the SEC to prevent initiation of a proposed public offering or to stop it after it has commenced, for reasons of inadequate disclosure. (see **materiality**).

syndicate, syndications A group of securities firms organized to undertake the specific offering and distribution of certain securities.

The Commission (see **SEC**).

underwriter A securities firm which commits itself either to sell a proposed securities issuance or portion thereof to investors, or failing that, to acquire it for its own account. (Also see **best efforts**).

underwriting The function being carried out by an underwriter pursuant to an underwriting agreement fixing the price, volume, and compensation arrangements of a securities offering being made by one or more securities firms comprising the underwriting syndicate or group.

underwriting agreement   The contract entered into between an issuer and an underwriter regarding a public offering of securities, setting forth the price and other relevant terms of the offering, including representations and warranties of the issuer, its covenants, and the conditions to be met at closing.

watered stock   Equity securities whose stated value or equity on the books of the issuer is diminished by the issuer making other sales or exchanges of the same security at lower prices, thus diluting book value or intrinsic value; or the process of artificially sustaining or increasing stated value or equity by writing-up or overstating the reasonably realizable value of the company's assets.

Wheat Report   An internal report of the SEC staff, under the chairmanship of then Commissioner Francis Wheat, published in 1969 under the title, *Disclosure to Investors: A Reappraisal of Administrative Policies Under the 1933 and 1934 Acts.*

Index